MILL AND MARX

PAUL SMART

Mill and Marx
**Individual liberty
and the roads to freedom**

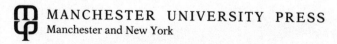
MANCHESTER UNIVERSITY PRESS
Manchester and New York

*Distributed exclusively in the USA and Canada
by* ST. MARTIN'S PRESS

Copyright © Paul Smart 1991

Published by Manchester University Press
Oxford Road, Manchester M13 9PL, UK
and Room 400, 175 Fifth Avenue
New York, NY 10010, USA

*Distributed exclusively in the USA and Canada
by* St. Martin's Press, Inc.,
175 Fifth Avenue, New York, NY 10010, USA

British Library cataloguing in publication data
Smart, Paul
  Mill and Marx: individual liberty and the roads to freedom.
  1. Liberty. Theories of Mill, John Stuart, 1806-1873. 2. Liberty. Theories
  of Marx, Karl, 1818-1883.
  I. Title
  323.44092

Library of Congress cataloging in publication data
Smart, Paul, 1957–
  Mill and Marx: individual liberty and the roads to freedom / Paul Smart.
    p.   cm.
  Includes bibliographical references and index.
  ISBN 0-7190-3333-0
  1. Liberty. 2. Marx, Karl, 1818-1883 – Views on liberty. 3. Mill, John Stuart,
  1806-1873 – Views on liberty. I. Title
  JC585.S527   1990
  323.44—dc20   90-37721

ISBN 0 7190 3333 0 *hardback*

Typeset in New Aster
by Koinonia Limited, Manchester
Printed and bound in Great Britain
by Billings Ltd., of Worcester

CONTENTS

Acknowledgements	*page* vi
General introduction	1

PART ONE HUMAN NATURE

1 Introductory comment – method and human nature 18

2 Mill and human nature 22
  1 Introduction 22
  2 The context 26
  3 Self-culture, free will and liberty 32
  4 Laws of the mind and the science of ethology 36
  5 Instincts 42
  6 Conclusion 45

3 Marx and 'homo faber' 48
  1 Introduction 48
  2 The continuity controversy 53
  3 Human nature, the productive individual and social relations 62
  4 Conclusion 85

PART TWO THE INDIVIDUAL AND FREEDOM

4 Introductory comment – the individual and freedom 90

5 Mill and individuality: the elite, the generality and democracy 95
  1 Introduction 95
  2 The principle of liberty and the concept of freedom 98
  3 The autonomous individual, happiness and freedom 104
  4 The elite, the generality and representative government 108
  5 Conclusion 114

Contents

6 Marx and the individual — 117
  1 Introduction — 117
  2. Marx on morality and justice — 121
    2.1 Marxian justice and communist morality — 124
    2.2 Marx against justice and morality — 133
  3 The *Grundrisse*, the individual and freedom — 144
  4 The individual, circulation and money — 149
  5 Self-determination, social freedom and revolution — 157
  6 Conclusion — 160

Concluding note — 163
Notes — 179
Bibliography — 193
Index — 199

ACKNOWLEDGEMENTS

Many people have helped with the production of this book, from thesis to final draft. Stanley Glass, Margaret Canovan and Andy Dobson at Keele University all gave excellent advice. Encouragement given by Jeremy Richardson and Dave Judge of Strathclyde University, and John Foster of Paisley College cannot be overestimated. I have also benefited from the valuable and constructive comments of Richard Bellamy, Richard Gunn, Desmond King, Nick Rengger and Jeremy Waldron. Along the way, Mark Cowling, Ian Forbes and Graeme Duncan have all offered useful advice.

Earlier versions of some chapters, or parts of chapters, have appeared in the following: 'Mill and Human Nature', Chapter 3 of *Politics and Human Nature*, ed. I. Forbes and S. Smith, Frances Pinter, London, 1983; 'Marx and the Individual in the *Grundrisse*' in *Approaches to Marx*, ed. M. Cowling and L. Wilde, Open University Press, Milton Keynes, 1989; and '"Some will be more equal than others", J. S. Mill on democracy, freedom, and the labouring classes', in *Archives for Philosophy of Law and Social Philosophy*, forthcoming, Winter 1990-91.

Finally, I would like to thank my parents and Lucy for their constant and invaluable support. I dedicate this book to them.

GENERAL INTRODUCTION

Mill and Marx: individual liberty and the roads to freedom
A proposal for a comparative critical reconstruction

1 Why compare?

Is there anything to be gained by comparing Mill and Marx? Despite their differences, did they share a common purpose? Were the originators of two notably distinct and competing ideologies inspired by similar visions of human emancipation? Even if the answer to each of these questions is 'yes', is not such a comparison merely *academic*; especially in the light of the apparent wholesale rejection by Eastern Europe of one of these visions and the adoption of the other? Not if you believe that there is a genuine point of comparison which is worth exploring, and which, furthermore, will have profound political consequences for those who too hastily claim a monopoly in the language of liberty.

In order to re-establish the pre-eminent status of freedom in the thought of Mill and Marx it is essential to clear away a thicket of partisan polemics which has only served to obfuscate and return to the authors' original statements of intention. And while I accept that with regard to the procedures applied to the study of the human condition there are considerable differences between Mill and Marx, I nevertheless believe that both were ultimately motivated by a commitment to establishing a society in which individuals could consciously realise their potential as humans through creative self-determination. In other words it was the pursuit of a particular kind of freedom which both defined the single purpose of the projects of Mill and Marx, underpinning the direction of their theoretical and practical politics, and was the ultimate justification behind their programmes for the transformation of society.

In adopting this perspective I have rejected those misconceived accounts that have attempted to place each thinker within a particular category or tradition because these relegate their commitment to freedom to the status of a secondary consideration. Such misconstruals have contributed to the general confusion which continues to plague many assessments of the merits and problems associated with modern-day liberalism and Marxism. I do not wish to claim that none have recognised that the true worth of Mill and Marx lies in their prescriptions for freedom. But, more often than not, such a conclusion is reached by those who seek to defend their own version of liberty while at the same time discrediting the opposition. We are all familiar with the following: 'Mill's theory of liberty reminds us of the dangers which accompany the socialism of a revolutionary, marxian persuasion.' Or: 'Marx's theory of alienation exposes the true nature of Mill's political economy as nothing more than an apology for laissez-faire capitalism.' That these views sadly prevail is reason enough to proceed from a different and, as I shall claim, a more authentic starting position. I do not, then, see Mill simply as a 'social democrat', nor just as a champion of the common good. Neither do I treat him as the promoter of the merits of free competition, nor view him as a social reformer. Similarly, I do not view Marx as a utopian communist, nor as a believer in the inevitability of history, and most definitely not as the scientific determinist *par excellence*. Granted, all of these interpretations may well have an element of truth about them, they may reveal particular facets of respective intellectual lineages, but to claim that any one of them is the fundamental basis for an appreciation of the true intention of either thinker is erroneous.

What did define the development of their systems was their unstinting belief in the cause of human emancipation. Not a negative freedom of the limited exercise of individual choice in present circumstances, but a self-motivated process of personal liberation exercised in a community of mutually recognitive and interdependent agents

Hence the primary aim of this study: to compare the theories of liberty – and the means of achieving it – articulated by the originators of the political philosophies which played a principal role in constructing the two competing ideologies of the late twentieth century – liberalism and communism. To claim that both

General introduction

systems were originally motivated by the cause of freedom is in itself a challenge to the conclusions reached by contemporary proponents of each commenting on the intentions of the other. To go on to suggest that each may have something to learn from the other is, in the eyes of some, the equivalent of committing intellectual adultery. Much of the recent debate on freedom in political philosophy has been a competition, a point-scoring contest of who can most successfully substantiate a conception of human emancipation derived from mutually exclusive systems. Each side has sought to strengthen its defences against the attacks of the opposition, repairing and reinforcing their respective positions in response to previous advances, digging in more securely, whilst rendering the ground between the redoubts uninhabitable.

Those who base their arguments for individual freedom on rights or utility nearly always presuppose that Marxism both attacks foundational principles irresponsibly and fails to offer an equivalent alternative, as if such an absence negates any effective contribution by Marxism to the debate on freedom.[1] In the counter-attack, liberal political theory has all too often been dismissed as nothing more than an apology for capitalism's tendency to dehumanise. Furthermore, it is usually claimed that there is little of a positive nature to be learned from the liberal heritage with regard to self-determination and the kinds of societal restraints that may inhibit its development.[2]

Some may now understandably insist that this intellectual standoff is no longer relevant. The dramatic revolutions of 1989, despite their unpredictable political consequences, have, so the 'triumphalists' would have us believe, unceremoniously jettisoned communism. And if the progeny is redundant then surely the progenitor has been exposed as a fraudulent millenialist? Surely, liberalism's version of democracy and freedom have successfully withstood and repulsed an aberration (a naive and dangerous presumption in itself)? However, even if this is accepted should it alone be any reason for uncritical celebration? I think not. Part of the purpose of this study is to reassess the roots of the liberal notion of emancipation and to suggest that, in one of its most celebrated and influential guises, there remain unresolved inconsistencies. That these jeopardised the viability of Mill's own project should have serious implications for those who today enthusiastically employ the same prescription, especially when they are chastising those who still insist that Marx may well have outlined the basis for a more thoroughgoing liberty. In other words, a heightening of the critical re-evaluation within and between liberalism and Marxism is a legitimate and crucial response to the collapse of old certainties, if only to guard against the replacement of one dead dogma with another. This study is a contribution to such a re-evaluation.

2 Similarities and differences

I do not pretend to offer a methodological concordance. This would be as pointless as insisting that Mill was a closet communist, or defending a libertarian Marx! Neither do I want to suggest that either Mill or Marx seriously considered, or incorporated into their own systems, the insights of the other. In the case of the latter the little attention that he did pay to his liberal contemporary was usually contained within the general criticisms of classical political economy. Beyond this there is the occasional grudging acceptance that Mill was perhaps a cut above the coterie of apologists for nineteenth century *laissez-faire* capitalism.[3] Mill, on the other hand remained in complete ignorance of his London neighbour.[4]

What I do concentrate on are the varied intellectual and circumstantial resources employed by both thinkers to construct social theories that have at their hearts a commitment to liberation. The ontologies and methodologies that emerged out of this process were partly the products of Mill's and Marx's critical evaluations of their respective mentors. But both also employed and incorporated into their systems the observations of others. Both, for example, worked within the same tradition of political economy, accepting many of its assumptions as legitimate starting points. And both, in their own ways, were profoundly influenced by French socialist political thought and materialist theories of social progress.

It may be suggested, with justification, that such observations could be made of any number of political thinkers one might arbitrarily choose to compare. Who has not modified and amended their intellectual inheritance? Who has not learned constructively from others? But I return to my original point of departure. These two luminaries from a century celebrated for its ambitious systems builders are arguably unique in one particular respect: they are today perceived by many theoreticians and practitioners, sides of the ideological divide, as the principal originators two *Weltanschaungen* which more than any other have shaped practical and theoretical agenda of modern day politics.

Furthermore, Mill and Marx saw themselves very much as 'scientists' of social relations; we only have to look at *A System of Logic* and *Capital* to realise that their authors were not interested in constructing yet more idealist moral prescriptions, nor purely descriptive, subjective, or normative critiques of a corrupt world. The sciences they elaborated sought to reveal the dialectic of change in ways which reflected a mid-nineteenth century certainty in the constructive power of human reason. For Mill it was Saint-Simon who had identified history as a dynamic process, the developments of which could be explained through the study of the interplay between critical and harmonious eras. Mill was under no illusion that he was living in a time of social calm; he revelled in the challenge of deducing order from the intellectual and social crisis of mid-nineteenth century Europe, attempting, via a constant process of eclectic synthesis, to combine the half-truths of competing doctrines in the hope of transcending their divisions. For Marx, of course, the writings of Hegel, stripped of their idealism and distilled down to their rational core, were the basis of his method, which when complemented with the materialism of the French socialists – Saint-Simonians amongst them – and British political economy, resulted in the materialist conception of history. Both accordingly believed in the irrevocable (though not irrepressible) tendency of societies to progress, especially their own society. Capitalism was, so far, the highest point of human development and, despite its inadequacies, it provided the potential for attaining both material abundance and a more equitable distribution of the social product, which, for both Mill and Marx were necessary prerequisites for human freedom. In other words, each of them believed that the continued economic and intellectual progress of human society was symptomatic of the more general and profound movement towards freedom, moreover it was a movement which could be understood 'scientifically', and could therefore be consciously controlled and rationally ordered.

The observation, that for Mill and Marx capitalism was the apogee, to date, of humanity's advance, makes the comparison

ng. Both writers observed and critically
...ysical evidence from a time of great economic,
...ange. They had each witnessed the precocious
...dustrial revolution in Britain. Each had also
...gnised the importance of the political
...e social dislocations which had accompanied
...ic advancement. In response to these epoch
making developments each of them emphasised the necessity of constructing theories of political economy, providing both an explanation of the basis of capitalism and an examination of its historical and progressive nature. In both cases the intention was not merely to describe prevailing socio-economic relations, but to change them. To this end, each saw his own insights as contributing to the pursuit of change and as providing the theoretical basis of practical action. They responded to the economic and spiritual impoverishment of the majority of the population – a condition generated, they both believed, by the industrialisation of society – by actively supporting (for admittedly different tactical and strategic reasons) campaigns for various causes, such as the reduction of the working day, the abolition of child labour, and the improvement of working conditions. Such activity was consistent with their shared belief that without an adequately structured, supportive and co-ordinated economic sphere, the future emancipation of the deprived generality would remain an impossibility. They also participated in oppositional and extra-parliamentary (as well as parliamentary, in Mill's case) political movements, pursuing radical political objectives. Both recognised and actively campaigned in support of the demand for universal franchise, not merely as an end in itself, but as part of the basis for the organisation of the disadvantaged. While at the same time each attacked the archaic institutions of political authority and the traditional elites that manipulated them for their own ends.[5]

However, the securing of political and social objectives on their own would not, they believed, guarantee emancipation. Mill and Marx recognised that without changes in the organisation of the relations of production and the alteration of the criteria of distribution, social freedom and individual liberty for the majority would remain unfulfilled.

But we must avoid the temptation of stretching this similarity too far. Of course, the methods each thinker believed would, through their practical application, secure these necessary restructurings differed considerably. Mill went no further than to encourage experimentation in various forms of production, particularly welcoming the initiatives of those workers who set up co operatives, while remaining opposed to the predominance of monopolies, and antipathetic to the widely disproportionate distribution of wealth.[6] Competition may have been central to his political economy, but only if it promoted efficiency and progress, avoided injustice, secured for as many as possible the chance for self-development, and was firmly based on as wide a possession of private property as possible. Marx viewed all such economic and social reform as inadequate and ineffective in the face of all-pervading competition and the pursuit of profit that was expressly founded on private property. As long as the predominant relation between individuals remained one of antagonism between capitalist and labour, between propertied and propertyless, genuine human self-determination was an impossibility. Only the revolutionary transformation of capitalism could overcome the unfreedom of alienation, and establish the conditions for social emancipation.[7]

So, despite their proximity, both spatially and intellectually, in spite of their common distaste for the consequences of rapacious materialism and egotistical competition, and regardless of their acceptance of the need for a unity of theory and action, each proposed widely differing means based on apparently incompatible methods and sciences. What, then, is there left to compare? The short answer is the validity of their prescriptions. In other words, an assessment of the strength of their theories of freedom, which should consider both the plausibility of their claims about the capacities individuals possess for self-determination, and the viability of their schemes for achieving the stipulated end.

Therefore, what underpins my comparison is the assumption that both thinkers developed views of freedom which, in terms of the image of what an emancipated existence might look like, are remarkably similar. The images that both project, of communities of creatively self-determining, mutually recognitive agents, share key features. For example, each conceived of the human being as an agent capable of self-motivated emancipation, and held that only the individual who voluntarily participated in the development of their own capacities could be said to be free. What is more, the process of individual self-determination could only be fully and successfully pursued in an environment comprised of like-minded individuals. Freedom, therefore, is both an individual and a social process of conscious creative activity, which relies upon the recognition by each of the other's ability to pursue conscious self-improvement, and hence rests on the assumption that freedom for individuals and society is the result of both semi-autonomous and collective action. The private and the public spheres are no longer mutually exclusive, while the false dichotomy between negative and positive liberty is transcended.

However, as has already been pointed out, although the ends may appear similar, the means which are recommended to achieve them, and the methods on which they are founded, appear irreconcilable. This particular comparison does not accept the exclusivity of either approach. Each may well contain insights that expose crucial inconsistencies and highlight glaring lacunae in each of the prescriptions. One way which might enable us to see these shortcomings for ourselves is firstly to resituate the notions of freedom propounded by Mill and Marx within their all-embracing social theories and then place them side-by-side. Whether we learn anything from the following juxtapositioning depends partly on the reader's willingness to question the explanatory exhaustiveness of each system, and, more problematically, on the same reader's preparedness to learn from a social theory which he or she may always have assumed is diametrically opposed to their own cherished beliefs.

3   The comparison outlined

So the following is an examination of what are usually perceived to be competing notions of freedom in the context of the overarching social theories from which they spring. This is consistent with the procedure adopted by both thinkers; they viewed the components of their systems as interdependent parts of integrated analyses, and they cautioned against the tendency to isolate aspects of their thought, whether textual or conceptual, from the integrality which gave them meaning.[8]

Admittedly, this is the prevailing method of analysis practised in most contemporary investigations of various issues and problems associated with the ideas of Mill and Marx. But such a sound approach rarely extends to the critical appraisals proffered by promoters of one thinker and his system when attempting to disassemble and devalue the ideas of the other. This is true of a number of liberal and radical scholars who reveal a woefully incomplete understanding of the methodologies of the 'opposition' whose views they attempt to debunk.[9] In an effort to side-step such pitfalls, I shall intentionally avoid treating particular works of each author as discrete and self-sustaining moments of their intellectual output. In so doing I also expressly avoid the tendency of elevating one book to a position of pre-eminence over others. Both of these errors inhibit a full appreciation of the importance and intention of particular works, whether they be considered seminal or second-rate. All too often contributions such as *On Liberty* and the first volume of *Capital* are taken as the definitive statements of their respective authors,[10] when in fact each is most definitely only one aspect of a system of thought which is constructed from inter-determinate elements.

With such thoughts in mind, I assume that, for example, Mill's evaluation of an individual's fitness to participate and to hold positions of responsibility in politics (as outlined in *Representative Government*), can only be fully appreciated if we have a good idea of his qualitative distinction between 'higher' and 'lower' forms of character (made in *A System of Logic* and *Utilitarianism*). The same goes for Marx when we need to delve into the density of the *Grundrisse* and its examination of the nature of 'categories', in order to make more sense of the cryptic notes on justice that appear in his polemical *Critique of the Gotha Programme*. Unless such methodical precautions are made, mistakes and misjudgements are all the more likely. Thus, in the pursuit of greater coherence, not only should Mill's and Marx's analyses of what constitutes individual and social freedom be considered, but also the methodologies and epistemologies which underpin their theories of liberty. I assume, then, that we cannot detach the conclusions from the method, for in the method lies the clue to a full appreciation of what each writer saw as the ability individuals have to change consciously their environment in the pursuance of self-development. There can be little doubt that without their exacting methods, neither Marx nor

Mill could have produced such enduring and alluring conceptions of emancipation. However, it must be admitted that within their respective 'scientific' examinations of human character lie problems, the presence of which helps to explain the shortcomings of each of these proposals concerning liberation. So, before anything else, there is a need to focus on the theories of human nature propounded by each thinker. This will be the purpose of the first section of my study.

Some of the tensions which I believe exist in each of the two theories of human nature stem from the eclectic character of the theories' origins. This is perhaps more apparent in the case of Mill, but has also given rise to disagreements concerning the true intentions of Marx. In both cases, the outcome of the intellectual synthesis attempted by the thinker resulted in the emphasis of particular aspects of human character at the expense of others. This invariably had effects on their critiques of alternative theories of freedom, leading them to dismiss, or ignore altogether, details of opposing views that did not appear to conform to their own conclusions. Such intransigence, I want to suggest, only served to compound the problems implicit in their own explanations of the human condition, problems which have all too easily been incorporated into the ideas of contemporary protagonists. So, even if we can dispel a number of the inadequacies commonly associated with Mill and Marx by equipping ourselves with a working knowledge of their ontologies, this will not account for all their shortcomings. Indeed it can be shown that origins of shortcomings in the theories of liberation championed by Mill and Marx can be traced back to the tensions that exist between respective methodologies and the application of these methodologies to examinations of the nature of human character.

In turning first to Mill, I show that the origins of his ambiguous and equivocal attitude towards the relationship between the capacity for self-improvement and the prospects for general emancipation, lie in his unsatisfactory approach to the compatibilist dilemma: how can we overcome the dead hand of determinism that accompanies a utilitarian, necessitarian epistemology without sacrificing our scientific empiricism to intuitionism and idealist metaphysics? Or to put it another way, is it possible to accommodate a concept of free will within a materialist account of human

General introduction

psychology? Mill's anguished attempt to achieve such a consilience leads him to conclusions, concerning the ability of individuals to emancipate themselves, that have a direct bearing on his proposals for social reform in general. In short, Mill was bridled by his continued faith in the explanatory efficacy of utilitarian individualism, but compromised its call for equality by suggesting that although all had a capacity for self-culture, only a minority, for the foreseeable future, would be able to exercise it to the best of their ability. The practical consequences of this position are exposed in Mill's defence of freedom which will be examined in the second part of my study. More on this later.

With regard to Marx, the major problem that I address is whether he escaped completely from the clutches of the universalist and teleological account of human nature which accompanied German idealism. Part of the solution can be found in an adequate account of the development of Marx's own critique of Hegelian metaphysics. This includes an assessment of the success of his attempt to shed the concept 'species being' through the application of his materialist method, along with an appraisal of his efforts to establish a theory of human agency that was unhindered by universalist claims. But if Marx ended up with an analysis claiming that individuals are nothing more than a reflection of the ensemble of social relations, then in what ways can they be alienated, and what are they alienated from? Did Marx still possess a paradigm of what emancipated existence might look like and did this continue to inform his social theory? If this was the case then how could one account for the capacity to engage in self-determination within a scientific materialism, particularly a materialism which claims that the dynamic which propels history has hitherto been an inevitable and uncontrollable dialectic? What I want to maintain is that Marx's understanding of human agency is quite distinct from his rejection of human nature. The latter, he believed, implied ageless character traits, such as self-interest or social sympathy, which led to bogus universalistic claims being made for what were in reality particular and contingent theories of freedom and equality. The former, however, made no such assumptions, claiming, rather, that human agents were distinct by nature of their ability to recreate consciously and develop the means of their own existence. But I believe a tension remains, even if we accept the open-ended consequence of Marx's views of human agency, between his claim for the individual's capacity for freedom and his recognition of the impact of impersonal historical forces on social relations.

In other words, the atomism of classical utilitarianism and the holism of hegelian metaphysics, although significantly modified by their inheritors, continued to weigh upon conclusions in ways that may not have been entirely propitious. Are these faults fundamental and irreversible? Can the theories be salvaged and the prescriptions sympathetically reconsidered? Or do the intentions of the authors remain at variance with the implications of their analyses?

In an attempt to answer these questions, it is necessary to follow through the concrete implications of each thinker's analysis of human nature via an appraisal of their respective views on the condition of the individual in contemporary society, and the various proposals that are made by each concerning the transformation of both social relations and the individual. In adopting such an approach I suggest the following in the second half of my comparison.

That the method and the science of human nature employed by Mill were inadequate for the task they were supposed to perform; rather than providing him with a sound theoretical basis for the universal emancipation of society as expressed in the early sections of *On Liberty* they led him to make recommendations which are inegalitarian and, in some cases, elitist. Much of the evidence for this charge lies in Book Six of *A System of Logic*, where Mill works out the theoretical basis for a theory of liberty, in the essay *Utilitarianism*, in which superior forms of human existence are recommended – this echoed in nearly all of his studies on the relationship between society and the individual. The practical implications of these conclusions are clearly discernible in his works on government, education, and the economy, where preferred character traits and the fortunate individuals who possess them are elevated to positions of real influence, at the expense of the generality, who, for the foreseeable future, will be encouraged to respect and defer to their intellectual and political superiors. So, although a vision of an emancipated existence had inspired Mill to write with conviction in *On Liberty* about the restrictions which inhibit the majority from pursuing virtuous lives, elsewhere the

General introduction

hard material evidence qualified his epistemological hypotheses and tempered his enthusiasm and his optimism, leading him to tone down his radical, egalitarian tendencies, compromising them with utilitarian arguments for elitist solutions such as the recommendation for sole kind of meritocracy or 'clerisy'.

On turning to Marx, I concentrate on his critique of what he took to be the liberal theory and practice of freedom and equality, along with his examination of the post-capitalist alternative that he believed would emerge from its disillusionment. This critique certainly went some of the way towards exposing the contradictions within prevailing arguments which accepted the predominant laws of production as the universal basis for establishing the realm of freedom. Mill, with reservations, would have counted himself amongst those who adopted such a position, therefore it can be safely assumed that Marx's criticisms apply to him. But in response it could also be said that Marx's revolutionary alternative reinforces the importance of Mill's observations concerning the tendency of numerical majorities to suppress those who do not conform to the generality's perception of the general interest. Or, to put the problem in the form of a question, is the individual sufficiently protected in Marx's system against the possibility of transgressions committed by the collective? Is the baby thrown out with the bath water? Does Marx dismiss all talk of rights too lightly when disassembling and rejecting it as a bourgeois apparition and nothing more than legitimating slogans? Marx's response to these doubts can be found in works which represent the culmination of his project, the *Grundrisse* and *Capital*. It is here where the conception of alienation is fully incorporated within political economy, allowing Marx to articulate a theory of freedom, combined with a metaethic, which insists that any universal rights claim only serves to limit liberty on the basis of *a priori* assumptions concerning the nature of the relationship between the individual and society, assumptions that are reflective of contingent duties, morals and obligations contiguous with prevailing social relations. But as with the supposed tension in his theory of human nature, doubts persist with regard to the extent of Marx's awareness of the possible dangers to individual freedom posed by the dictatorship of the proletariat. These doubts are only reinforced by Marx's infamous reticence on the organisation of post-revolutionary society.

Unfortunately, these perceived inadequacies are often used by critics from opposing camps to dismiss the entire contribution made by each thinker. The more constructive procedure would be to recognise the positive contribution made by each system to the pursuit or freedom, and subsequently to engage in a critical reappraisal of those aspects of each system which do not withstand the test of close scrutiny. This is the advantage of a comparison; we can assess both systems and their intrinsic value while at the same time conducting an open-ended dialogue between the two.

What might be the results of such a dialogue? Firstly, as has already been suggested, it does, I believe, reveal a remarkable similarity between the projections offered by Mill and Marx of what a fully emancipated existence may well look like: a society of free, consciously creative, mutually recognitive and interdependent self-determining agents. Secondly, the examination of the widely differing methodologies and epistemologies employed by each thinker, exposes the varying degrees of their effectiveness in promoting the achievement of the common end. The individualism of Mill's utilitarian compatibilism is most certainly bedevilled by normative assumptions concerning the agent's capacity for and ability to achieve freedom, these weaken considerably Mills claims for scientific neutrality and, in fact, indirectly impose a revised idealist morality. Whereas Marx's method, based as it is on a concept of humanity as a species which distinguishes itself by virtue of its ability to recreate consciously its material existence, rejects, rather too recklessly it might be claimed, evaluative prescriptions and universal *moral* claims. The result of such a non-ethical approach is an open-ended or 'extensive' view of freedom, which seeks to overcome the traditional dichotomy of theory and practice by urging revolutionary praxis. Therefore, for Marx, self-emancipation was direct and immediate participation in the collective process of social transformation. But for Mill the initial modification of the circumstances conducive to liberty would be the responsibility of those of confirmed virtue. The generality would be, for some time to come, inadequately equipped for such a task and should be encouraged to defer in favour of those already enlightened in the 'science' and 'art' of the general good.

So although the idea of freedom and the activity of liberty may well be shared by both thinkers, the routes taken in pursuit of the end are widely divergent, to the extent that one approach may well end up being more consistent than the other when attention is turned to the adequacy of the means proposed for achieving emancipation. Or, to put this problem another way, I believe that the genuineness of each thinker's commitment to universal *and* individual freedom can be gauged by his willingness to consider seriously qualifications to his overall strategies; qualifications which may well compromise the freedom of the many, while at the same time enhancing the liberty of the few. Such qualifications, I want to maintain, would reveal a reluctance to accept the unpredictable consequences of universal emancipation and a tendency to resort to paternalistic and undemocratic remedies. Mill is inflicted with this dilemma; for him the problem appears in two distinct, though interrelated guises: (l) how can we restrict the damage wrought by the uncultivated generality's misuse of liberty without denying them the educative and emancipating benefits of a representative democracy? And,(2) how can the services of the enlightened be secured for the benefit of the community without estranging the majority from the processes of political authority? For Marx such a dilemma is symptomatic of the problem faced by all political philosophers who are not prepared to accept the practical, contradictory consequences of their most cherished hypotheses. But Marx is himself open to the charge of blind optimism on those rare occasions when he turns to the capacity of the oppressed to engage successfully in revolutionary activity, paying little attention either to the effects of post-capitalist political, social and economic turmoil on the impoverished and the dispossessed, or to the basis of resolving conflicts of interest in an emancipated world. So although Marx's commitment to universal freedom may indeed be more genuine than Mill's more reserved conclusions, perhaps the latter's reservation is his greatest strength, and the former's 'heroic silence' his most notable weakness.

What follows, then, is principally a work of comparative exegesis, but it is one which I believe in its own way serves a contemporary purpose. Despite recent fundamental changes to the political map the prevailing intellectual mood remains one of mutual misunderstanding and systemic exclusivity. However, there is a small but growing field of research – that has undoubtably received a fillip from the break-down of cold war certainties –

which is reassessing, in an open and comparative fashion, the intellectual legacy of liberalism and marxism. This has taken two general forms: one has been the incorporation, into re-evaluations of the contemporary worth of each 'classical' theory, of aspects usually associated with its opposite number; the second is an attempt to develop a synthesis of the two systems, combining the strengths and jettisoning the weaknesses. What follows will indicate why the second trend may well be misguided and ultimately unsuccessful, and why the first is potentially far more rewarding as a procedure for testing the validity of the claims and counter-claims made by each system and for pursuing the goal of freedom as being self-determination in a world of mutual recognition and co-operative interdependence. To this end references will be made to contemporary debates only when they are directly relevant to the discussion of Mill and Marx on human nature, the individual and freedom.

PART ONE

Human nature

CHAPTER 1

Introductory comment–method and human nature

Why start with human nature? Is there any point of comparison between thinkers who appear at first to be so diametrically opposed to one another on the question of the origins of human character? Surely, there is little to be gained from juxtaposing a theory of society which obtains its first principles from laws determining the formation of an individual's character with an analysis which insists that human essence is the ensemble of social relations?

One response to these understandable doubts might begin by suggesting that the methodologies of Mill and Marx are both examples of the reductionist school of thought, and that the purpose of any comparison would be to assess the strengths and weaknesses of their respective versions of methodological individualism. It may come as a surprise to learn that Marx could be counted amongst the company of other revolutionary individualists such as Hayek and Nozick, but over the past decade there has emerged a growing body of literature (principally American for one reason or another) which claims that Marx's methodological starting point is the individual. Two recent exponents of this view, D. F. B. Tucker and Jon Elster,[1] have gone so far as to say that unless we view Marx in this light we cannot hope to make full sense of his social theory, or to salvage the positive elements of his thought from those that are historically outdated. If this 'rational choice' prognosis is true then a comparison between the two similar methods of Mill and Marx might well prove fruitful, and we could end up with an amalgamation of the better parts of both, an aim which I believe the marxian individualists are themselves pursuing, especially those who claim that Marx was employing a sophisticated utilitarian psychology. This, to my mind, is a false start.

Method and human nature

Mill most certainly was a methodological individualist, he himself said as much in *A System of Logic*, but Marx, as we shall see, equated such an approach with other forms of speculative abstraction which isolated certain aspects of human character from their social context and elevated them to the status of explanations. By the same token, however, our recognition of this difference should not lead us to the opposite extreme, adopted by the likes of Isaiah Berlin and Karl Popper,[2] of condemning Marx as a methodological holist of a determinist persuasion who had little or no time for the individual. To do so would be to deny the clear evidence in all of Marx's major works of his continued concern for the individual as an agent capable of self-determination. Much of his early intellectual exploration was in the form of a critical re-appraisal of hegelian holism with its belief that individuals were nothing but the emanation of 'spirit'. For Marx the consequence of this 'settling of accounts' was a materialist method that incorporated individuals in social relations as the concrete presupposition, and which sought to expose the fallaciousness of bourgeois freedom.

If we cannot compare like with like, (Mill and Marx as methodological individualists), nor usefully contrast atomism and holism, surely the whole enterprise is pointless? To this the answer has to be no. Mill and Marx were both committed proponents of human freedom, and the roots of this commitment can be found in their respective analyses of human agency. However, when one elaborates on this theme by suggesting that both thinkers were inspired by a notion of freedom as self-determination, and that this notion was to play a central role in the formation of their social theories, then one ventures into the realm of controversy. Often, the debate on this issue has been conducted along the inhibiting lines of the competing claims of positive and negative liberty. But if you believe, as I do, that this distinction fails to capture the essence of Mill's and Marx's understanding of the self-realising agent, then we have to begin a comparison from a different point of departure. The point I have chosen is one from which the origins of their respective theories of self-determination can be charted.[3]

As Steven Lukes[4] has pointed out with his customary eloquence, both thinkers were inheritors of the romantic vision of individuals as self-developers, and as such, both elaborated theories which emphasised the uniquely human capacity for self-improve-

Human nature

ment. But, equally, Mill and Marx took pains to take the analysis of this capacity out of the hands of the idealists and each sought to situate it within his general sciences of society, for without it these sciences would have remained examples of the crude determinism which had denied the existence of the ability to take personal control of our own lives.

The identification of this capacity was to serve a threefold purpose for both thinkers. Firstly, it enabled them to articulate theories of history which placed the self-determining agent at the centre of their explanations for human progress. Secondly, it was the basis for their indictments of unfreedom in bourgeois society. And thirdly, it informed their proposals for an emancipated society of liberated individuals. What is more, Mill and Marx were both convinced that the capacity for self-realisation was itself a product of the ever-changing material existence and accumulated practical experience of individuals in social relations. In effect, both believed that the individual, human society and human history were all scientifically explicable, and both consequently rejected Kantian claims for universal reason, regarding them as being nothing more than the product of unsubstantiated speculation. Human nature, therefore, was just as open to scientlfic explication as any other phenomenon. Mill and Marx, in their own ways, came to the opinion that all that is palpable is all that we know, and all that we know can be controlled.

The next two chapters will critically chart the development of these 'sciences' of human nature along the following lines:

In the first chapter, Mill's account of the formation of human character will be broken down into four distinct, although interrelated, parts for the following reasons: Firstly, in order to support his claim that human progress is the result of individual self-improvement, in particular the consequence of advances made by individuals in the realm of ideas, Mill needed to provide himself with a notion of free will that was compatible with a materialist epistemology, in the hope that he could liberate his system from the determinist confines of orthodox utilitarianism, while at the same time avoiding an 'intuitionist' and hence unscientific view of human agency.[5] Secondly in true classical materialist fashion, Mill presumed that all social phenomena can be reduced to simple laws concerning human psychology, and through a judicious, utilitarian

Method and human nature

use of the principle of association he equipped himself with universal laws of the mind. These laws were to be incorporated in his science of ethology, Mill's theory concerning the formation of character. This was an area of crucial importance, because Mill maintained that if we understood the processes at work when individuals interact with outside circumstances, then these processes could be made to work for the improvement of humankind. Finally, Mill incorporated into his analysis an account of human instincts. These instincts were considered as being biological, animal traits, which at their passionate worst could threaten the stability of society, but at their controlled best contributed to the foundations for a lasting system of justice.

In turning to Marx, I want to suggest that although he categorically denied the existence of a universal human nature, he nevertheless constructed out of his critique of speculative philosophy and political economy a fairly detailed picture of the self-determining human agent. It was a picture based on a number of facts concerning the ways in which humans act upon nature in order to satisfy their needs. These facts were not directly attributable to humankind's biological constitution and as such distinguished it from all other species in the following ways: Firstly, humans are creative; they have developed an increasingly sophisticated capacity for modifying and shaping nature to an individually and/or a socially preconceived plan, to the extent that this activity itself has become a need. Humans are productive agents motivated by the requirement to satisfy needs, and these needs are in turn re-shaped by the forms that production and consumption take. Secondly, human needs are socially given, pursued in social relations, and are constantly modified by the changing conditions of their production and consumption. Thirdly humans evolve a consciousness both of themselves and of their species; in other words they have developed self-consciousness and species-consciousness. Both forms of consciousness are mutually reciprocal in that individuals recognise in themselves and in others a capacity for manipulating nature, for applying a creative project in the world of objects in order to satisfy needs. Humans in this regard are mutually recognitive, they are capable of recognising in other capacities they themselves possess, and of distinguishing each other as subjects as opposed to objects.[6]

CHAPTER 2

Mill and human nature

1   Introduction

What this chapter seeks to reveal is the conditioning link between Mill's theory of human nature as detailed in *A System of Logic* and concept of freedom articulated in his later essays on liberty, utilitarianism and government. The reason for this approach? To reinforce the claim that will be made in the second section regarding Mill's defence of a particular form of individuality and the illiberal implication this defence has when set along side his support for an elitist solution to the problem of democratic tyranny. In adopting this approach I take Mill at his word when he said that subsequent to 1840 he had 'no further mental changes to tell of.'[1] In other words he had reached a stage in his mental development which was to serve as the bases for all his later studies, in short, he had equipped himself with a method, an ontology and an epistemology. This view of the evolution of Mill's thought is not new, eminent 'Mill-ologists' such as Anschutz, McCloskey and Ryan[2] have all subscribed to the opinion that he was a scientific system builder in the true Victorian fashion. But what I am going to suggest is that, not only did Mill construct to his own specifications the foundations for a science of society in the *Logic*, but, he also convinced himself that individuals possessed a capacity for self-improvement, in spite of causal psychological laws, and that this capacity could be exercised to achieve qualitatively superior forms of character. Furthermore, Mill came to believe that 'none but a person of confirmed virtue is completely free', i.e. the only truly liberated individual was one who had successfully exercised the capacity for self-improvement.[3] It was this belief that informed

Mill and human nature

Mill's argument, particularly in the essays on *Utilitarianism* and *Liberty*, for elevating the unhindered pursuit of 'higher pleasures' to the status of the dynamic of history, an argument that had a not unimportant corollary in his lifelong promotion of intellectuals as deserving of public approbation and political authority.[4]

The problem with his novel approach was that Mill was faced with a dilemma: how can a materialist, utilitarian account of human nature successfully incorporate into its associationist epistemology a capacity for autonomous self-development, without succumbing to an intuitionist explanation for reason? Some of the earliest, hostile responses to Mill's proposed solution quickly dismissed 'compatibilism' as ill-conceived and untenable. James Fitzjames Stephen, for example, insisted that a principle of liberty based upon a notion of self-improvement could never be accommodated by a utilitarian morality.[5] More recent proponents of this view have sought to dismiss Mill's unfortunate preoccupation with liberty by explaining it as either by a passing flirtation,[6] or a secondary consideration to his primary preoccupation with utility.[7] Both these perspectives are defended with reference to his tendency to consider sympathetically the ideas of his contemporaries, to extract what he wanted from them, and to include these 'half-truths' in his own works: the muddled eclectic *par excellence*. Essentially, the argument goes, Mill was disheartened and disillusioned by what he perceived to be the consequences of the single-minded promotion of utility in its Benthamite form and turned to the 'opposition' for solace, ending up with a theory of liberty in *On Liberty* that was, in terms of his materialist roots, indefensible.

More recently, others have concentrated on Mill's essays on utilitarianism and liberty in the belief that it is within these texts that the 'true' Mill resides. In these pages, it is maintained by the likes of Gray and Ten, we can find a sufficient and self-sustaining statement of his concept of individuality and a more than adequate explanation of his utilitarian preference for qualitatively superior forms of happiness.[8] More importantly, it is here the principle of liberty is at last elevated to its proper status of *primus inter pares*, with utility playing a vital, although ultimately supporting role. Unfortunately, little reference is made to the possible inconsistency between the free-choosing agent favoured by the Mill-as-libertarian view, and the virtuous, moral and superior self-improver of Book

VI of the *Logic*, who, as we shall see, becomes the legislator and the guarantor of progress in *Representative Government*. Equally absent from the 'new orthodoxy' of a coherent Mill is any proper assessment of the obvious tension that exists within his writings between, on the one hand, the protection of the endangered liberty of self-cultivating agents and, on the other, the pursuit of an enduring and progressive set of social circumstances conducive to general utility (a tension that dogged Mill's mature project from start to finish). Why these apparent oversights?

At this stage, I think it is important to begin by recalling Mill's own words when he said in the *Autobiography*: 'The *Liberty* is likely to survive longer than anything else that I have written (with the possible exception of the *Logic*)'.[9] For me this statement is very revealing because I believe it reveals Mill's preparedness to view both works as equally important examples of his thought, contributions that he felt would stand the test of time. And his reason for making such a claim? The answer is in the *Logic* where Mill demarcates the boundaries between 'Science' and 'Art', i.e. theory and practice, and in so doing indicates to his readers that it is necessary for social reformers and self-improvers, himself amongst them, to equip themselves with both a sound method with which to make sense of the world, and a set of practical responses to its problems. Simply, the much vaunted, empowered self-emancipator was to apply utilitarian prescriptions to an unenlightened generality.

Mill believed that an important element in the equation of self-improvement and social change was a thorough understanding of human psychology. It is surprising, then, that little has been written by the modern proponents of Mill's principle of liberty on the relationship between his own theory and practice, or to be more specific, between his theory of human nature and his concept of freedom. The only notable exceptions to this rule have been the contributions of those who are sceptical of the coherence of Mill's system. Ryan and Smith,[10] for example, have both expressed serious doubts about the asymmetry between Mill's philosophical and political writings, and have employed an extensive knowledge of his methodological works to expose what they believe are weaknesses in his attempt to reconcile free will with determinism. They have also noted the detrimental effect this has on the validity of Mill's claims to an empirical explanation for the capacity of 'individuality' so central to his argument in *On Liberty*. In pursuing this line, the sceptics have taken account of the following facts about Mill's system: (1) Mill himself believed that it was not enough just to claim that liberty was under threat from a number of dangers; those engaged in the task of championing freedom also had to have a systematic scientific explanation of the human condition to enable them to put their theories into practice, empowering them to create the circumstances conducive to emancipation and utility, hence the necessity for Art *and* Science; (2) Mill's work is best understood in terms of a set of interconnected and interdependent parts, each concerned with a particular aspect of human existence, for example *A System of Logic* is both a philosophical response to the critics of empiricism and the methodological basis for the scientific explanation of human behaviour and social relations; (3) much can be learnt about Mill's own view of the *activity* of freedom from works which are not directly concerned with the demise of liberty and the threat to intellectual endeavour.

So, why should it be the case that in a number of recent works which have attempted to re-emphasise the importance and the continued validity of Mill on liberty, the linkages between *On Liberty* and his methodological works have not been more fully explored? Is it because those who have chosen to champion a particular view of Mill's concept of freedom are confronted by anomalies in his position when they turn to other works which do not conform to their own reading? Are the consequences of taking on board a view of freedom present in works other than the celebrated 'Essay' too damaging to the received view of Mill as the progenitor of modern liberal democratic thought?

What I want to suggest in this chapter, partly as a response to these questions, is that Mill constructed a theory of human nature which formed the basis of a broader conception of freedom not entirely reliant upon a utilitarian epistemology, whether the utilitarianism is of the 'stretched' variety or not,[11] and that this theory enabled him to make the claim that only those who were responsible for their own, virtuous self-determination could be said to be truly free. Furthermore, with respect to his aspirations as the inspirer for social reform, Mill wished to provide the philosophical foundations for his political programme. This programme rested on the following assumptions: that the nature of individuals was

Human nature

ascribable, primarily, to causal laws (the other intervening factor being the biological constitution of the species as a whole); that these laws were themselves the basis for a science of society, (a methodological individualism) which, in turn, could inform the direction of social reform; and that only those of confirmed virtue should be entrusted with the crucial task of furthering the advancement of humanity, i.e. intellectual, meritocratic social reformers.

And the results of this approach? In anticipation of the conclusion, a couple of points are worth mentioning: *On Liberty* does not contain the definitive version of Mill's Doctrine of Liberty[12] nor an exhaustive account of his concept 'individuality' *qua* self determination; we cannot isolate or elevate one part of Mill's system at the expense of others, for in doing so we exaggerate the function of that part in relation to the whole and distort the aims of his project; as regards the importance to Mill of utilitarianism and liberty, we need to rebalance the scales to something approaching their original equilibrium; in other words we must remember that Mill attempted to combine and harmonise enlightened reform in the name of the general good with the protection and promotion of liberty.

2   The context

John Stuart Mill's study of the multifarious human condition should be seen as a direct response to several major concerns he believed were crucial: the bankruptcy of classical utilitarianism; the challenge of idealist German metaphysics, and its domestic offshoot, English romanticism; the continued, irrepressible advance of science; the inestimable value of freedom; threats posed by burgeoning mediocrity and prejudice born of ignorance to the continued advance of civilisation. Hence his analysis of human nature and character formation, just as any other part of his system, should be viewed in the light of these preoccupations. With this in mind, this chapter will concern itself with several aspects of Mill's enquiry: the freedom of the individual in a determined world (and the concomitant justification of the freedom of the will); the universal laws of the mind of Mill's utilitarian psychology; the formation of character and his science of ethology; and his ambiguous discussion of human instincts.

But first a brief, though not unimportant digression on the nature of the preoccupations mentioned above and their relevance to my enquiry into Mill's theory of human nature.

Up to, and probably before, his celebrated 'mental crisis' of 1826-27 Mill had had serious doubts about the adequacy of Benthamite psychology, but these uncertainties never led to a total abandonment of utilitarianism. So, even though he recognised, from the benefit of hindsight, the folly of the dogmatic fanaticism to which he had succumbed in his youth, and despite the 'sectarian spirit' of the 'little knot of young men of whom I was one' who professed allegiance to the creed of the Philosophical Radicals,[13] Mill remained convinced of the *general* efficacy of Bentham's observations concerning the formation of human character. In the *Autobiography* he clearly signals his debt to Bentham whose:

> fundamental doctrine [in psychology] was the formation of all human character by circumstances, through the universal Principle of Association, and the consequent unlimited possibility of improving the moral and intellectual condition of mankind by education.[14]

Furthermore, of all Bentham's doctrines none was more important than this, or needs more to be insisted on'.[15] However, in the same work Mill reflected that his youthful enthusiasm for the pursuit of utility for its own sake had been shattered with the revelation that under its explanatory auspices he was nothing more than a determined being,

> I felt as if I were scientifically proved to be the helpless slave of antecedent circumstances – as if my character and that of all others had been formed for us by agencies beyond our control, and was wholly out of our power.[16]

Coinciding with this disturbing conclusion was the realisation that Bentham had not provided a sufficient explanation for the existence of self-consciousness, rather, he and Mill's father had attached 'almost exclusive importance to the ordering of outward circumstances' and had little conception of, and practically no regard for the 'internal culture of the individual'.[17] In preferring to account for most human thought and action in terms of pleasure and pain, Benthamites believed that all conduct was governed 'partly by the different modifications of self-interest, and the passions commonly classified as selfish, partly by sympathies, or occasionally antipathies, towards other beings'. And once they were satisfied that this had been established their 'conception of human nature stops'.[18] For Mill this approach could only ever explain one half of the processes leading to the formation of character, and, consequently, provided only one part of our understanding of the individual as a moral being; the other half – self-culture, self-education – remained a blank in Bentham's system, much to utilitarianism's cost.[19]

Whether Mill turned to the insights of English romanticism before, during, or after his intellectual depression is not important, the fact is that he did so at all, however, is vital to our understanding of his mental development. His assimilation of the artistic and philosophical observations of the likes of Wordsworth, Coleridge, Sterling, Maurice and Carlyle only served to reinforce the young Mill's belief in the capacity for self-improvement, as well as his growing realisation that individuals, if liberated from the strictures of habit, custom and psychological fatalism, could be almost entirely responsible for the formation of their own characters. However, Mill drew the line of his commitment at the intuitionist foundations of the home-grown inheritors of German idealism. Although they praised the existence of a self-perfecting inner culture, and celebrated the emotions, they remained for Mill exponents of a metaphysic that he had no time for;[20] in fact, the philosophical school to which they owed allegiance was anathema to his own empiricist upbringing, and he spent the rest of his life attacking what he saw as the greatest intellectual threat to the primacy of a materialist rationale: 'the German, or *a priori* view of human knowledge, and of the knowing faculties, [which] is likely for some time longer to predominate amongst those who occupy themselves with such enquiries'.[21]. As a consequence Mill's self-professed role became that of the synthesiser, or practical eclectic, whose intention was to 'harmonise the true portions of discordant theories'.[22] This is not to say that he set out to establish a wholly new explanatory system; two things remained constant during his cerebral travails, one was has continued faith in a revamped utilitarianism with its accompanying scientific pretensions, and the other, his unfailing opposition to intuitionism. Thus, the *System of Logic* was nothing more than 'a text book of the opposite doctrine – that which derives all knowledge from experience, and all moral and intellectual qualities principally from the direction given to the associations'.[23] Self-culture was to be captured and tamed by an expanded associationist epistemology, and put to work in the service of a utilitarian pursuit of progress.

Mill's objective, it should be re-emphasised, was change, the progressive transformation of individuals and society. And the predominant motive force of such progress? Intellectual endeavour, the forming of new ideas and the pursuit of knowledge in all spheres. During his own lifetime Mill had witnessed dramatic advances in the natural sciences which had given rise to technological innovation, productive abundance and the potential for material prosperity. All this had reaffirmed Mill's confidence in the ability of humanity to reach a higher realm of civilisation freed from the dead hand of necessity: 'Every considerable advance in material civilisation has been preceded by an advance in knowledge'. Indeed, he went so far as to claim that:

> each of these [intellectual movements] has been a primary agent in making society what it was at each successive period, while society was but secondarily instrumental in making them, each of them (so far as causes can be assigned for its existence) being mainly an emanation not from the practical life of the period, but from the previous state of belief and thought.[24]

However, there was one area of knowledge that remained in its infancy, languishing within the sphere of random empirical observation: the study of humanity, that 'most complex and most difficult subject of study on which the human mind can be engaged',[25] and unless substantial progress was secured in this crucial field, the continued improvement of the species would remain problematic. Such a study, Mill recommended, should be subject to the same processes of enquiry employed in the verification of laws governing simpler phenomena; in other words, what was required for the elaboration of the sciences of human nature and society, was a method, and Mill little doubted his ability to furnish the psychologist and sociologist with what he believed they needed,

> the only thing that I believe I am really fit for is the investigation of abstract truth, and the more abstract the better. If there is any science which I am capable of promoting, I think it is the science of science itself, the science of investigation – of method.[26]

Human nature

This intention was reaffirmed by Mill in *A System of Logic*, the purpose of which was to supply a 'Connected View of the Principles of Evidence and the Methods of Scientific Investigation'.[27] Modestly, his ambition did not stretch to providing the definitive science, he preferred to liken his role to that of a guide, 'to point out the way' for future examinations of the human condition.[28] But this task was no less important because:

> he who can throw most light on the subject of method will do most to forward that alliance among the most advanced intellects and characters of the age, which is the only definite object I ever have in literature or philosophy, so far as I have any *general* object at all.[29]

Mill was convinced that if he could supply a unifying method for a multi-dimensional study of humanity he would be making no small contribution to an imperative of historical dimensions: the forging of an alliance between the intellectual luminaries of the age to ensure the continued progressive development of civilisation. Again, we return to Mill's preoccupation with change and his faith in humanity's ability to control it purposefully. This enthusiasm of his for social progress had originally been given analytical force by the theories of history propounded by Saint-Simon and his followers (especially Gustave d'Eichtal):

> I was greatly struck with the connected view which they for the first time presented to me, of the natural order of human progress; and especially with their division of all history into organic periods and critical periods.[30]

Critical periods were of particular interest to Mill, because, apart from anything else, he believed that he was living through one. It was an era of intellectual, social and political confusion; a time characterised by competition in the realm of ideas, as well as in the market place; a period of philosophical and spiritual malaise. But, it was also an epoch of dynamism and frenetic creativity, of experimentation and discovery, the birth place of a new, organic order. And although he was later to shed the rigid distinction between the critical and the organic,[31] Mill continued to insist that if we as a species were to continue to advance then we should be prepared to allow the maximum expression of individual talents and initiatives, which after all, were the driving force of history.

To find this amalgamation of utilitarianism, idealism, science and history we need look no further than Book VI of a *A System of Logic*, for it is here that Mill articulates his analysis of psychology, his science of society and his theory of history, all very much in that order. The end result was, for Mill, a unifying analytical procedure, the importance of which should not be underestimated when we turn to other works that initially appear devoid of method. The 'inverse deductive, or historical method' was one which 'involves observing uniformities in nature, e.g. from a study of history, and inferring them back to known psychological causal laws'.[32] This, he believed, would explain the formation and dynamics of human society, an explanation which relied upon the formulation of sciences of the mind and the formation of character, of social life and of social change:

> all phenomena of society are phenomena of human nature, generated by the action of outward circumstances upon masses of human beings and if therefore, the phenomena of human thought, feeling and action, are subject to fixed laws, the phenomena of society cannot but conform to fixed laws..[33]

Once armed with such a method the agents of progress could get on with the real business of social change. And the identity of these illustrious harbingers of change? Free, self-determining, virtuous individuals, who, through their pursuit of liberty, would have gained a better understanding both of themselves – their limitations and their possibilities – and of their community. So, from the ranks of the self-cultured would be drawn the enlightened, dispassionate legislators, who presumably would possess a superior knowledge of Mill's proposed sciences of human nature and society, who would be equipped with his notion of utility in its 'largest sense', and would consequently be able to provide the general prescriptions for general improvement. The inevitable progress of humanity would, for the first time, be harnessed by humanity itself.

Mill insisted that the basis for all scientific analyses of social phenomena was a theory of human nature, and that before we could begin to contemplate practical reform he urged us to equip ourselves with an understanding of human psychology, and that is where we shall start from.

3 Self-culture, free will and liberty

Free will, or the desire to change one's character, was, for Mill, central to the analysis or individual human nature. Without a full appreciation of this concept, any contemplation of freedom would be totally inadequate. His examination begins with a question:

> Are the actions of human beings, like all other natural events, subject to invariable law? Does the constancy of causation, which is the foundation of every scientific theory of successive phenomena, really obtain among them?[34]

This, it transpires, is only the preamble to a general discussion of the celebrated controversy of free will and determinism, or as Mill termed it, 'Liberty and Necessity'. This debate reveals Mill as an eclectic at work, employing countervailing systems of thought and combining 'half truths' in the formulation of new hypotheses. However, far from creating a completely original and unique system of thought which transcended the malaise of half truths, Mill placed himself squarely in the realm of necessity. His utilitarian background remained secure in spite of all as a basis for his analysis of humanity: 'I found the fabric of my old and taught opinions giving way in many fresh places, and I never allowed it to fall to pieces, but was incessantly occupied in weaving it anew'.[35]

With regard to the study of human nature, this 'weaving anew' resulted in Mill adopting the concept of free will but within a necessitarian methodology. His approach, in reconciling what he saw as conflicting theories, provides the reader with Mill's perception of human nature (as it appears in the *Logic*). He begins his investigation of liberty and necessity by posing the question as to 'whether the law of causality applies in the same strict sense to human actions as to other phenomena'.[36] In response, a defender of necessity would assert that an individual's ability to choose and act for him or herself is necessary and inevitable, that the capacities and characteristics of all individuals are reducible to causal agencies. According to Mill, this affirmative answer to the original question is opposed by the idealist, 'metaphysical' philosophers who would claim that the will is not determined by antecedents, but determines itself, such that our own volitions are not the effects of causes. Mill viewed this approach with a considerable degree of sympathy. As far as he was concerned, the doctrine of necessity was a direct successor to the materialist, empiricist philosophies of the eighteenth century, and, by the time Mill was writing, had become, much to his regret, a dogmatised discipline. The 'utopianists' in particular, and especially the followers of Robert Owen, were he believed, culpable of such an offence. And it was Bentham and, more damagingly for Mill, his proselytisers who had apparently condemned humanity to an existence determined by outward circumstances.

Having himself been a temporary victim of Bentham's shallow psychology,[37] – 'The description so often given of a Benthamite, as a mere reasoning machine, was during two or three years of my life not altogether untrue of me' [38] – Mill well understood the response of the metaphysical philosophers, who were reacting against the image created by the necessitarian determinists of a 'manufactured man'. Even though he saw this idealist rejection as essentially a misguided one, Mill nevertheless believed that it provided a useful service in exposing many of the crude misinterpretations of the doctrine of necessity adhered to by most of its supporters and practitioners.

> I do not deny that the doctrine, as sometimes held, is open to these imputations; for the misapprehension in which I will be able to show that they originate, unfortunately is not confined to the opponents of the doctrine, but is participated in by many, perhaps we might say by most, of its supporters.[39]

What Mill attempted to do was to answer the criticisms of the metaphysicians by establishing beyond reasonable doubt that free will was consistent with a correct reading of the doctrine of necessity. At the same time, he attempted in the *Logic* to rescue necessitarianism from its 'fatalist' assumptions and conclusions in an effort to posit a semi-autonomous agent capable of participating in the process leading to the formation of character. Mill's 'compatibilism' in the *Logic* was his attempt at reconciling the ostensibly irreconcilable:

> The metaphysical theory of free –will, as held by philosophers (for the practical feeling of it, common in greater or less degree to all mankind is in no way inconsistent with the contrary theory) was invented because the supposed alternative of admitting human actions to be necessary was deemed inconsistent with everyone's intuitive consciousness, as well as humiliating to the pride, and even degrading to the moral nature of man.[40]

Human nature

Apart from the assumption of a moral human nature, both Mill's interpretation of necessity, and that of its misinterpreters, held in common the general premiss of the doctrine – that if we knew an individual thoroughly, knew the motives that influenced that person's mind, taking into account the character and disposition of the subject – 'the manner in which he will act might be unerringly inferred', and that if we knew all the inducements which act upon the individual, 'we could foretell his conduct with as much certainty as we can predict any physical event.'[41] But Mill had parted company with his former necessitarian colleagues because he was not prepared to accept their fatalist conclusions. Necessitarians of this persuasion believe that human actions are determined by the human character which itself is conditioned by extraneous circumstances, i.e. existing social relations, physical restraints and antecedent collective experience. The necessitarian accordingly believes: '...that his nature is such, or that his circumstances have so moulded his character, that nothing can now prevent him from feeling and acting in a particular way, or at least that no effort of his own can hinder it...'[42] The most extreme exponent of this doctrine is inevitably a fatalist because he is convinced that '...His character is formed *for* him, and not *by* him; therefore his wishing that it had been formed differently is of no use, he has no power to alter it.'[43] Mill believed that this 'grand error' should be rectified if we were to obtain a truer depiction of human character and of the processes leading to its formation. His contribution to this cause consisted of postulating a process of character formation which adds to the factors of causation the ability to alter one's own character. Central to his analysis is the concept of self-culture, an integral, causal element of the human character which, in conjunction with 'outward circumstances', should be taken into consideration during the course of any enquiry into the formation of human nature. Individuals therefore have, to a degree, a power to alter their characters, and only through a free expression of this power can they ever hope to achieve genuine individual freedom:

> [Man's] character is formed by his circumstances (including amongst these his particular organisation), but his own desire to mould it in a particular way is one of those circumstances, and by no means one of the least influential.[44]

However, this desire cannot be used at will. It may be a propensity possessed by all humans, but it is a characteristic that is rarely evident in the process of character formation, because either we are not aware of its potential, or we would deny its very existence:

> We cannot, indeed, directly will to be different from what we are ... we, when our habits are not too inveterate, can, by willing the requisite means, make ourselves different ... we can place ourselves under the influence of other circumstances. We are exactly as capable of making our own character, *if we will*, as others are of making it for us.[45]

Therefore, 'if we will', we can change our character. This capacity appears to take on the form of a metaphysical free will, an innate propensity of human nature. Notwithstanding, Mill retrieves his postulate from the realms of idealism, and seeks to replace it firmly within a materialist framework by explaining that our capability to change our characters is formed for us by experience: 'experience of the painful consequences of the character we previously had, or by some strong feeling of admiration or aspiration accidentally aroused.'[46] This suggests that our desire to change our characters is explicable through an application of the traditional utilitarian principles of pain and pleasure. It is another circumstance, all be it an internal one, which has a conditioning impact on our response to outward experience. Either the painful consequences of a previous character, or the pleasurable expectations aroused by an appraisal of alternative examples of individual characters, appear to be the stimuli which form the desire to change. But experience and desire would appear to be two separate elements in the process that leads to character formation, and Mill's analysis does not allow for an *a priori* intermediate process (reason?) which transforms the raw material of experience into the specialised, individuated desire for character change. In short, for Mill the mind is apparently a receptacle for experience which is inexplicably transformed into an individual desire to change one's character. His inductive scientific method can take him no further than this unless he is prepared to consider the existence of a capacity for individual self-improvement that is uniquely outwith the empiricist parameters which he believes are central to all other explanations. For Mill to leave it at this appears all the more unsatisfactory when we consider the fact that he sought to elevate individual self-improvement to the status of paramount importance.

The personal propensity to reform one's character became an integral element of Mill's view of a future liberated age, to the extent that this capacity became for him a conscious sentiment of moral freedom. Moral freedom, therefore, is the achieved desire to modify our character, itself explicable through an understanding of the causal nature of experience. 'A person feels morally free who feels that his habits or his temptations are not his master but he theirs'.[47] But who or what is the ultimate determinant? If the desire to change our character is reliant upon the causal nature of experience, and that desire is our feeling of moral freedom, our moral freedom is, in the last analysis, determined for us.

As such, Mill posited a *semi-autonomous* individual, one who, in the first instance, is determined by circumstances, education and experience, but one who also possesses a capacity for personal change that is exercised in conditions of complete freedom from restraint.

> It is of course necessary, to render our consciousness of Freedom complete, that we should nave succeeded in making our character all we have hitherto attempted to make it; for if we have wished and not attained, we have, to that extent not power over our character – we are not free.[48]

4 Laws of the mind and the science of ethology

Self-culture, free will, or the desire to change one's character, is, Mill believed, a capacity which, as with other elements of human nature and character formation, is – potentially – scientifically explicable, and it is a purpose of Book VI of the *Logic* to provide a secure methodological base for the future scientific investigation of human nature. Mill identifies in the *Logic* two sets of laws, which not only explain the formation of individual human character, but also are necessary in the formation of a General Science of Society, itself the prior condition for any effective reform of society:

> The actions and feelings of human beings in the social state, are, no doubt, entirely governed by psychological and ethological laws: whatever influence any cause exercises upon the social phenomena, it exercises through those laws.[49]

To understand social phenomena one has to understand human

Mill and human nature

nature, especially the laws of its formation, the laws of the mind and the laws of ethology. Indeed 'Ethology itself ... is the immediate foundation of the Social Science'.[50]

For Mill, the silence of human nature would be an intermediate science, one which would be capable of establishing general laws of causation, that would provide a complete explanation, if there were no other intervening causes. But observation and experimentation show us that there are a whole number of secondary causes, which on their own appear insignificant, but in combination are in a position to change the effects of the general causal laws. However, as with sciences such as 'Tidology', Mill believed in the efficacy of general laws of causation 'which effect the phenomenon in all cases, and in a considerable degree'.[51] This could never be an exact science in the sense that the thoughts, feelings and actions of all individuals could be predicted with complete certainty. Any investigation would find it impossible to identify all the circumstances in which each individual might be placed, but for the purpose of general prediction of human behaviour in particular circumstances, approximate truths concerning causation would be sufficient.

Thoughts, emotions, volitions and sensations are all states of mind, each contributing to what is commonly perceived as human nature, but the interpretations as regards their origin differ considerably. Therefore, as with liberty and necessity, Mill attempted to steer a course between two extremes, German idealist metaphysics and necessitarianism:

> The majority of those who speculate on human nature prefer dogmatically to assume that the mental differences which they perceive, or think they perceive, among human beings, are the ultimate facts, incapable of being either explained or altered ... The German school of metaphysical speculation ... has had this among many other injurious influences.

Thus, the view of human nature as universal and historical is opposed by an analysis which insists that there are no laws of the mind in the sense that Mill employs the term, and all workings of human consciousness are, in principle, reducible to physical, bodily processes over which individuals have no control. Positivists such as Comte regarded mental science as a 'mere branch, though the highest and most recondite branch, of the science of

37

Human nature

physiology'; Comte went even further and not only 'claims the scientific cognisance of moral and intellectual phenomena exclusively for physiologists', but also 'denies to psychology, or mental philosophy properly so called, the character of a science'.[53] As with his discussion of a correct understanding of free will, Mill, recognising the dangers of crude necessitarian analysis – evident in both his view of human nature, and the threat to individual liberty apparent in its programmes for the future – tempered the determinism of the traditional utilitarian interpretation by providing an explanation of the formation of states of mind. This, in turn, established general laws of mind which formed the basis of Mill's explanation of the formation of human nature.

Mill admitted that each mental state may indeed have an antecedent nervous state, but that our knowledge of the latter is so incomplete that for a long time to come we must rely upon the more accurate information concerning the 'uniformities of succession among the states of mind' obtained through observation and experiment. Psychology or the science of the mind may well be a derivative science, reliant upon physiological laws, and Mill insisted that this must be borne in mind when studying mental states. But, for the present, a science of the mind must be pursued as an independent enquiry. Mill again attempted to encompass within the eclectic analysis divergent interpretations, situating within each individual mind laws of mental activity, which *may* be the result of physiological laws, but, for the time being exist as independent laws in their own right. These laws rely, in the first instance, upon circumstances which supply the mind with a variety of impressions exciting in the agent a state of consciousness. Once such an impression has been made it can be recalled as a state of consciousness that resembles the original state of consciousness or impression, and can be achieved without the presence or the original cause or impression. 'This law is expressed by saying in the language of Hume, that every mental *impression* has its *Idea*.'[54] As well as the laws of mental activity there were the 'laws of association' which Mill saw as being the other main group of 'simple or elementary Laws of Mind' and he recommended that the reader should refer to James Mill's 'professedly psychological work', *Analysis of the Phenomena of the Human Mind*.[55] Here, the laws of ideas are examined in some depth, especially the 'principal laws of

Mill and human nature

association, [which] along with many of their applications, are copiously exemplified, and with a masterly hand.'[56]

These simple laws of mind, Mill believed, generate all the complex laws of thought and feeling. They are laws that are universal elements of Mill's philosophy of human nature, serving to explain the workings of the human mind and providing the laws by which mental and physical impressions, whether received simultaneously or successively, are assimilated and processed into mental states, both simple and complex. 'the general laws of association prevail among [the] more intricate states of mind, in the same manner as among the simpler ones.' Therefore, 'a desire, an emotion, an idea of the higher order or abstraction, even our judgements and volitions when they have become habitual, are called up by association, according to precisely the same laws as our simple ideas'[57] What emerges from Mill's examination is a view of the workings of the human mind which is still essentially necessitarian in outlook, in that human character is the product of outward, empirically verifiable, causes, but each individual operates according to universal laws of mind. Mental differences, as well as mental similarities, are hence made explicable by employing these general laws, and all who speculate on the origins of mental states (as well as, no doubt, all those engaged in social reform) should "take the trouble of fitting themselves, by the requisite processes of thought', and before implementing any change 'referring those mental differences to the outward causes by which they are for the most part produced, and on the removal of which they would cease to exist.'[58]

Although for Mill human beings are not merely biological machines (as envisaged by Comte), they are for the most part conditioned by education, circumstance and the related causal laws of mind, determinants which were held to have direct implications for the vision of a future society. Therefore, if, through the application of the correct procedures as outlined by Mill, we comprehend the roles of each in forming human nature, we can mould systems of education (understood in its most general sense which includes the inculcation of superior norms and higher character traits) and the circumstances of social relations into forms which serve the general purpose of encouraging the development of both emancipated individuals and an enlightened society.

Human nature

However, a knowledge of the laws of the mind alone was insufficient for the purpose of change. Mill insisted that a science of the formation of character was also required. He chose to call this science ethology, and it was to be the link between the universal laws of the mind governing individual human character and the science of the 'actions of collective masses of mankind, and the various phenomena which constitute human life.'[59] Empirical laws provided Mill with observations of human affairs within a particular realm of experience. They were illustrations of the consequences of the causal laws of human nature and nothing more. These empirical laws were not to be taken as 'ultimate laws of human action; they are not the principles of human nature, but the results of those principles under the circumstances in which mankind have happened to be placed.'[60] Unfortunately, Mill observed, it was the common practice for metaphysical philosophers, economic theorists and capitalists to adopt transitory, empirical laws of human nature as universal truths, basing their respective analysis on these 'truths'. Mill criticised the economists for 'regarding not any economic doctrine, but their experience of mankind, as of universal validity; mistaking temporary or local phases of human character for human nature itself.'[61] Capitalists also made a misconception, in that they viewed the

> normal state of human beings [as] that of struggling to get on ... that the trampling, crushing, elbowing, and treading on each other's heads, which form the existing type of human life, are the most desirable lot of kind, or anything but the disagreeable symptoms of one of the phases of industrial progress.[62]

For Mill, ethology goes beyond this circumstantial, historical picture of transitory human nature, providing us with laws of causation, which explain the formation of the wide variety of human feelings and actions. 'In other words, mankind have not one universal character, but there exist universal laws of the Formation of Character.'[63] Although the laws of ethology are 'derivative laws, resulting from the general Laws of Mind', as a science it remained independent of the science of psychology.[64] Where psychology concerns itself with the elementary laws of mind, ethology is the subsequent science which largely determines the type of character formed by the interaction of the general laws of mind and the specific set of circumstances. But this science of character formation, Mill admitted, can never be an exact one. This, however, is not a failing; as a science, it need only inform us that 'certain means have a *Tendency* to produce a given effect, and that others have a tendency to frustrate it'.[65] Ethology, therefore, would be the science of the hypothetical laws which affirm tendencies rather than unequivocal facts, tendencies which assert that a given cause will produce a particular reaction as long as the process operates uninterrupted. Mill believed that this limited 'scientific' knowledge would be enough to equip enlightened reformers with the tools to change circumstances:

> When the circumstances of an individual or of a nation are in any considerable degree under our control, we may, by our knowledge of tendencies, be enabled to shape those circumstances in a manner much more favourable to the ends we desire, than the shape which they would of themselves assume. This is the limit of our power; but within this limit the power is a most important one.[66]

Ethology provided Mill in the *Logic* with his *axiomata media*, the middle principles, which lie between the laws of common observation and those of the highest generalisations, between the practical knowledge of humanity in particular circumstances and the science of the laws of mind. The purpose of such a science is to prepare the way for a practical application of the middle principles through the agency of education in its broadest sense. 'According to this definition, Ethology is the science which corresponds to the art of education; in the widest sense of the term ...'[67] And despite his eventual abandonment of any further investigation into the laws conditioning the formation of character, Mill never doubted the necessity of a clear understanding of how individuals interact with one another and with outward circumstances for those engaged in the crucial task of reforming society. Likewise, he always maintained that the structure of any society could only be fully comprehended if we were equipped with an extensive analysis of human nature in general. However, there were certain aspects of human existence which Mill never incorporated successfully into an all-embracing science of human nature.

Human nature

5 Instincts

While discussing the human condition in the *Logic*, Mill paused to consider a number of 'mental facts' that do not appear to conform to those modes of explanation which furnished the laws of mind. These facts are the 'various instincts of animals, and the portion of human nature which corresponds to those instincts'.[68] Mill admitted that these instincts are beyond the realms of an explanation that rests on psychological causes alone. He appeared to be far more favourably disposed towards a genetic explanation of their existence. 'There is great reason to think that they have as positive, and even as direct and immediate, a connection with physical conditions of the brain and the nerves, as any of our mere sensations have.'[69]

Not only, then, are there universal laws of mind, but also, Mill seemed to suggest, there are universal physiological predispositions which partially determine human character. Mill left it at that; humans possess a number of animal instincts, and although he added that these instincts may be modified or 'entirely conquered', he failed to identify the nature of those instincts and the extent of their influence in the formation of human character. Mill attempted to formulate physiological laws of mind peculiar to humankind, universal laws that would provide the basis for an understanding of the workings of human nature. However, in the *Logic* he appears to have left a whole area of human activity uncharted, and, maybe more importantly, he chose not to discuss the interrelationship between these instincts and the universal mental laws of causation.

Elsewhere, however, especially in his later works, Mill's discussion of propensities, desires and impulses and their effect on human character formation is, perhaps, more enlightening. Innate human sentiments, he suggests, do exist and are discernible from those elements of character directly ascribable to the laws of mind, particularly the principle of association.

Just as the history of humanity provides us with evidence of a transitory human character so it also informs us about enduring characteristics, which according to Mill have been of vital importance to human progress. One such characteristic is the faculty of speculation, which, when all things are considered, 'Is the main determining cause of the social progress'.[70] Although Mill thought it a 'great error' to claim that this faculty is 'among the more powerful propensities of human nature', he did not deny that it is a propensity, a natural tendency or disposition.[71] He made little attempt to establish the origin of this propensity which is central to Mill's belief in progress) but he did note that some advances in the investigation of mental states were being achieved in the field of cerebral physiology. No doubt such enquiries would presumably provide an explanation for two other propensities which regularly appear in Mill's studies and remain essentially unexplored; those related to *self interest* and *social sympathy*:

> ... the strongest propensities of uncultivated or half cultivated human nature (being the purely selfish ones, and those a sympathetic character which partake most of the nature of selfishness) evidently tend in themselves to disunite mankind; not to unite them – to make them rivals, not confederates; social existence is only possible by a disciplining of those more powerful propensities, which consist in subordinating them to a common system of opinions. [72]

Mill regarded self-interest as a major threat to the general happiness of the community and the workings of good government.[73] In *On Liberty* he addressed himself to the problem of uncontrolled desires and impulses which 'are as much a part of perfect human being as beliefs and restraints', and concluded that 'strong impulses are only perilous when not properly balanced', since

> ... one set of aims and inclinations is developed into strength, while others, which ought to co-exist with them, remain weak and inactive. It is because men's desires are strong that they act ill; it is not because their consciences are weak.[74]

Social conscience is itself attributable to what Mill termed social sympathy, an innate element of human nature, which was also at the root of justice and morality. In *Utilitarianism*, when discussing the ultimate sanction of the principle of utility, Mill established what he believed to be the natural basis of sentiment for utilitarian morality.

> This firm foundation is that of the social feelings of mankind; the desire to be in unity with our fellow creatures, which is already a powerful principle in human nature, and happily one of those which tend to become stronger, even without express inculcation, from the advancing civilisations.[75]

Human nature

An individual's own social conscience would be one of the checks and balances limiting the dangerous excesses of the more powerful propensities. But this social conscience once supplemented and strengthened by a system of ethics, would not only reinforce humanity's natural susceptibility for social feeling, but also reinforce the moral tenor of society as a whole.

Therefore, morality itself is not innate, as the intuitionists would have us believe; but, according to Mill the social feelings, and the accompanying 'social state [are] at once so natural, so necessary, and so habitual to man'.[76] In the same work, in a chapter entitled 'On the Connection between Justice and Utility' Mill employed both the self-regarding and the sympathetic propensities of human nature in his examination of justice. The sentiment of justice consists of two major elements, 'the desire to punish a person who has done harm, and the knowledge or belief that there is some definite individual or individuals to whom harm has been done'.[77] Mill maintained that both these elements emanate from two sentiments, 'both in the highest degree natural, and which either are or resemble instincts; the impulse of self-defence and the feeling of sympathy'.[78] Humanity shares with all animals these sentiments, but to a higher degree, in that we are able to sympathise with all human beings and that our more developed intelligence provides us with a wider qualitative range to our innate propensities. It is this more developed intelligence – itself the product of a natural inquisitiveness enhanced by the laws of mind and the principles of association – which prevents our natural instinct for retribution from becoming indiscriminate. Here the principle of association encourages through education and experience the moralising potential of our social feelings; it disciplines those natural qualities which threaten the peaceful co-existence of free individuals while cultivating those propensities beneficial to the community and the individual.[79]

For Mill, instincts, or innate sympathies, appeared to have a considerable degree of influence in the formation of human character. Potentially, they were also constructive, providing they were harnessed correctly, controlled and channelled by civilised rules of behaviour. Once more Mill urged those who would take up the challenge of reform to be fully conversant with the mysteries of human nature, to take advantage of the raw material of pliant natural traits and to be wary of those desires that could disrupt the successful pursuance of the project.

6   Conclusion

Mill began his systematic investigation of human nature in the *Logic*. This enquiry was partially a response to two distinct yet interrelated dilemmas, one personal, the other philosophical. While under the influence of Bentham, Mill was committed more than most to the philosophy of necessity and the doctrine of utility. During his formative years, the general happiness principle remained paramount; the determining elements of pain and pleasure, linked with the view of humanity as essentially selfish, conditioned the young Mill's view of human nature. The simple prescription for the attainment of a good and happy society was the enlightened ordering of outward circumstances.

His 'mental crisis' put paid to his youthful enthusiasm for a system of thought that had appeared so rational and yet, apparently, was so susceptible to withering attack from social scientists and philosophers alike. Macaulay had questioned perceptively the limited premises employed by Mill's father in his *Essay on Government*,[80] which placed in doubt the efficacy of his philosophical method. For their part, the 'Colridgians', especially Maurice and Sterling, challenged the utilitarian assumption that human nature was solely determined by outward circumstances, reasserting a belief in the individual as an autonomous being, capable of self-culture. Prompted by his own anxiety, Mill began to doubt the efficacy of the pursuit of individual happiness as an end in itself: 'All my happiness was to be found in the continual pursuit of this end. The end had ceased to charm, and how could there ever again be an interest in the means? I seemed to have nothing left to live for'.[80]

The Logic became a reasoned attack on the conservative doctrines of idealist metaphysics, but an attack made from a standpoint which itself was a product of a critical re-evaluation. Mill had noted with despair the development of a popular, yet crude, interpretation of necessitarianism, a doctrine with an admirable eighteenth century pedigree. Therefore, in conjunction with his critique of idealism, Mill set out to refurbish the premises and methodology of an otherwise sound doctrine, providing it with

Human nature

a progressive historical perspective. The purpose was not only to explain the present nature of individual character and human society, but also to provide a scientific theory of humanity's progress. Inseparable from a theory of history was an exhaustive science of human nature, and Mill elucidated what he believed constituted the causal laws of such a science.

The laws of mind (encompassing those of the formation of original ideas and of association) and the derivative laws of character formation were intended to provide the predominant determinants of human nature. According to this analysis while human nature *per se* is transitory (which, for Mill, served scientifically to disprove the metaphysicians' claim that human nature is universal and ahistorical) the laws governing the formation of character are not, since they constitute the enduring elements of human nature. Armed with these precepts, the virtuous reformer, spurred on by the *Logic* could probably agree with Mill's conclusion: 'It is certain that, in human beings at least, differences in education and in outward circumstances are capable of affording an adequate explanation of by far the greatest portion of character'.[82]

However, sixteen years after the publication of the first edition of the *Logic*, he was prepared to admit that:

> Human nature is not a machine to be built after a model, and set to do exactly the work prescribed for it, but a tree, which requires to grow and develop itself on all sides, according to the tendency of inward forces which make it~living thing.[83]

He had already attempted to accommodate within his revised necessitarian framework a concept of free will, a provision which sought to explain an individual's ability to choose – the cornerstone of his belief in self-emancipation. By the time he was writing *Utilitarianism* and *On Liberty* he had moved on to a view of human nature that incorporated the formative role of instincts and propensities. Some of these dispositions were shared with other sentient beings, others were peculiar to humanity (such as the species' distinctive ingenuity and its heightened capacity for self-awareness and self-education). As has been illustrated, these propensities assumed the position of sanctions in Mill's justification of the efficacy of a utilitarian morality. This was in direct response to his age-old rivals, the intuitionists or metaphysical philosophers, who had challenged the premises of his adopted and revised doctrine, necessity. Nevertheless, in the *Logic* Mill attempted to assimilate into his own analysis such universal concepts as free will, while at the same time insisting on the essential malleability of human nature. Ethology and the principle of association were based on the assumption that human nature is malleable, but Mill eventually held a position that appeared to confuse matters by alluding to phenomena that were not dissimilar to universal principles.[84] The possible difficulties resulting from such an alliance seem not to have concerned Mill; suffice to say that any individual engaged in the pursuit of change would require an extensive knowledge of what became a complex phenomenon, namely the science of the human condition. But even Mill himself admitted that such a science could never be exhaustive. Such an an admission jeopardised the possibility of attaining any useful understanding of the relationship between individuals and society, so necessary, Mill had initially believed, for an enlightened restructuring of society. Scientific certainty when applied to human nature was, in the end, severely compromised by Mill's earnest attempt to incorporate facets that failed to satisfy the rigours of his own empiricist method. Whether these be connected with 'volition' or will, or with instincts and sentiments, the end result was an inconsistent analysis that persistently undermined Mill's adherence to a causal, empiricist explanation. Ironically, Mill sought to provide enlightened reformers with the scientific methods he believed were necessary for lasting social reform, and yet was ultimately incapable of explaining, through the application of those same scientific methods, the human capacity of self-cultivation, the full development of which was an essential qualification for any budding social reformer.

CHAPTER 3

Marx and 'homo faber'

1 Introduction

'Marx and human nature'. Until relatively recently the conjoining of these two would have stimulated howls of derision from an audience imbued with the scientific certainly of dialectical materialism. Once the furore had died down there would have been the chanting of the mantra: 'The essence of man is no abstraction inherent in each single individual. In its reality it is the ensemble of social relations';[1] followed by the reprise: 'It is not the consciousness of men that determines their being, but, on the contrary, their social being that determines their consciousness.'[2] With this reassuring and textually faithful rendition having weakened the case for a more open-ended view of Marx's analysis of human nature the misguided interlocutor would receive the *coup de gras*: 'circumstances make men just as much as men make circumstances.'[3] The meeting would adjourn secure in the knowledge that once again Marx has seen off those who would seek to encumber him with a anachronistic philosophical notion of 'species essence', and that He had reaffirmed the inevitability of historical change; fate was in the hands of the impersonal dialectic and its guardian, the Cominform. Enter state left (circa 1930s): *The Economic and Philosophic Manuscripts* of 1844 accompanied by assorted unpublished extracts and lengthy exegetical meanderings (e.g. *Grundrisse, The German Ideology, Critique of Hegel's Philosophy of Law*[4]). After an initial gestation period, these works reinforced the post Second World War political disenchantment with 'Marxism-Leninism', providing a theoretical re-evaluation of the development of the great man's intellect, the content of the 'classic' texts, and the validity of the received, Third International, revolutionary programme. The perceptive insights of Korsch, Lukács and the Hegelian Frankfurters appeared vindicated. For the first time the 'official version' was confronted with the chapter-and-verse refutation by the originator himself of much of its deterministic fatalism. This was particularly significant in the west, where the movement had the luxury of tearing itself apart – although Yugoslavia also experienced similar academic ructions.[5] The practical repercussions of the battle between the competing inheritors of the 'word' made themselves more than apparent in that legendary period of revolutionary revivalism, 1968. The consequences? A divided marxian intelligentsia and a disputatious revolutionary party. In one corner, the philosophical humanists, who continued to claim that the answer lay in the juvenilia of 1844; in another, the old guard relying for solace on the *Manifesto, Capital* and Engels; and in the third, the dialectical discipline of Althusser and Poulantzas, whose rigorous *diamat* was elevated by their followers to its 'rightful' explanatory exclusivity, although theoretically, the account was no more than a elaborate re-affirmation of the old-fashioned inevitability doctrine.

Structuralism accounted for the persistence of Hegelian and idealist concepts and terminology in the later works as unintended and unimportant vestiges of Marx's intellectual adolescence, while the early, pre-Theses writings could be dismissed as the utterings of an unreconstructed bourgeois radical. 'Forces' and 'relations' were reinstated to theoretical primacy, the individual demoted to the status of conditioned consequence, and humanism and human nature banished to the realm of sentimentality. The epistemological break appeared irreparable. But there remained in the structuralists' cherished texts the nagging irritation of certain categories which could not be so easily explained away; alienation, estrangement, fetishism, essence, the individual, all of which harked back to an unscientific political philosophy that emphasised conscious, creative subjectivity as well as social relations and forces of production.[6]

The revised 'continuity thesis' sought to pick up the pieces and reconstruct what it believed was the genuine Marx, in a large part as a response to the structuralists' involuntarism. Marx, the thesis argued, did continue to use methods, concepts and categories reminiscent of his youthful idealism in ways that were not entirely subsumed by his sciences; he may well have constructed a damning

Human nature

indictment of capitalism, but he did so with the aid of a political philosophy that contained more than a trace of a normative response to human impoverishment. The problem, then, was to develop an analysis that would harmonise what appeared to be countervailing tendencies evident between many of Marx's works, and even within some of them. A plethora of observations on alienation[7] (and related matters) was the result, that by quantity, if nothing else, appeared to bury the structuralist aberration once and for all. And what we were left with was a Marx who may well have possessed some kind of ethic, who did have a fairly clear idea about the oncoming millennium, and who maintained that the revolutionary moment could be a peaceful transition.[8] In other words a late twentieth-century, post capitalist Marx. More recently this viewpoint has been complimented – some might say unnecessarily complicated – by the meteoric rise of analytical/rational choice marxism, which has attempted to bring Marx into the mainstream of political philosophy by saddling him with the accoutrements of the liberal tradition: methodological individualism, rational maximisers, distributive justice; in sum, we are left with a Marx, who, if he did but know it, was a market socialist.[9]

What has all this to do with human nature? Each of the above views comes equipped with an exposition on the marxian theory of human nature which is compatible with a particular explanation of Marx's system as a whole. The variety of approaches can, with a few exceptions, be divided into two main groups: those that reject entirely the opinion that Marx entertained any concept of universal human nature; and those that say that he did incorporate an idea of human essence in his latter works, and that the origin of this idea lies in the pre-1845 writings. Both groups insist that their own reading of Marx liberates him from traditional, 'conservative' notions of human nature (e.g. individuals as bearers of uncontingent, inalienable rights, or as utilitarians, etc.), and subsequently allows him to articulate the epistemological basis for our own liberation. But in effect both assessments end up by resituating Marx within philosophical traditions he himself believed he had transcended, with the result that his 'radical departure' is delayed and his views of freedom compromised.

The first approach is what I would call the 'orthodox' standpoint, orthodox in the sense that it believes itself to be the inheritor of the 'official' dialectical determinism of Engels and Kautsky:[10] it relies almost entirely upon the 'iron laws' of history and the inevitability of capitalist self-destruction, with individual subjectivity taking a back seat, while class struggle remains the principal medium of social emancipation. The most celebrated recent exponent of this thesis is Louis Althusser:

> The Economic-Philosophic manuscripts have nourished a whole ethical or (what amounts to the same thing) anthropological interpretation of Marx - making *Capital*, with its sense of perspective and apparent 'objectivity', merely the development of a youthful intuition which finds its major philosophical expression in this text and in its concepts.[11]

Althusser responds to such an unfortunate and misleading development with the observation that the 1844 manuscripts are philosophical 'in *the same sense* as that which Marx later linked *an absolute condemnation*'.[12] It was the same condemnation that led to his rejection of all theories of history and politics which rested on a theory of human essence, and his dismissal of the problematic based on the assumption that there was a universal human nature and that it was an attribute of each individual.[13]

In contradistinction to the orthodox approach, there is the 'humanist' or 'ethical' account. One way or another, its proponents rest their case on a version of the continuity argument, accompanied by claims either for a marxian teleology, or an ethic of liberation, both of which rely upon a metaphysic, itself grounded on a univer-salist conception of human nature. For the adherents of this view the origins of their Marx can be discovered in the early works; and with little if any alteration, the concepts, categories and terminology of this period (especially those relating to human nature) continued to underwrite the content of all the later, seminal writings. Com-mentators well disposed towards this position such as Ollman and Geras are not averse from making the following statements: 'the men who act and interact in Marx's later writings are no different from those who appear in his early works. The conception of human nature with which he began has hardly altered'.[14] While Geras asks,

> 'One Marx or two?' The real picture is of a theoretical development marked in places by genuine novelty and change, but marked equally by some stability of conception, by definite continuities and strong

Human nature

> ones ... he subscribed to the supposition of a common human nature from beginning to end.[15]

And with a final flourish he summarises, 'Marx did not reject the idea of a human nature. He was right not to do so.'[16]

Now with two such diametrically opposed explanations, the task of discovering the 'genuine' Marx would appear to be doomed from the start. The choice appears to be a stark one: scientific socialism or philosophical humanism, break or continuity, contingency or universality. The choice, I believe is a bogus one. Neither option reflects the totality of the marxian system, and both represent epistemologies and methodologies that Marx himself rejected; dialectical determinism is a not too distant cousin of the fatalistic materialism of Feuerbach, dispensed with in nearly all of Marx's 'transitional' works:

> The materialistic doctrine that men are products of circumstances and upbringing, and that, therefore, changed men are products of other circumstances and changed upbringing forgets that it is men that change circumstances and that the educator himself needs educating.[17]

While humanist teleology closely resembles the 'True' socialism roundly deprecated in the *Communist Manifesto* where it is charged with not representing 'the interests of the proletariat, but the interests of Human Nature, of Man in general, who belongs to no class, has not reality, who exists only in the misty realm of philosophical fantasy.'[18]

What are we left with? The cryptic response might be everything and nothing; everything in the sense that both the scientific and the humanist readings together describe, but do not explain, the whole range of Marx's own analysis of human nature (in fact they may reveal some telling inconsistencies in his analysis); nothing because each approach, on its own, either fails to take into account or dismisses entirely those factors that are in direct opposition to the commentator's chosen conclusion, but which are crucial for a fuller understanding of the problem as Marx himself perceived it. Is there a way out of this impasses? If we combine the half-truths of each interpretation, while at the same time, and in true marxian fashion, transcending their particularity, yes.

The proposed alternative allows Marx to speak for himself, and in doing so may well leave some questions unanswered. For example, I believe there is no systematic normative dimension to Marx's theory of human nature, and to look for one, or to attempt to construct one for that matter, is a fruitless task (see the efforts of Geras, Buchanan, Brenkert, Elster, Husami, etc.[19]); neither can one make the claim for an exclusive explanatory model along the lines of a structuralist or a functionalist account of history or human nature (see attempts along these lines by Venable, Althusser, Cohen, etc.[20]). What can, and should, be done is the re-combination of Marx's unique assessment of human agency with his evaluation of the dynamic interrelationship between forces and relations of production. The former, he insisted, cannot be understood without the recognition of the centrality of the latter, which itself is meaningless unless the nature of the individuals engaged in recreating the conditions of their own existence is comprehended. We must recall that Marx was intent on linking theory with practice, and to isolate one from the other was for him tantamount to denying our uniquely human capacity for revolutionary subjectivity.

In order to set the stage for my own exposition of Marx's critique of human nature and his alternative, I first of all want to develop further the nature of the continuity/break debate, and by looking at texts employed as evidence by both sides suggest that both positions are based on false premises about Marx's epistemology. Secondly, via a restatement of Marx's own methodology as found in his 'mature works', I wish to show that individuals in social relations remain the point of departure for his critique of bourgeois society, despite his apparent concentration on modes of production.

2   The continuity controversy

I believe that an examination of Marx's critique of human nature should begin with his writings of 1845-46, in particular with the *Theses on Feuerbach* and *The German Ideology*. Both sides of the continuity/break dispute have used these texts to establish the validity of their respective positions, but there is ample evidence here to challenge the claims of each of them, and on which to base a more open-ended appraisal of Marx's own interpretation.

It was during this period that Marx built the foundations for

Human nature

his study of capitalism and formulated an epistemology which equipped him with a unique and original view of human history. At the same time Marx and Engels were attempting 'to settle accounts with our former philosophical conscience',[21] to go beyond the ineffectual Hegelian idealism of Bauer and Stirner, and transcend the fatalistic phenomenology of Feuerbach. However, Marx stopped short of the outright rejection of this heritage, and he never denied the positive impact that these influences had had on the development of his world view. Writing over fifteen years after his brush with the radical hegelians in the *Preface* of 1859 he noted his debt to the angry young men of the early 1840s. He recalled, as a notable step in his discovery of historical materialism, that as early as 1843, in the *Contribution to the Critique of Hegel's Philosophy of Law*[22] he had arrived at the idea that legal relations and the form of the state can only be explained by setting out from 'civil society', the anatomy of which must be sought in political economy.[23] But from the closer proximity of the *German Ideology*, although he saw his work of 1843-44 as necessary preparation for the formulation of a materialist conception of history, he nevertheless realised that these writings were still coloured by the concepts and method of an idealist philosophy. Of course, such a critical self-appraisal of the impact of influences on his intellectual development is all grist to the mill for those who seek to defend either Marx the consistent or Marx the changeling. Therefore, I feel it necessary to give my own view (which I suggest is Marx's own!) of the results of the period of transition and, especially, how they affected the formation of his theory of human nature.

We have already seen that the conception of humankind we find in the 1844 *Manuscripts* is held up by those who stand by the thesis of the unbroken continuity of Marx's intellectual development as being the 'correct outline', where we find the key to a correct reading of the mature Marx. The self-criticism of 1845-46, the argument continues, was nothing more than the fine tuning of the materialist method adopted after 1843. From these early writings, we are told, we obtain a fundamental principle of Marxism: human kind is not reducible to the relations of production but is always defined by free choice and the universal *gattungwesen*.[24] It is in such youthful philosophical humanist themes, that argument continues, that we find the principles which reveal the true content of the man's mature texts.

The theory of continuity appears attractive in its elegance and simplicity, but I believe it rests upon a mistaken view of the development of Marx's ideas and gravely underestimates the fundamental changes they went through in 1845-46. This period marks a clear transition evident in the mixture of youthful discourses characterised by philosophical speculation and more mature 'scientific' texts based on the all important positing of humankind in social relations, particularly the social relations of capitalism. The 'alienation' of 1844 was transformed as a concept and demoted as an explanation after 1845, although it was never abandoned. The *Manuscripts'* vivid description of the dehumanised existence experi-enced by the propertyless of bourgeois society was to be incorporated in all of the later, classic texts under such names as 'estrangement' and 'fetishism'; but the methodological basis of the early works, in which the concept of alienation played a key determinate role, was inverted and subsequently transcended. Consequently, the theory of alienation expounded in Paris should be viewed as the high point of Marx's speculative enquiry which held that human essence was to be understood in terms of the ideal 'species man' and that the unfolding of human history was the objective realisation of abstract individuality. So, in true speculative tradition, the Marx of 1844 explained the relationship between social relations (understood here in the guise of private property) and alienated labour (the deformed human essence) in terms which attributed to human essence the states of the fundamental (or determinant) moment. A few extracts serve to illustrate this point:

> Through *estranged, alienated labour*, then, the worker produces the relationship to this labour of a man alien to labour and standing outside it. The relationship of the worker to labour creates the relation to it of the capitalist (or whatever one chooses to call the master of labour). *Private property* is thus the produce, the result, the necessary consequence, of *alienated labour*, of the external relation of the worker to nature and to himself.
>
> *Private property* thus results by analysis from the concept of *alienated labour*, i.e. of *alienated man*, of estranged labour, of estranged life, of *estranged* man.

So, it is *not* particular forms of exploitation which create specific forms of alienation, but 'estranged life' that gives rise to private property.

> True, it is as a result of the *movement of private property* that we have obtained the concept of *alienated labour* (of *alienated* life) in political economy. But analysis of this concept shows that though private property appears to be the reason, the cause of alienated labour, it is rather its consequence, just as the gods are *originally* not the cause but the effect of man's intellectual confusion. Later this relationship becomes reciprocal.[25]

Later in the same manuscript the distinction and origins of alienation are made even clearer.

> How, we now ask, does *man* come to *alienate*, to estrange, his *labour*? How is this estrangement rooted in the nature of human development? We have already gone a long way to the solution of this problem by *transforming* the question of the *origin of private property* into the question of the relation of *alienated labour* to the course of humanity's development.[26]

For the mature Marx it was extracts such as these which revealed the upside down nature of his young hegelian method. These writings were still primarily ideological speculations, which asserted a circularity between concrete circumstances and alienated labour, a relationship where the starting point was 'human essence' or 'species being' (*gattungwesen*), i.e. human nature conceived abstractly. Alienation is here still the concrete expression of a universal essence that had more in common with an idealist, speculative philosophy and not, as later on, a description of human existence that accompanies an economic explanation of capitalist exploitation. The *Manuscripts* were not the foundation of the mature analysis because they started off with an inversion of the relationship between alienation and social relations. From such a philosophical humanist standpoint, historical development and social relations were explained in terms of the objective manifestation of 'species man', whereas after 1845 Marx never hesitated in maintaining that social relations were determined by the nature of productive forces. This also serves to explain the absence from his youthful meditations of the fundamental concepts of his mature political economy, for example, value, labour power and surplus value, all of which he later believed were essential for a full understanding of humanity in modern social relations.

Marx and 'homo faber'

So, despite their importance as transitional works which herald the beginning of a new, historical, economic and scientific approach, the *Manuscripts* were still 'tainted' with a speculative humanism that was only set aside by Marx when he adopted the materialist method of 1845 and after. Marx believed that he had set the record straight with *The Theses on Feuerbach* and *The German Ideology* wherein capitalist exploitation is said to give rise to concrete forms of alienation. In these two works we have the first articulation of his radically revised methodology: no longer are we to understand social relations via a phenomenology of human essence, and as the Sixth Thesis of Feuerbach states, 'the human essence is no abstraction inherent in each single individual. In its reality it is the ensemble of social relations'.[27] From now on, then, Marx's analysis was to be situated firmly in social relations. He rejected the 'idealistic humbug' of his forebears and established to his own satisfaction that revolution in the form of a 'practical overthrow of the actual social relations' was the real and only alternative to the idealistic view of history which 'in every period [looks] for a category' and 'explains' practice from the idea. Marx's critique continued: 'the idealists believed "that all forms of products of consciousness" could be dissolved by mental criticism, by resolution into "self consciousness" or transformation into "apparitions", ("spectres") "whimsies".' Such criticism, he insisted, was most definitely not the driving force of history, this role henceforth was to be the preserve of revolution. Social revolution revealed 'that history does not end by being resolved into "self-consciousness" as "spirit of the spirit", but that in it at each stage there is found a material result':

> a sum of productive forces, a historically created relation to nature and of individuals to one another, which is handed down to each generation from its predecessor; a mass of productive forces, capital funds and circumstances which on the one hand is indeed modified by the new generation, but on the other also prescribes for it its conditions of life and gives it a definite development and special character.

The implications for an understanding of human nature are made clear.

> This sum of productive forces, capital funds and social forms of intercourse, which every individual and generation finds in exist-

ence as something given, is the real basis of what the philosophers have conceived as 'substance' and 'essence of man'.[28]

Here, Marx's rejection of the concept 'essence of man' is manifest, a concept that he clearly adhered to in the 1844 *Manuscripts*. The 'scientific' marxists would claim that the break is irreparable. But is it that simple, can we exclude so easily from our analysis the important strides made by Marx prior to 1845-46? If we did so, surely this would lead us to the other extreme of the structuralists' theoretical anti-humanism with its central claim that what happened after 1845 was a radical and irreversible departure, with Marx transforming the basis of his analysis from the human essence to social relations. We would have little alternative but to accept their conclusion, that before he could establish the validity of his new theories of historical materialism and scientific socialism, Marx had to reject completely his former conceptual framework as this was characterised, some would say contaminated, by a speculative attitude. It was a speculative attitude in which a *concept of man* was given a primary ontological status that required the pole-axe blow of the sixth *Thesis in Feuerbach* which established that the 'human essence' resides in the 'ensemble of social relations', not in the individual; in this sense individuals personified social relations and henceforth this was to be their only role in mature Marxist thought. So that by the time we turn to the preface to the first German edition of *Capital* Volume One the *volte face* appears com-plete because it is here that Marx dispelled any lingering hopes that he had not rejected entirely his idealist credentials: 'individuals are dealt with only in so far as they are the personification of economic categories, embodiments of particular class relations and class interests.'[29]

The anti-humanists thus maintained that in his mature works Marx discovered that what *exists* theoretically speaking is not humankind as species being, as theoretical individual, but social relations. From this interpretation historical progress has human meaning only in the guise of the succession of social formations; history does not culminate with the realisation of the universal human essence but with the resolution of contradictions between social structures; it is historical materialism and political economy that has replaced the philosophical humanism of Marx's work prior to 1845.

Marx and 'homo faber'

The idea of a break at one time appeared unassailable; Marx had been saved from the clutches of the neo-hegelians and the ethical socialists, and the exposition of this position did raise some important issues concerning his status as a political philosopher. But it has to be said that in misinterpreting and underestimating the relevance of the early writings its analysis of the mature works remain flawed. To the Althusserian anti-humanist nothing (except temporary, inconsequential after effects) was carried over from 1844, hence there was no continuity in the development of Marx's thought between the youthful and mature works. His unequivocal adoption of a materialist, scientific method, we are told, killed off once and for all his romantic inclinations.

The choice appears a stark one; which analysis should we accept, the idealism of the philosophical humanist or the theoretical anti-humanist determinism of the dialectical materialist? Neither; a more accurate evaluation of Marx's work must consist of a combination of themes raised by both these schools of interpretation while at the same time transcending their one-sidedness. I do not deny that ruptures can be detected in the continuity, but that is inevitable if any theory is being continually restructured, and such restructuring was an integral component of Marx's intellectual development. His aim along with Engels was an attempt to master an 'unchanged domain of the real', that is real society, real social relations and the individuals that inhabited them. It was to be carried out with the transformation of concepts and methods on the way, a process that subsequently gave rise to modifications of the analysis as a whole, occasions confirmed in later works such as the *Preface* of 1859 where Marx indicated that 'in the Spring of 1845' he and Engels 'resolved to work out in common the opposition of our view to the ideological view of German philosophy . . . The resolve was carried out in the form of criticism of post-Hegelian philosophy',[30] a philosophy which had tutored them both. But as we have already seen this same work also appears to reinforce the argument for continuity. This is further reinforced by the evidence that Marx was constantly referring to earlier writings when composing the later works, using the concepts and categories of the former in a reconstituted way. For example, the four-way description of alienation familiar to us in its 1844 form reappears, barely altered, in the *Grundrisse*.[31] As to the

Human nature

relevance Marx attached to the pre-1845 material in later life, a letter to Engels provides evidence: 'I was pleasantly surprised to find that we do not need to be ashamed of this work [*The Holy Family* of 1844] although the cult of Feuerbach produces a very humorous effect upon one now'.[32]

What can we conclude from this discussion? All, I believe, we can be sure about is that once Marx realised as folly the attempt to discover the source of alienation in 'human essence' and recognised the sterility of a concept of universal human nature, he never veered from the course firmly re-plotted in 1845-46. Alienation remained an intrinsic and vital element of Marx's theories, but it was not incorporated in the analysis of concrete social relations, and not in an abstract philosophical concept of human essence. However, the individual did not disappear entirely, human volition was not subsumed under the deadweight of determining circumstances. After all, each human agent through their own actions contributed to the construction and reconstruction of those very same social relations which were now the focus of Marx's analytical attention; 'the social history of man is never anything but the history of their individual development, whether they are con-scious of it or not.'[33] Alienation only served to emphasise the antagonism present in those human-made relations of production based on exploitation, a theme Marx returned to constantly in the Grundrisse:

> The *most extreme form of alienation*, wherein labour appears in the relation of capital and wage labour, and labour, productive activity appears in relation to its own conditions and its own product, is a necessary point of transition – and therefore already contains in *itself*, in a still only inverted form, turned on its head, the dissolution of all *limited presuppositions of production*, and moreover creates and produces the unconditional presuppositions of production, universal development of the productive forces of the individual.[34]

In *Capital* we not only have many illustrations of 'separation' and 'estrangement', but also the antithesis of alienation - social production:

> The Capitalist system pre-supposes the complete separation of the labourers from all property in the means by which they can realise their labour. As soon as capitalist production is on its own legs, it not only maintains this separation, but reproduces it on a continually extending scale.[35]

This is the consequence of 'modern industry', which revolutionises both the technological basis of production and the variety of functions performed by the labouring force. However, despite its development of the variation of work, under capitalism, modern industry serves merely to compound the iniquities of the 'ossified particularisation' of 'the old division of labour' and to create 'that monstrosity, an industrial reserve army, kept in misery in order to be always at the disposal of capital'. This is when alienation is experienced in all its extremes,

> in the incessant human sacrifices from among the working-class, in the most reckless squandering of labour power, and in the devastation caused by a social anarchy which turns every economic progress into a social calamity.

This, Marx continues with uncharacteristic understatement, 'is the negative side'.[36] But on the other hand modern industry can be the productive base enabling the 'greatest possible development' of the labourer's varied aptitudes, indeed,

> Modern Industry ... compels society under the penalty of death, to replace the detail-worker of today, crippled by life-long repetition of one and the same trivial operation and thus reduced to a mere fragment of a man, by the fully developed individual, for a variety of labours, ready to face any changes of production, and to whom the different social functions he performs are but so many modes of giving free scope to his own natural and acquired powers.[37]

In *Theories of Surplus-Value* Marx once again returns to his abiding concern for individuals, their inseparable link with social relations and the eventual control of these relations by a future generation: 'at first the development of the capacities of the *human* species takes place at the cost of the majority of human individuals and even classes', but eventually the development of human capacities accompanies the breakdown of this contradiction and 'coincides with the development of the individual; the higher development of individuality is thus only achieved by a historical process during which individuals are sacrificed.'[38]

The 'individual' was clearly never abandoned by Marx in 1845-46, on the contrary, the conscious objectifying agent lived on, reworked, situated in social relations, affecting and being affected by their historical development. Marx believed he had escaped the clutches of hegelian dualism and in so doing had freed himself and all humans from the constricting deity called 'species being', 'reason', 'essence'. In its place he constructed the materialist analysis of history. But by the same token, it was not a materialism that determined the existence of individuals, on the contrary, Marx attempted to keep active human agents in concrete relations at the centre of his explanatory stage.

3 Human nature, the productive individual and social relations

Marx's examination of these active agents and their role in his analysis of human history was, firstly, incorporated within a critique of the speculative abstraction 'man', secondly, contained in his indictment of bourgeois political economy, and finally, central to his argument for revolutionary subjectivity. For the remainder of this chapter I shall follow the first two aspects of this examination, leaving the discussion of the human subject and revolutionary subjectivity to the chapter on Marx and freedom. What underlies this exposition is the view that Marx sought to liberate individuals and society from blind determinism. Whether this was the determining dialectic of Hegelian metaphysics, or crude 'scientific' empiricism, Marx wished to reassert the primacy of human agency to an understanding of history and social change. That most now accept that Marx was not just another materialist is to be welcomed. But there is a growing tendency for contemporary analysts of Marx to swing too far in the other direction and saddle him with a teleological ethic. The return of 'world spirit'? Even though Marx was equally scathing in his attack on all forms of idealism as he was in his condemnation of empiricist determinism, some are still not deterred from seeking to equip him with a moral foundation. The following discussion should be viewed, in part, as an attempt at a refutation of this tendency.

As we have already seen, Marx clearly wished to distinguish his own historical analysis of the development of human character from those theories that maintained that history was nothing more than the working out of a universal human essence. This was partly the reason for his reformulation of the theory of alienation after 1845, a theory he had hitherto equated with a distorted expression of species-being, or species-essence pursuing its true identity through time. Once he believed he had overcome this obstacle he applied the same critique to capitalist political economy, tackling head-on its 'ageless' categories and abstractions which had been applied with the same universalist zeal as had characterised the activities of the promoters of idealism. What is clear in all of Marx's work after 1845 is the reversal of the speculative relationship between essence and existence, form and content, abstract and real.[39] In all cases the former had conditioned the latter in idealist metaphysics, and thus the perceived contradiction between the two could, quite simply, be resolved in the head of the intellectual. With the adoption of a materialist method, Marx revealed to his own satisfaction the up-side-down perspective of idealism, and consequently the ineffectiveness of its cerebral critique. The resolution of contradiction was from now on to be the business of self-actualising men and women:

> The transformation, through the division of labour, of personal powers (relations) into material powers, cannot be dispelled by discussing the general idea of it from one's mind, but can only be abolished by the individuals again subjecting these material powers to themselves and abolishing the division of labour.[40]

The theory of change was to be derived from the realm of practice, practice was to inform theory which in turn would instruct practice. Similarly, the procedure of abstracting from the concrete to concretising the abstract would, Marx believed, expose the true content of concepts and categories employed to legitimate universalist philosophies. It was a procedure first applied to the speculative concept 'man' and subsequently to 'production'. But as production was the mode of existence unique to humanity, 'man' was not dismissed altogether by Marx, rather it was, as we will see, incorporated into his critical appraisal of capitalism.

Interestingly, the first moves in this direction can be detected in the pre-1845 *Critique of Hegel's Philosophy of Law*[41] where Marx takes Hegel to task for misrepresenting the origins of the dialectical movement in human history. Actual contradictions in social relations were considered by Hegel from the perspective of their reflection in thought, to the extent that they were reduced to the status of a logical abstraction which, once the relationship was inverted, itself became the essential essence and indeed the origin of what

Human nature

was in truth an empirical contradiction. For Marx, Hegel had committed the double mistake of making the idea, i.e. the speculative abstraction, the real subject, and in so doing claiming for this 'subject' a position of explanatory exclusivity for all empirical relations:

> Subsequently the actual subject appears as a result, whereas one must start from the actual subject and look at its objectification. The mystical substance, therefore, becomes the actual subject, and the real subject appears as something else, as an element of the mystical substance. Precisely because Hegel starts from the predicates of the general description instead of from the real *ens* [subject], and since nevertheless, there has to be a bearer of these qualities, the mystical idea becomes this bearer.[42]

Hegel therefore forced empirical facts to conform with speculative abstractions, and in so doing ignored the practical contradictions of the concrete, resolving these antagonisms via their abstract expression in thought. As a consequence Hegel's system remained uncritical of *existing* conditions. But for all this, as far as Marx was concerned, the Hegelian analysis was a *reflection* (all be it an inverted one) of reality; if only we could put everything back on its feet again by insisting that the dialectic was the reflection in thought of the real movement of human history (and not its determinator), while at the same time maintaining that the dialectic was not a general speculative abstraction but the 'specific logic of the specific subject',[43] then the real basis of the movement of human history could be understood. This is just what Marx set out to do in the *German Ideology*, the *Grundrisse* and *Capital*, it was an approach which was to have an undeniable impact on his critique of human nature.

From the *German Ideology* onwards Marx made a clear distinction between 'Human Nature' and the natures of men and women. The former, he believed, alluded to some universal, enduring, metaphysical quality, or qualities, attributable to the human race as a whole and residing in each individual representative of the species, i.e. an abstract determination. It mattered little to Marx whether the metaphysical ontologies that underpinned universalist notions of human nature were idealist or empiricist; for him both speculative philosophy and contemporary political economy relied on the explanatory primacy of abstractions, one of which was the abstraction 'man'. Both approaches had managed to invert the relationship between the concrete and the abstract so that actuality became subservient to the idea, to the extent that for the idealist the concrete was an expression of the idea unfolding itself through time, whereas for the political economist actual production should be brought closer to its ideal form of unimpeded free competition. But according to Marx the consequence of either approach was one of inaction, and hence conservatism, because both retreated to the sterile domain of the personal intellect, as had the prime target of *The German Ideology*, Feuerbach, who 'remains in the realm of theory and conceives of men ... not under their existing conditions of life ... he never arrives at the actually existing, active men, but stops at the abstraction "man"'.[44]

Marx believed that by relying upon such abstractions political philosophy and political economy alike both relegated material existence to a secondary status of objective datum, mistaking the activity of real individuals in changing circumstances for the workings out of abstract categories, whether they be 'human essence' or 'production'. History, from this standpoint, therefore became the history of the category or idea and not the history of actual relations between individuals pursuing new and ever-changing forms of productive activity. So, instead of allowing human history to speak for itself it was made to conform to *a priori* abstract conceptualisation.

In the face of this mystification and in spite of his intellectual debt to hegelian holism and empiricist atomism, Marx attempted to invert this relationship by establishing a diachronic perspective through a critical examination of the concrete evidence around him, i.e. the *results* of a historical process both in terms of the raw facts of contemporary human existence, and in terms of their expression in thought as enshrined in the categories and abstractions of prevailing philosophies.[45] Consequently, Marx claimed that his premises were the opposite of those applied by the ideological supports of bourgeois society:

> The premises from which we begin are not arbitrary ones, not dogmas, but real premises from which abstraction can only be made in the imagination. They are the real individuals, their activity and the material conditions of their life, both which they find already existing and those produced by their activity. These premise can thus be verified in a purely empirical way.[46]

Human nature

Such a perspective when applied to the development of human nature revealed, Marx maintained, a constantly changing human character, both in terms of the species as a whole and of individual men and women, inseparably linked with a continually developing relationship between human needs and the means of satisfying these needs.[47] Initially, humans satisfied needs through their contact with nature much as any other species of animals, but humanity divorced itself from other animals when it began to create through this interaction with nature new needs as well as new means for their satisfaction. This departure is central to Marx's first premise concerning all human existence:

> namely, that men must be in a position to live in order to be able to 'make history'. But life involves before anything else eating and drinking, housing, clothing and various other things. The first historical act is thus the production of the means to satisfy these needs, the production of material life itself.[48]

This is a 'fundamental fact' for Marx, central to any conception of history, a fundamental condition 'which today, as thousands of years ago, must daily and hourly be fulfilled merely in order to sustain human life'. Within the space of a paragraph Marx reiterates this point but from a different perspective: 'the satisfaction of the first need, the action of satisfying and the instrument of satisfaction which has been acquired, leads to new needs; and this creation of new needs is the first historical act.'[49]

But this fact means nought if it is not understood in terms of further circumstances that characterise historical development. Two other moments, or primary historical relations must be recognised; firstly there is the reproduction of the species, the relation between man and woman, which for Marx is the first social relation, although by no means the only one. The development of increased and changed needs gives rise to new social relations that subordinate the family, however its status as the first social relation is unaffected. Secondly, as a consequence of the aforementioned aspects 'which have existed simultaneously since the dawn of history and the first men, and which still assert themselves in history today', the production of life whether it be one's own life or another life brought about through procreation, existed and continues to exist, as a:

two-fold relation: on the one hand a a natural, on the other as a social relation – social in the sense that it denotes the co-operation of several individuals, no matter what conditions, in what manner and to what end.⁵⁰

And it is this crucial social dimension of production that becomes for Marx the key to the analysis of human history and of the natures of men and women. Therefore, each mode of production, i.e. the particular ways of satisfying human needs is automatically accompanied by a certain form of co-operation, which is itself a 'productive force'. It is but a short step from here to Marx's materialist epistemology:

> Further, that the aggregate of productive forces accessible to men determines the condition of society, hence the 'history of humanity' must always be studied and treated in relation to the history of industry and exchange.⁵¹

Marx was unequivocal, from the start humans have satisfied their material needs through forms of social interaction, and it is the way in which the needs are created and satisfied via a mode of production that conditions the characters of those engaged – in whatever capacity – in social relations; it is an interrelationship 'which is as old as men themselves'. Only when he believed that he had hammered home this point did Marx then go on to consider the origins of human consciousness.

Once more the conditioning influence of the creation and satisfaction of needs plays the principle role: 'language, like consciousness, only arises from the need, the necessity, of intercourse with other men ... Consciousness is, therefore, from the beginning a social product'.⁵² But consciousness does not spring fully developed from the satisfaction of the first need, it evolves out of the constantly changing circumstances of human material existence. Consciousness of ones self and of others develops both synchronically and diachronically alongside the growing awareness of 'nature', and it is in this relationship that Marx situated the origins of abstraction. Specifically, it is the division of labour into material and mental labour that signifies the moment when for the first time 'consciousness can really flatter itself that it is something other than consciousness of existing practice, that it really represents something without representing something real',⁵³ the way is open for the mind to 'free' itself from

Human nature

the concrete and to create, unhindered by material constraints, 'theology, philosophy, morality, etc.'[54] However, no sooner has consciousness established its autonomy than it inverts the conditioning relationship between it and its material beginnings; from now on the abstraction becomes the 'explanation'.

To summarise: for Marx both the character and the satisfaction of human needs are historical (and not naturalistic), being the result of a process that has continually developed and continues to develop; and it is in this process that he situated the origins of human progress, for the creation and satisfaction of needs through social relations was for him a continuous dialectical pursuit.

> [Humans] begin to distinguish themselves from animals as soon as they begin to produce their means of subsistence, a step which is conditioned by their physical organisation. By producing their means of subsistence men are indirectly producing their actual material life . . .
>
> This mode of production must not be considered simply as being the reproduction of the physical existence of the individuals. Rather it is a definite form of activity of these individuals, a definite form of expressing their life, a definite *mode of life* on their part. As individuals express their life, so they are. What they are, therefore, coincides with their production, both with *what* they produce and with *how* they produce. The nature of individuals thus depends on the material conditions determining their production.[55]

This, in its barest form, was for Marx the foundation for any examination of 'human nature' in any historical epoch; similarly it served as the starting point for the theory of class struggle and revolutionary subjectivity, for understanding estrangement in all its guises and, eventually, to the labour theory of value.[56] Of course, the relationship between needs and their satisfaction is nothing peculiar to the human species, it is one that it shares with other animals. All animals have need and each species satisfies them in ways that are unique to that species. But what makes the human species unique is its historical development of the capacity for self-determination – the capacity exercised by individuals in social relations for the reproduction of the conditions of human existence through a transformative, creative interaction with nature. It is the products of this self-determining activity – the material objects created by the process and the social conditions in which they were created - that are the basis for further reproductive activity and hence for further varied expressions of human character.

This view was in direct contrast to that of Feuerbach and the empiricists had insisted that consciousness is nothing more than a conditioned passive process of cognition, reflecting, for Feuerbach, an essence, and for the empirisists, the environmental condition of humanity's existence. But, despite their shared faith in the inevitable progress of history, the optimism of Feuerbach and the materialists was, Marx believed, undermined by their underestimation of humanity's capacity for self-determination. Consciousness was for them a determined consequence of external conditions, so humanity would always be incapable of liberating itself and society because it was impossible for it to engage in self-conscious activity. The fatalistic conclusion that humans could not change the world because they did not make it in the first place was one that Marx could not accept and he signalled his disagreement in the third thesis on Feuerbach:

> The materialist doctrine that men are products of circumstances and upbringing, and that, therefore, changed men are products of other circumstances and changed upbringing, forgets that it is men that change circumstances and that the educator himself needs educating.[57]

Marx renewed his attack on the hapless Feuerbach and his fatalism in *The German Ideology*. Here the weapon was heavy irony, the opponent being assailed with his own terminology in an attempt to ridicule the defeatism of his epistemology:

> [Feuerbach] develops the view that the being of a thing or a man is at the same time its or his essence, that the determinate conditions of existence, the mode of life and activity of an animal or human individual are those in which its 'essence' feels itself satisfied.

Here the old duality of existence and essence reappears, with essence holding the position of primacy while existence remains its placid expression in reality. If the two are in harmony then actuality will be devoid of contradiction, however if there should be an anomaly whereby the concrete expression of the essence is distorted there is little that the 'thing' or 'human individual' can do about it bearing in mind Feuerbach's gloomy view of human agency:

> Here every exception is expressly conceived as an unhappy chance, as an abnormality which cannot be altered. Thus if millions of proletarians feel by no means contented with their living conditions, if their 'being' does not in the least correspond with their 'essence', then ... this is an unfortunate misfortune which must be born quietly.[58]

There are echoes of Hegel in Marx's resolution of the apparent fatalism in the materialist method, for it is from this idealist *par excellence* that he inherited the view that reality is not external to humans, confronting them as an all-conditioning unchanging world of objects but that humanity actively shapes and modifies nature. However, as has already been noted, Marx departed from the speculative orientation of Hegel's doctrine with its premise that the objective counter-point to human consciousness is itself illusory, being a creation of distorted 'Spirit', when he stated that it is a necessary condition for the creative activity of the human subject to have a concrete reality, the world of objects.[59] If we return to the *Theses on Feuerbach*, and specifically the first thesis, this new methodological stance can be deduced from Marx's criticism of 'hitherto existing materialism':

> The chief defect of all hitherto existing materialism – that of Feuerbach included – is that the thing (Gegenstand), reality, sensuousness, is conceived only in the form of the *object* or of *contemplation* but not as *human sensuous activity, practice*, not subjectively. Hence it hap-pened that the *active* side, in contradistinction to materialism, was developed by idealism – but only abstractly, since, of course, idealism does not know real, sensuous activity as such. Feuerbach wants sensuous objects, but he does not conceive human activity itself as *objective* activity.[60]

From this it can be deduced that Marx believed that the nature of human consciousness is not limited to merely inactive cognition, a passive acceptance of reality, but that the human subject intervenes directly in the process of the restructuring and modifying of reality; in becoming involved with reality, either through productive activity or reflective thought, humanity automatically shapes and changes it, stamping it with the mark of the species. Henceforth Marx believed that he had transformed the epistemology of 'all hitherto existing materialism', based as it was on reflective cognition, postulating it instead as a theory of interdeterminancy amongst the human subject, society and nature. The view of history that emerged out of this analysis was one that relied on 'starting from the material production of life itself - and comprehending the form of intercourse connected with and created by this mode of production ... as the basis of all history'.[61] Such an exposition also served to explain the origins of all the forms of consciousness, whether they be expressed as religion, philosophy or morality. The end result, i.e. production, history, consciousness, could thus be depicted in its totality (and, therefore, to, the reciprocal action of these various sides on one another)'.[62] This recognition of the reciprocal interaction of the various moments of any particular epoch clearly indicates Marx's attempt to view human history as a totality comprised of differences, each of which affects the other in a variety of ways. It is an interconnectedness that is constantly modifying its own basis, the mode of production, which itself consequently conditions the subsequent premises of the further interconnecion between the various moments (amongst which must be counted individuals). The result was an analysis of human nature that attempted to transcend the classic dichotomy between subject and object by a synthesis and transcendence of the materialist and idealist doctrines which themselves had both sought to separate the 'moments' of their own time in order to place one of them (usually the 'idea' or the 'concept') in a position of explanatory exclusivity.

Marx was prepared to admit that the classical materialist account of human nature, faithfully reiterated by bourgeois economists, was adequate enough as a description of alienated existence in present circumstances; as long as bourgeois society continued to exist so too would the deformed and incomplete forms of human character that were its product. But as an authori-tative account of human nature *per se* it was, he insisted, as mis-leading as any idealist notion of a universal species-being. Both deprecated the real, active individual's ability to determine his or her own existence, and if there was one thing that Marx never underestimated it was the human capacity for self-determination. Indeed he was constantly at pains to emphasise humanity's intimate relationship with nature, for he believed that nature cannot be severed from human action, but nature as it presents itself as an object of potential human cognitive action has already been affected by the actions of previous generations. Humanity constantly 'humanises' nature which in turn, as modified reality, conditions the character of subsequent modification and shapes the social relations in which the modification is performed. Throughout this process it must be remembered that for Marx the predominant moment is always productive activity:

> This conception of history thus relies on expounding the real process of production – starting from the material production of life itself – and comprehending the form of intercourse connected with and created by this mode of production ... as the basis of all history,

and further,

> that each stage (of history) contains a material result, a sum of productive forces, a historically created relation to nature and of individuals to one another, which is handed down to each generation from its predecessor; a mass of productive forces, capital funds and circumstance, which on the one hand is indeed modified by the new generation, but on the other also prescribes for it its conditions of life and gives it a definite development, a special character. it shows that circumstances make men just as much as men make circumstances.[63]

Feuerbach and the materialists insisted, by comparison, that the 'sensuous world' around them was a never-changing certainty 'a thing given direct from all eternity', such a view was myopic, it could see no further than its own epoch which was, as was every other epoch, a 'product of industry',

> an historical product, the result of the activity of a whole succession of generations, each standing on the shoulders of the preceding one, developing its industry and its intercourse, and modifying its social system according to the changed needs. Even the objects of the simplest 'sensuous certainty' are only given him through the social development, industry and commercial intercourse.[64]

Marx's proposition was that the anatomy of human history should be understood in terms of the ever-changing interdeterminancy between humanity and nature, and it is in this context that any examination of human nature should be conducted.[65] Individuals were not to be devalued by this approach, indeed Marx continued to emphasise their central importance in the construction of productive forces. Individuals have always had to enter into relations with one another by virtue of their needs and the methods employed to satisfy those needs. As a consequence of this individuals have never confronted one another as 'pure egos', their interrelationship has always been defined by the 'definite stage of the development of their productive forces', and

> since this intercourse, in its turn, determined production and needs, it was, therefore, precisely the personal, individual behaviour of individuals, their behaviour to one another as individuals, that created the existing relations and daily reproduces them anew.[66]

The development of an individual is intimately connected and conditioned by the development of all those individuals with whom he or she is associated, and Marx continues, it follows that the 'physical existence of the later generations is determined by that of their predecessors', who also bequeath productive forces and social relations, thus determining the mutual relations of the succeeding generation. In short . . . the history of a single individual cannot possibly be separated from the history of preceding or contemporary individuals, but is determined by this history'.[67]

The resulting formula appeared simple enough: the concrete world is shaped by active humans/the humanised world conditions future human activity (the predominant moment being productive activity); but for Marx its implications were highly subversive. The idealist foundations of speculative philosophy were undermined and rendered inapplicable by the day to day activity of real individual humans in concrete social relations, while the universal, legitimating categories of classical political economy were reduced to the status of contingent, descriptive abstractions when faced with the hard evidence of transitory relations of production.[68]

To Marx then, human rational cognition of the world is not the unchanging predominant moment, it is the consequence of the productive activity of individuals. Therefore, human cognition is transformed as the world is shaped by human activity, i.e. the meaning attached to objects changes as those objects acquire different functions and satisfy new needs within altered forms of production; the world of objects is no more autonomous than the human capacity for rational cognition because both are ultimately conditioned by the constantly changing reproduction of the means of human existence. The existence of individuals in social relations, their productive interaction with the world of objects and each other conditions their natures, and all is subject to the dynamic,

Human nature

dialectical process of human historical development, so that 'it is not the consciousness of men that determines their being, but, on the contrary, their social being that determines their consciousness.'[69]

Subsequently, Marx was to concentrate his intellectual energies on a lengthy discourse on this 'social being', which was to encompass the totality of differences that was the bourgeois mode of production. Individuals and their natures were not to be disregarded but were to be incorporated as productive agents (in the broadest sense of the term) in his critique of conventional political economy. The stage for all this had already been set in *The German Ideology*.

> The social structure and the state are continually evolving out of the life-process of definite individuals, however, of these individuals, not as they may appear in their own or other people's imagination, but as they actually are, i.e. as they act, produce materially.[70]

But the analysis was to reach its maturity in *The Grundrisse* and in *Capital*. It is here that the focus of analysis moved irrevocably from 'man in general' to 'production', and it is in these writings where the explanatory, critical method developed in the works of 1845-46 was applied to what Marx believed was the predominant moment of human relations, productive activity. In particular, it was the contemporary form of production that interested Marx, especially its theoretical expression, bourgeois political economy. He proceeded to unwrap the abstract categories and concepts employed by the political economists of the day by means of the same process of inversion that he had applied to the abstractions of speculative philosophy, ending up with the same general conclusion: that political economists, just as speculative philosophers, generalised through the use of abstraction the characteristics they already believed were common to all historical forms of production, then claimed universality for the abstraction in order to legitimate their claim that there is only one ahistorical mode of production, which was of course their own.

According to Marx, many had been lured by the clean simplicity of this approach, even the utopian socialist Pierre Proudhon had been susceptible to the universalist claims of the 'bourgeois' materialists. In particular, although Proudhon had not directly stated that 'bourgeois life' was for him 'an *eternal truth*', he states it indirectly by deifying the categories which express bourgeois relations in the form of thought'.[71] Indeed, he did what 'all good bourgeois do':

> They all tell you that in principle, what is considered as abstract ideas, competition, monopoly etc., are the only basis of life, but in practice leave much to be desired. They all want competition without the pernicious effects of competition. They all want the impossible, namely, the conditions of bourgeois existence without the necessary consequences of those conditions. None of them understands that the bourgeois form of production is historical and transitory, just as the feudal form was. This mistake arises from the fact that the bourgeois man is to them the only possible basis of every society; they cannot imagine a society in which men have ceased to be bourgeois.[72]

In sum, they set out from a preconstructed *idea* of commodity production synonymous with the capitalist mode, and sought to 'discover' the idea in every past and present form. For Marx, this was nothing less than the 'Eternalisation of historic relations of production'[73] which only served to obscure the actual antagonisms and contradictions that characterised the reality of capitalism, while at the same time refusing to recognise 'that all history is nothing but a continuous transformation of human nature'.[74]

In our turn, if we are to obtain a clear picture of Marx's mature analysis of human nature, we must follow his critique of political economy in so far as it concerns itself with the characters of the social individuals who inhabit the world of commodity production. From the beginning, the approach bears many similarities to that employed in *The German Ideology*. First of all Marx distinguishes his analysis of production from that of others, utilising the same labels but redefining their meaning, so that whenever he refers to production it is to a form of production that accompanies a certain stage of social development – 'production by social individuals'.[75] But in much the same way as his earlier critique of the abstraction 'man', Marx then goes on to discuss 'Production in general', a category which serves to bring together characteristics common to all epochs of production. It appears at first glance that he is engaging in the same speculative abstraction that he had condemned in others, however he soon clears up this misapprehension by insisting that 'production in general' is a rational abstraction which incorporates generalisations in order to indicate 'nothing more than the essential moments of all production'.[76] In fact, these generalisations are reducible to a 'few very simple characteristics, which are hammered out into flat tautologies',[77] for example: 'No production possible without an instrument of production, even if this instrument is only the hand',[78] 'No production without stored-up, past labour, even if it is only the facility gathered together and concentrated in the hand of the savage by repeated practice',[79] 'All production is appropriation of nature on the part of an individual within in and through a specific form of society',[80] and 'every form of production creates its own legal relations, form of government, etc.'[81] As 'flat tautologies', the argument goes, they tell us very little about the character of specific forms of production, so we will often have to look elsewhere for the origins of the distinguishing features of different epochs. Marx believed there were many different determinations that gave each historical epoch its distinctive character and not all of these were common to every period, therefore the task was to sort out common elements from facets unique to a particular era; and if the common elements turned out to be nothing other than tautologies then the focus of attention should be the historic (i.e. contingent) determinations:

> There are characteristics which all stages of production have in common, and which are established as general ones by the mind; but the so-called *general preconditions* of all productions are nothing more than these abstract moments with which no real historical stage of production can be grasped.[82]

From this position Marx begins his first skirmish with bourgeois political economy, and it is conducted in much the same way as his earlier attack on speculative philosophy. Both systems inverted the rational abstraction which subsequently became the universal abstraction; with the philosophers it was human essence, for the economists it was replaced with 'production in general' so that they chose to:

> present production – see e.g. Mill – as distinct from distribution etc., as encased in eternal natural laws independent of history, at which opportunity *bourgeois* relations are then quietly smuggled in as the inviolable natural laws on which society in the abstract is founded.[83]

There are further echoes of this rebuttal of idealism in Marx's critical response to the economists' universalist claims, indeed he did not hesitate in comparing the philosophical inversions of Hegel with the methodological procedures of political economy. In a section entitled 'The Method of Political Economy'[84] Marx leaves us in little doubt about the radical departure his approach represents. Rather than starting off from a perceived concrete whole, e.g. population, one should commence from the simplest of relations and ascend to the more complex, even though the concrete totality remains the real presupposition. The former analysis is initially confronted by a chaotic collection of phenomena which makes up the totality, this it attempts to make sense of by analytically descending from the chaos to ever simpler determinations, all the time seeking the illusive family of simple concepts which, when 'found', are then transformed into abstract determinations. Such is the fate of 'exchange', 'division of labour', 'price', etc.. For Marx these simple abstractions are his starting point, from where he begins a journey the purpose of which is to discover the interconnections between the various moments of simple relations, extending this analysis to more complex phenomena, and finally arriving at the 'population' again (or in Marx's case, the 'world market'). But this totality no longer appears as chaotic, it has become a unity 'of many determinations and relations'.[85] In effect the procedure was reversed by Marx so that instead of evaporating the totality in order to obtain an abstract determination, it was the abstract determinations which led 'towards a reproduction of the concrete by way of thought'.[86]

In other words:

> The concrete is concrete because it is the concentration of many determinations, hence unity of the diverse. It appears in the process of thinking, therefore, as a process of concentration, as a result, not as a point of departure, even though it is the point of departure in reality and hence also the point of departure for observation [*Anschauung*] and conception.[87]

Therefore the only way that thought can make sense of the concrete and reproduce it in the mind is by setting out from the abstract, but it almost goes without saying that 'this is by no means the process by which the concrete itself comes into being', and it must be remembered that 'the real subject retains its autonomous existence outside the head just as before ... the subject, society, must always be kept in mind as the presupposition'.[88] Political economy had consistently failed to recognise this, preferring to invest in the

Human nature

abstract generality 'production in general' the quality of real essence, i.e. the objective point of departure. In the face of this all historic differences were extinguished, and as we have already seen, without these Marx insisted that 'no real historical stage of production can be grasped'.[89]

How does humanity fit into all this? Firstly, in attacking the fallacious basis of bourgeois political economy, Marx was also questioning the image of humankind which accompanied it, exposing the contingency of such 'ageless' human characteristics as greed and utility. Secondly, in elaborating his own materialist political economy, Marx refined his analysis of the development of human character throughout history, and as expressed in parti-cular epochs. Individuals were to be situated within the concrete totality of bourgeois economic and social relations, and in their capacity as active agents, incorporated as a presupposition, or moment, of the many different determinations within the unity of capitalism.

The sixth Thesis on Feuerbach, wherein the human essence in its reality 'is the ensemble of social relations, remained the touchstone for Marx's appraisal of the nature of individuals in bourgeois relations: 'Society does not consist of individuals, but expresses the sum of the interrelations, the relations within which these individuals stand'.[90] What more proof, it has often been said, is required of Marx's disinterest in the fate of the individual? Surely, the prosecution continues, this is sufficient evidence for condemning him as an unreformed determinist? But I believe that to come to this conclusion is to ignore most of what has gone before and thus make as erroneous a claim as that made by those who wish to bring Marx back into the fold of mainstream metaphysics. The individual is most definitely not cast aside by Marx in the later works, in fact the picture that emerges of the human agent reproduces in detail the conscious, active, and productive social being who inhabits the pages of the *German Ideology*, and who therefore, by definition, exists in the real world. Marx reiterates the point that individuals can only be understood in the context of the social relations in which they interact, and if we try to isolate them from society, which is after all the product of their interaction, we deny them their humanity. Individuals are 'a product of history',[91] a history constructed by their predecessors and reconstructed by the present generation for the future, i.e. individuals are the product of their own social individuality.

The Marxian scientific study of history is at the same time the historical study of the development of individuals, the two go hand-in-hand, because for Marx, history is itself the product of the 'essential moment' of individuals interacting through particular social relations, 'the *main force of production* [is] *the human being himself*'.[92] As a consequence the historical development of productive forces and the historical development of human capacities and characteristics are contiguous. In the last analysis it is true that the relations of production are relations between men and women engaged in productive activity of one form or another, but this is not to say that individuals enter into these relations already fully equipped with the capacity for interactive production, quite the reverse. Men and women find themselves in pre-existing relations of production which underpin the social basis of their life processes. However, this does not mean that humans are conditioned by the relations between things, for Marx this was nothing but 'crude materialism' which he believed had failed to realise that it was the relations between human beings that constituted the real essence of the relation between things that constituted the real essence of the relation between things. But the materialists continued to express their faith in an inverted relation, only serving to highlight the alienation of the social relations between individuals:

> the economists ... say that people place in a thing (money) the faith which they do not place in each other. But why do they have faith in the thing? Obviously only because that thing is an *objectified relation* between persons; because it is objectified exchange value, and exchange value is nothing more than a mutual relation between people's productive activities ... [money] can have a social property only because individuals have alienated their own social relationship from themselves so that it takes the form of a thing.[93]

In bourgeois political economy the individual is lost amongst the relations between things; this is the logical consequence, according to Marx, of the approach of economists who:

> regard as the *natural properties* of things what are social relations of production among people, and qualities which things obtain because they are subsumed under these relations, [which] is at the same time just as crude an idealism, even fetishism, since it imputes social relations to things as inherent characteristics, and thus mystifies them.[94]

Human nature

Such is the case with the category 'commodity production', an abstraction peculiar to bourgeois relations of production. Here was an abstraction which Marx believed, had been transformed by political economy from a logical, descriptive category of actual existence, into a mystical idea that objectified itself through concrete relations between humans and thus obtained the status of an explanatory, legitimatory universal. But in carrying out this manoeuvre political economists had lost sight of the actual relations between individuals which had given rise to the abstraction in the first place; 'The *production of capitalist and wage labourers is thus a chief product of capital's realisation process.* Ordinary economics, which looks only at the things produced, forgets this completely.'[95] The committing of this error only serves the purpose of obscuring the antagonistic relationship between those who sell their labour power and those who purchase it. Hence the contradiction that is at the heart of capitalism is forgotten even by 'some socialists' who claim 'that we need capital but not the capitalists', and Marx reminds us that 'the concept of capital contains the capitalist'[96] and by the same definition also contains the alienated wage labourer. This obviously has direct implications for Marx's observations concerning the nature of the human character in bourgeois social relations. The productive interaction between labour and capital relies upon the constant renewal, through personal consumption, of labour power, a process which Marx regarded as an integral moment of the reproduction of capitalism as a whole. Of course, the ways in which labour power is reproduced are defined by the parameters of capitalism's conditions of existence, therefore the human character which is itself an immediate product of this relation will almost inevitably reflect the prevailing, dominant traits synonymous with this mode of production. For the individual this will mean that the capacity for self-determination exercised through personal consumption will be viewed merely in terms of the reproduction of one living labour capacity for another.[97] So the individual worker by reproducing his or her capacity for work despite being directly engaged in the reproduction of the forces of production and the related social relations, is still regarded by capital solely as a means for producing value. It is a view of the individual agent that bourgeois political economy seeks to eternalise by universalising its theory of commodity production, but it is

Marx and 'homo faber'

a view, in Marx's eyes, that is inseparable from the contradictions that prevail in social relations based on the exploitation of living labour power. These same contradictions are lived out through an alienated existence which is mistaken for ageless 'human nature' by those who believe in the immortality of capitalism

For Marx the contradictions of capitalism are of course the evidence for its eventual demise, an end that will be, as with all other historical transitions, the consequence of humankind continuously transforming itself through the process which he characterises as the 'reproduction of the physical existence of individuals';

> This *reproduction ... is at the same time necessarily new production and destruction of the old form...* Not only do the objective conditions change in the act of reproduction, e.g. the village becomes a town, the wilderness a cleared field etc. but the producers change, too, in that they bring out new qualities in themselves, develop themselves in production, transform themselves, develop new powers and ideas, new modes of intercourse, new needs and a new language.[98]

This same view underpinned Marx's analysis in Capital, and this must be constantly born in mind, lest we be led astray by comments which, when taken out of context, appear to catapult us right back to Paris and 1844.

'We presuppose labour in a form that stamps it as exclusively human'.[99] From this it might well be deduced that just as in the *Economic and Philosophical Manuscripts*, Marx in *Capital* is providing us with a 'philosophy of man', fully equipped with its distinguishing characteristic 'creative labour'. The temporary aberrations of the imprecise jottings of 1845-46 and 1857-58 are replaced by a resurgent speculative humanism. This view appears to be reinforced by a further comment: 'At the end of every labour-process we get a result that already existed in the imagination of the labourer at its commencement', after all this is what separates humans from bees.[100] The obvious conclusion is that human labour is defined by consciousness. This is an erroneous conclusion.

As with *The German Ideology* and the *Grundrisse*, Marx takes the trouble in *Capital* to clear up some possible confusion concerning his method. He begins by outlining three broad generalisations, or rational abstractions concerning the labour-process. 'The elementary factors of the labour-process are (1) the personal activity of man, i.e. work itself, (2) the subject of that work, and (3) its instruments.'[101] But this has not been the character of human labour for all time, it is the consequence of a long historical development:

> We are not now dealing with those primitive instinctive forms of labour that remind us of the mere animal. An immeasurable interval of time separates the state of things in which a man brings his labour-power to market for sale as commodity, from the state in which human labour was still in its first instinctive stage.[102]

Marx is clearly suggesting that the character of human labour has changed through time, and that at one stage it was no different from any other animal interaction with nature. The gradual evolutionary development of humankind's relation with nature was therefore accompanied by a transformation of consciousness. So, by appropriating the fruits of the natural world in ways conditioned by the individual's wants, this same individual by 'acting on the external world and changing it ... at the same time changes his own nature'.[103] Consciousness is most definitely *not* the the primary determinlng moment for Marx, it is as much a product of the material existence of humans as are their changing needs.

Why the need, then, to outline three elementary factors of the labour process? Marx's intention was to describe the *nature-imposed* conditions of human existence which he believed were common to every social phase of that existence.[104] But, as with his use of generalisations in earlier works, their utility was limited to nonspecific explanations, i.e., as long as Marx was not dealing with a concrete understanding of a determinate economic formation, then broad, tautological, generalisations sufficed. However, when he considered particular economic formations, his understanding of them relied upon the employment of concepts and categories which took him ever further away from those rational generalisatlons concerning 'labour in general'. As we have already seen, this was especially the case with his critique of capitalism and its political economy. Here in *Capital* Marx was concerned almost entirely with critical analysis of the large number of different determinations characteristic of capitalism already identified in the *Grundrisse*. He believed that only by comprehending scientifically these different determinate moments, could we then go on to understand the complex interdeterminancy of the workings of capitalism, that most advanced form of production separated by an 'immeasurable interval of time' from the first halting steps of human labour.

With regard to the impact of the above on the Marxian analysis of human character its theoretical basis was, as before, situated firmly in the social relations of capitalism. Actual individuals in concrete social relations could only be understood if we went beyond the limited constraints of 'labour in general'. To settle for thie latter as the foundation for the analysis of humankind would only confine us to a similar approach as that adopted by those who set out from the realm of abstraction and end up staying there. It was this approach that Marx was attempting to disprove via his complete inversion of the relationship between abstraction and actuality. *Capital* should be seen in this context for it is a critique of the political economy which had reduced the productive relations between active, social individuals to the level of mystified abstraction.

But there are those who, for various reasons, wish to equip Marx with an ageless conception of human nature which they believe would reveal the true inspiration behind his political philosophy. Putting to one side the substantial body of evidence that points directly to a methodology which uses as its presupposition a concrete stage of human social development, those who desire to return Marx to the speculative fold highlight remarks in the 'classics' in support of their dramatic claims, for example: Marx responds to Bentham's efforts to reduce all human actions to the principle of utility with the following comment, 'he that would criticise all human acts, movements, relations, etc., by the principle of utility, must first deal with human nature in general, and then with human nature as it is modified in each historical epoch'.[105] Norman Geras, that most recent exponent of Marx as speculative philosopher, uses this comment, amongst others, to defend the notion of a marxian theory of ageless human nature.[106] However, in isolating it from the wider context of Marx's critique of utilit-arianism, Geras succeeds only in obscuring the meaning of the original quotation.

The sentence appears in a footnote on Bentham, during a typical no-holds-barred assault by Marx on the champion of the English shopkeeper who is described as 'that insipid, pedantic, leather-tongued oracle of the ordinary bourgeois intelligence of the nineteenth century'.[107] Not only does Marx take Bentham to task for broadcasting the 'dogma' that conceived of social capital 'as a fixed magnitude of a fixed degree of efficiency'[108] but also for being a poor pupil of the eighteenth century materialism of Helvetius 'and other Frenchmen'. They had insisted that the correct approach for a utilitarian would be one that commenced with general propositions concerning human nature before invoking the principle of utility; e.g., 'To know what is useful for a dog, one must study dog nature. This nature is not to be deduced from the principle of utility'. This is immediately followed by the contentious sentence concerning humans. The comparison that Marx makes here is an echo of a similar discussion carried out in *The German Ideology*.[109] He claimed that both Helvetius and Holbach had applied the broad category of utility to a generalised, abstract notion of human nature in an attmept to universalise its applicability.

Subsequently, the procedure was to observe how the general utilitarian disposition appeared ln different guises in different historical epochs. But as with idealism, the utilitarian empiricists had isolated a category by way of abstraction from actual social relations, inverted the relationship, and then maintained that actual social relations were a manifestation of the category, 'a wholly metaphysical method of procedure'.[110] Marx understood this urge to universalise an abstraction in historical terms. Helvetius and Holbach were intellectual opponents of the *ancien regime* and sought universality for a notion that they believed was true for *all* individuals; their theory of utility was:

> the historically justified philosophical illusion about the bourgeoisie just then developing in France, whose thirst for exploitation could still be regarded as a thirst for the full development of individuals in conditions of intercourse freed from the old feudal fetters.[111]

Once freed of these feudal fetters, and having established the dominance of capitalist economic relations, the bourgeoisie, especially their intellectual 'oracles', incorporated the princlples of utility as part of the legitimatory doctrines of political economy. In the process, the subject of utilitarianism was transformed from the idealised image of humanity in general to the bourgeois individual fully equipped with capital's desires for competition and exploitation. For Marx, Bentham had been the chief architect of this transformation. The meaning of the original quote concerning human nature in general should now be clear; Marx was most definitely not indulging in the mysticism which he so abhorred in others, he was merely recalling *en passant* the origins and distortions of utility. He noted that the abstract idea of human nature present in the philosophy of Helvetius and others had been deftly by-passed by the likes of Jeremy Bentham and James Mill who 'with the dryest naivety' had taken the 'modern shopkeeper, especially the English shopkeeper, as the normal man. Whatever is useful to this queer normal man, and to his world, is absolutely useful', a yard stick which is then applied to 'past, present and future'.[112]

The actual consequence of this not entirely unimportant diversion is a reinforcement of Marx's own critical approach to the theories of human nature offered by others. In the above this took two forms. Firstly, Marx outlined the historical development of bourgeois philosophy and political economy, with particular reference to the changing fortunes of the principle of utility, and related all to the socio-economic developments of France and England. Secondly, he employed once more his critique of mysticism in an attempt to expose the contingency of the 'ageless' concepts employed by those who viewed contemporary society as one based on 'universal principles', principles which were, Marx insisted, nothing more than abstractions gleaned from a concrete historical totality and inverted to explanatory primacy.

4 Conclusion

Does Marx have a theory of human nature? If we mean 'does he have a theory about the development of human character?', the answer is most definitely 'yes'. On the other hand, if we are looking for a notion of human nature founded on universal principles, the answer is an unequivocal 'no'. It must be admitted that Marx did employ the term 'human nature' in ways not entirely related to his critiques of speculative philosophy and of bourgeois political economy. But at least in the mature works his concept of human nature is very narrowly defined, being used to describe the biological basis of all human existence regardless of time and place, and inspite of the impact of social relations upon individuals. In *The German Ideology*, Marx explains this biological basis in terms of the

Human nature

'physical organisation' of individuals, i.e. their physical attributes and their natural needs.[113] A similar definition reappears in the *Grundrisse* and again in *Capital*, where, as it has already been noted, the 'natural being' is presented as nothing more than a rational generalisation concerning humankind in general, and as such is but a tautology. Such a limited notion of human nature is in stark contrast to those enployed by idealists and materialists alike, who, as far as Marx was concerned, built up elaborate explanatory theories on foundations of thought alone, and to this end took as their model of ageless humankind the socially developed individual of their own times.

Marx was adamant that the explanation for those things which we identify as exclusively human characteristics are the products of history, the results of the continuous transformation of social relations; they are most certainly not the effusions of some 'natural given'. The 'natural individual' who populates the pages of speculative philosophy and political economy alike, in reality arose historically.[114] But if the individual was nothing more than the product of history, is there any place left for him or her as a particular and unique expression of the species in Marx's world view? Let us recall Marx's and Engels's statement on their transition from the realm of Hegelian speculation to that of the materialist conception of history, when they insisted that they would still be dealing with the *unchanged* domain of the real, i.e. the same material reality, a reality inhabited by individual human agents. This always remained the concrete presupposition for Marx, even during the most prosaic moments of his analysis of the intricate workings of capitalism, so that each *theoretical* element or concept employed by him in his mature analysis corresponds, in one way or another, to an aspect of the lives of actual individuals. But are the humans who appear on the pages of Marx's writings merely the bearers of economic functions? This would certainly be the view of those who adopt an anti-humanist stance, who would turn to *Capital* for their supposedly incontestable evidence where Marx said himself that individuals are only dealt with here as the 'personification of economlc categories', i.e. as abstract social agents. The supporters of this claim will then often turn to the sixth thesis on Feuerbach which serves to confirm Marx's 'rejection' of humanism, where it suggests that history produces individuals.

Marx and 'homo faber'

Why, then, should Marx insist in the third thesis on Feuerbach that 'men make circumstances'? Surely this contradicts the determinist tendencies of thesis six? Perhaps the philosophical humanist view of Marx is correct, 'man' does make history afterall, maybe he did incorporate an image of an ideal human agent in his epistemology, and maybe to him history is nothing but the workings out of a universal human essence. Unfortunately, such widely divergent conclusions are the result of fundamental misunderstandings concerning Marx's own approach. What both sides of the controversy have failed to recognise is the *reciprocity* between humans and history, this provides us with an equation of interdependency in which the first historical act is the production of the means to satisfy the needs of human life, 'the production of material life itself'. The equation, according to Marx, should thus read: Humans make History – History makes Humans – Humans make History. where humans are, in the first instance, little more than animals satisfying basic, natural needs. The speculative abstraction 'Man' plays no part in this equation, Marx and Engels had dispensed with it in *The German Ideology*, not in order to replace it with a simple-minded determinism, but to assert the centrality of actual individuals to their understanding of revolutionary subjectivity. The individuals who make history are always at the same time the products of history, therefore if these humans engage in revolutionising social relations, this would not be due to the promptings of an innate creative essence, nor to an ageless notion of freedom synonymous with 'man in general', but would be the response to the contradictions and antagonisms of a particular set of social relations.

The ensemble of social relations may well be the basis of human essence, but this does not remove individuals as human agents in their own right from Marx's analysis of these social relations. Even when he deals with economic categories and treats individuals as the personification of these categories, he does so having stated that it is only in this particular case that individuals are considered in this way, hence the use of the word 'here', i.e. in this particular instance.[115] Social relations are of course the relations between living, active men and women, therefore, whenever Marx analyses concepts that relate to economic relations such as need, consumption, labour and freedom he is at the same time

Human nature

dealing with concepts that have a direct bearing on the individual human agent. This only reinforces the view that the interdeterminate reciprocity between individuals and social relations is always the presupposition that underpins Marx's critique, in other words, there are always two interrelated sides to the marxian understanding of reality. Productive activity is both a social and an individual activity, social in the sense that it is social relations that defines the procedures and the content of this productive activity, individual because such activity is a fundamental aspect of any human agent's life-process.

Humans in social relations make their own history. This was for Marx both the basis for his appraisal of the historical development of an ever-changing human character, and the foundation for revolutionary subjectivity. As such it undermined the static universalism of political philosophies which sought to idealise existing expressions of human character, while revealing that individuals in social relations were, of their own accord, capable of freely and consciously creating and recreating the conditions of their own existence. Marx believed he was right to abandon all talk of 'Man' and to reject elaborate notions of human nature, for in doing so he returned reality from the mind of the intellectual to the hands of actual indlviduals.

PART TWO

The individual and freedom

CHAPTER 4

Introductory comment – the individual and freedom

How is it that society is comprised of individuals who each possess the potential for self-determination and yet are prevented by that same society from exercising it? What are the chances of establishing a society which will enable most people to explore the different facets of their humanity in concert with others, and what are the processes that might bring about such a society? Mill and Marx in their own ways were inspired by and believed they had answers for all these questions, and each of their answers incorporated or implied a systematic critique of existing institutions, attitudes, values and morals, and were informed by their own theories of social progress.

As has been shown, the analyses of human nature developed by Mill and Marx each formed an integral part of their theories of social progress. For both of them, history was only explicable in terms of the ways in which the human capacity for self-determination had been exercised in the past and was being utilised in the present. And when it came to the future, this was to be of humanity's own making, secured through the conscious exercise of the uniquely human ability to constructively create the circumstances of existence. In this sense, Mill and Marx were both inspired by a Promethean image of the human agent, an image of individuals as creators, surrounded by the fruits of their labours (both intellectual and material), engaged in the constant and extensive development of their personalities and needs, and realising the potentialities of their own characters along with those of society as a whole.[1]

But as regards the means by which this future was to be secured, Mill and Marx most definitely parted company. For the

The individual and freedom

former, a programme of legal, political, social and educational reform, inspired by the foresight of an enlightened and influential few – already benefiting from the exercise of self-culture, would be the only alternative to a system suffering from baleful prejudice, ignorance and short-sighted self-interest. For the latter the only positive alternative was the revolutionary transformation of the existing conditions of production, and the accompanying social relations, carried out by those who had suffered most from exploitation and servitude.

Both of these solutions to the problem of unfreedom in contemporary society must be seen in the light of each thinker's belief in the possibility for the continuance of human progress, and I think here lies a clue to the reasons why some have believed that the theories of freedom propounded by Mill and Marx are compromised. Both believed that there were distinct and recognisable causes behind the advancement of human society, and both in their own ways were at times susceptible to the notion of inevitability. It was the means chosen to harness the dynamic of progress which have led some to claim that Mill and Marx were prepared to compromise individual liberty for the sake of a better future for society as whole. Did each take sufficient precautions against the potential for the abuse of freedom by the 'Clerisy' or the 'dictatorship of the proletariat'?

We have already seen that Mill was impressed by the Saint-Simonian dialectic, inherited and improved by Comte, i.e. the belief that history could be compartmentalised into organic and critical periods, the former being times of social harmony characterised by consensus, a legitimate status quo and uncontested principles, while the latter suffered from social dislocation, political uncertainty and moral malaise. Mill was certainly convinced that he was living through a time of crisis, indeed, he saw it as his duty to contribute to the on-going intellectual inquiry which he regarded as the way forward to a new era of certainty. But, he recognised that such path-breaking endeavours were under constant threat from the ignorance and prejudice of the uneducated mass who consistently failed to appreciate the beneficial consequences of the pursuit of self-improvement. As a consequence of this predicament Mill was faced with a dilemma: how do we guarantee the pursuit of progress and freedom – which will of

The individual and freedom

course be to the benefit of all – while at the same time protecting those who will do most to advance the cause – the unconventional, the challenging and the eccentric? Mill's solution reflects a caution and a fear, caution in the sense that his earlier utilitarian radicalism and enthusiasm for an undiluted universal franchise had been tempered by worries about the tyranny of the majority, fear that without due care the delicate flame of truth might be extinguished by stupidity and cowardliness.

How to guard against these baleful prospects became, I believe, Mill's chief concern and one evidenced in all of his major works. Others have recognised the same dilemma and have sought to explain apparent inconsistencies in Mill's writings in the light of his 'failure' to reconcile countervailing tendencies that emerged from his search for a solution. Richard J. Arneson,[2] for example, claims that Mill resorted to a Benthamite utilitarian paternalism when it came to his proposals for the implementation of representative government, in stark contrast to his clarion call for freedom in *On Liberty*. Others have gone the whole hog and suggested that Mill lost hope in the ability of the generality to raise themselves up from their mental and material penury, insisting that he came to view the state not as an improver but as an 'umpire between the majority of fools and the minority of Socrates', incapable of overcoming the stubborn distinction between them.[3] Whereas William Thomas[4] argues that Mill's ideal became a pedagogic one, with society structured along the lines of a classroom, 'where the teachers justify their leadership by imparting their knowledge freely, and the pupils give obedience and respect to those who most deserve it'.

Although there is much to commend each of these viewpoints – and there is certainly ample evidence to support them in Mill's work – they all underestimate Mill's conviction that times will change, probably for the better, given a supportive environment. He was of the opinion that the initial institutional elitism would eventually wither away and be replaced by an enlightened social consensus. However, I believe that his ever-cautious approach comes close to being fatalistic, so that he was more prepared to accept the devil he knew than the one he did not understand. In effect, he was confined by his own prejudices about the labouring classes (and for that matter, the middle classes) and blinkered by

The individual and freedom

his conviction that only those who resembled his own ideal, virtuous, self-improver were suitable candidates for being entrusted with real authority. Further, when it came to the general happiness Mill appeared to vacillate between 'rule' and 'act' utilitarianism, depending on the circumstances. He was more than prepared to recommend rules and laws for actions that failed to conform to his own moral standpoint, but was also of the opinion that those who took advantage of self-culture should be free to experiment with higher and lower orders of pleasure, secure in the knowledge that all would ultimately choose the former, much as he had done. Far from being an 'indirect utilitarian' Mill was quite willing to suggest intervention if it would secure circumstances for the cultivation of general happiness, while guaranteeing freedom for those who wished to pursue it.

Marx was of course inspired by a different dialectic, one that was the product of social individuals engaged in the constantly changing satisfaction of needs via conscious productive activity. The sad reality was that this potential source of individual liberty and social emancipation was in his own times being squandered by an economic system that extracted wealth from the majority in order to satisfy the distorted appetites of the few. Nevertheless, the antagonisms and contradictions of capitalism would eventually generate, he believed, the circumstances for social transformation, creating a climate of revolutionary expectation amongst the dispossessed and exploited. The bourgeois relations of production were, Marx believed, pregnant with the basis of a new order, providing insights of what might be once the the massive resources built up by capital are consciously utilised for and by the mass of self-determining, mutually recognitive agents.

It cannot be denied that Marx's indictment of capitalism was both powerful and detailed, and that his vision of an emancipated existence still manages to inspire many. But he did leave it very much up to ourselves to bring about the revolutionary moment (despite the persistence of those who are convinced that he was nothing more than unreformed determinist). Marx was most reluctant to provide us with a set of objectives, or with a system of values and norms with which we could convince others of the rightness of our cause. He also appeared to possess an incurable faith in the ability of all individuals to take charge of their own destinies. These two factors when combined generate a certain unease in those who would otherwise consider Marx's proposals plausible. Steven Lukes, for one, finds Marx's sceptical view of the 'rights of man' a 'narrow and impoverished' one[5] in that it is too easily prepared to dismiss all rights talk as bourgeois nonsense and as a veil behind which capital continues to expropriate. Alasdair MacIntyre expresses a genuine concern when he notes that Marx never discussed the 'question of what principles of action are to inform the working-class movement', neither did he consider the 'morality of socialist and communist society ... he is at best allusive on this topic'.[6]

The reason for these understandable concerns is in part related to the experience of revolutionary reality, when the supposed lacuna in Marx's work concerning morality is held as being partly responsible for the excesses of cruelty and repression in post-revolutionary societies. If this does not lead to outright rejection of the marxian system it does at least beg the question: can marxism have a morality, and if it does can its origins be found in the originator's writings? I believe that the query can be answered adequately by assessing the relationship between Marx's method and its application to his critique of existing moral theories, systems of justice and political economy. And furthermore, that Marx's own impressions of an emancipated existence emerge out of his critique, in the same way as he himself believed our own expectations of freedom would develop out of our own practical struggle against oppression. Whether the profoundly estranged masses of capitalist society would ever possess the committed, collective motivation to radically restructure society is a concern that requires its own response.

The implications these lines of thought have for both thinkers' professed commitment to liberty are assessed in the following chapters.

CHAPTER 5

Mill and individuality: the elite, the generality and democracy

1 Introduction

For Mill representative democracy was both an end in itself and a means to an end. As an end in itself it was the most desirable political system, characteristic of only the most advanced and progressive societies. As a means to an end it would be an invaluable institutional aid to the development of free individuals. Mill initially believed that both these facets were mutually compatible, neatly dove-tailing to give citizens the best of all possible worlds. And yet, the practical priorities of establishing representative democracy, and the need to defend it from abuse tended to gain precedence over the laudable aim of freeing the masses from ignorance. Mill's youthful, radical championing of the universal franchise was eventually replaced by a pragmatic defence of elite-led gradualism. What explains this apparent change of emphasis?

I want to argue that Mill's eventual preference for a meritocratic reformism had its roots in both his political and his philosophical writings. In *On Liberty*,[1] Mill combined a hierarchical categorisation of pleasure and happiness with criteria for distinguishing between superior and inferior forms of human character. His 'happiness hierarchy' lay at the heart of *Utilitarianism* and underpinned his preference for a fulfilling life of 'poetry' and his disdain for those who would rather play at 'pushpin'. While his examination of human nature in Book VI of *A System of Logic*[2] sought to incorporate a notion of free will within a materialist methodology, for without an explanation of self-direction Mill's call for a defence of liberty would remain unsubstantiated.

Mill ended up not only seeking to demarcate a sphere of individual liberty which is inviolate, but also insisting that there is

The individual and freedom

a preferable form of self-determination, incorporating the higher aspects of human character and the qualitatively superior forms of happiness. Such self-determination (or 'individuality' as Mill terms it in *On Liberty*) was, he believed, the vital dynamic force in any 'civilised' society, without which progress would be impossible. Hence the need to protect those of 'higher character' from the detrimental side-effects of an unbridled universal franchise: the celebration of mediocrity and the tyranny of the majority.

In this light *Considerations on Representative Government* can be regarded as providing the justification for giving governmental authority to the intellectually superior. Mill expected that in such hands the future democratic political system would itself become an agency for general education and social progress. But perhaps most controversially, he also believed that the meritocracy would by their actions perform an instructional role. He hoped that the generality would come to deferentially respect, and emulate those who had so clearly benefited from self-cultivation.

Admittedly, Mill did recognise the demand for suffrage, and went further than most in campaigning for a universal rather than just a 'manhood' form. Nevertheless, he continued to believe that in the hands of the uncultivated and unvirtuous the legislative and executive institutions of democracy would be abused. The long term pursuit of the common good would be discarded in favour of short sighted material gain via the disruptive redistribution of wealth. His proposed solution to this potentially destructive situation was to place the governance of society in the hands of the enlightened few until such time as the generality were fit to govern themselves. It is a solution that reveals much about Mill's views on the state of his own society and its adequacy as the basis for continued human advancement. He recognised that the vast majority were currently unprepared for the responsibility of guaranteeing liberty through popular sovereignty. While, at the same time, he accepted that there was a need to legitimate a system of government which would vest real authority in the hands of a virtuous, liberated intelligentsia.

To understand the origins of Mill's evaluation of the capacity of society to progress, and, more specifically, his preference for both universal franchise *and* elitism, it is necessary to start with a re-examination of his analysis of liberty. To this end I will begin with the proposal that in *On Liberty* Mill was not simply defending a negative principle of liberty but was also seeking to promote a positive ideal of freedom, situating both within a broader conception of the explanatory worth of utility. Such a manoeuvre, he hoped, would avoid both the narrow determinism of orthodox utilitarianism and the charge of intuitionism, at the same time as highlighting the voluntary nature of self-improvement. But a tension still remained in this particular compatibilist solution, which, I believe, has been incorporated in the writings of those who have sought to restore Mill to the status of *the* negative libertarian.

Secondly, I will show that Mill's enthusiasm for the fullest expression of positive individual freedom in *On Liberty* reflects a qualitative categorisation of human activity based on the qualitative examination of happiness found in *Utilitarianism*. Such a capacity for individual freedom, Mill believed, would, initially, only be fully realised by an intellectual elite, who, by virtue of their high level of self-determination, would be the only individuals adequately equipped to occupy a position from which to enlighten the generality. This generality, Mill assumed, would be incapable of, or indifferent to, the pursuit of the higher virtues, certainly for the foreseeable future.

Thirdly, in turning to *Considerations of Representative Government*, I will outline Mill's arguments for providing those of proven ability and virtue with a political authority enabling them to influence, persuade and legislate in pursuit of the common good, as they themselves would have perceived it, while at the same time minimising the damage of majority rule. Finally, by way of conclusion, I will note a few of the illiberal consequences of Mill's compatibilism. In particular, I shall point to its elitist connotations and its inegalitarian political implications; showing that this only served to reinforce his unresolved oscillation between an optimism born out of his analysis of human nature and the 'discovery' of the capacity for self-determination, and a pessimism which accompanied his appraisal of the potential for social emancipation in his own society

The individual and freedom

2 The principle of liberty and the concept of freedom

Mill wished to assert;

> one very simple principle ... that the sole end for which mankind are warranted, individually or collectively, in interfering with the liberty of action of any of their number, is self protection. That the only purpose for which power can be rightfully exercised over any member of a civilised community, against his will, is to prevent harm to others.[3]

To those who would wish to dress Mill in the guise of a negative libertarian, nothing could be clearer by way of a defence of allowing individuals to do that which they want to do without fear of coercion, legal penalty or moral reprobation. As long as these individuals do nothing to harm the vital interests of others, the argument goes, they can satisfy their multifarious wants, and pursue their personal pleasures. This interpretation would appear to place Mill within the utilitarian, empiricist tradition, championed by his tutor/father, and by his mentor, Bentham; i.e., that the best way to secure individual, and consequently general, happiness is to guarantee for want-maximising, pleasure-seeking agents a realm of freedom in which they can pursue, generally unimpeded, their personal desires. And it is on the basis of such an interpretation that the 'traditional' critique of Mill sets out to condemn him as an inconsistent and muddled eclectic. Fitzjames Stephen and his latter day inheritors – Berlin, McCloskey, Honderich,[4] to name but a few – all adopt a similar position which suggests that Mill's defence of a negative liberty, grounded on the principle of utility, soon gave way to a positive view of freedom as self-determination based on a belief in free will, an analysis which, in terms of an orthodox utilitarian psychology, was both inexplicable and dangerously intuitionist. Essentially, a morality based on the principle of utility has no room for a principle of liberty which rests upon a theory of self-culture, and by attempting to conjoin the two, Mill ended up with a compromised utilitarianism and a confused epistemology.

Recent attempts to defend Mill from these attacks insist that he adopted a broader concept of utility which perceived the pursuit of happiness as much more than mere want satisfaction; 'utility in the largest sense, grounded on the permanent interests of a man as a progressive being'.[5] Writers such as Ten, Gray and Berger[6] have suggested that for Mill, individual and general happiness would only improve if individuals were recognised as being capable of autonomous choice, and that the principle of liberty was a necessary prerequisite for individual and social happiness as it protected autonomous self-development. In other words, unless such autonomous individuality were given a free rein, within the constraints laid down by the principle of liberty, society – as well as the individual – would be the loser:

> It is not by wearing down into uniformity all that is individual in themselves, but by cultivating it, and calling it forth, within the limits imposed by the rights and interests of others, that human beings become a noble and beautiful object of contemplation ... In proportion to the development of his individuality, each person becomes more valuable to himself, and is therefore capable of being of more value to others ... when there is more life in the units ; there is more in the mass which is composed of them.[7]

This 'revisionary' argument (a term used by Gray to categorise all those who have attempted to rescue Mill from the clutches of his detractors[8]) is fine as far as it goes. It does reinstate Mill's broader understanding of the utilitarian associationist epistemology, incorporating as it does the capacity for choice making, (understood in terms of an ability to change our character, if we so wish, by placing ourselves under the conditioning influence of different circumstances); it also attempts to free Mill from the supposed inconsistency, suggested by Berlin, of pairing a 'positive' view of freedom as rational self-development with a 'negative' principle of liberty, *without* inferring a connected morality discoverable through rational thought and action. But despite its attempt to iron out some of the inconsistencies traditionally associated with Mill's eclecticism in terms of a modified utilitarian method, the 'revisionary' account fails to explain adequately Mill's preference for a particular kind of autonomous, self-developing individual, one who exhibits those faculties and qualities which Mill equates, in *A System of Logic* and elsewhere, with virtue.[9] Hence my feeling that a tension remains within the 'revisionary' rebuttal of the 'traditional' critique of the 'muddled eclectic'. In the former's attempt to redefine Mill's utilitarianism, widening it in the pursuit of coherency, it still fails to account for Mill's preference for a virtuous way

The individual and freedom

of life, embodying a morality which is not entirely explained by his reworking of the principle of utility. What I want to suggest is that Mill developed and needed a theory of freedom as virtue which then allowed him to defend both a particular kind of individual, i.e. the individual of confirmed virtue, and that individual's favoured position in the constitution of a representative democracy. Further, Mill believed that his compatibilist solution to the free will/determinism dichotomy had furnished him (and social reformers as a whole) with a social theory that both legitimated the defence of individual liberty in the name of progress, and recommended that the guardians of the general good should be appointed from the ranks of those who had gained the heights of excellence in their chosen field. To make these moves, Mill had to modify and, at the same time, go beyond a purely utilitarian epistemology. What were the results of this manoeuvre?

Much of the recent literature on Mill's utilitarianism wrestles with the problem of whether he was an act or a rule utilitarian, or something in between.[10] The 'revisionists' have themselves adopted positions concordent with one or other of these reassessments in an attempt to engineer a rapprochement between liberty and utility, for without it they cannot hope to claim coherency for Mill.[11] Orthodox utilitarians have no need of such soul searching, for them the case is clear: individuals are want maximisers, who, in satisfying their wants, obtain happiness, and as long as favourable conditions exist which defend such a pursuit of utility, the general good will be guaranteed. However, for those who have chosen to bite the bullet and explain Mill's preference for particular types of character and his predilection for certain personal traits in terms of a stretched general happiness principle, the problem remains one of incompatibility. Simply put, the principle of utility was inadequate for the tasks Mill expected it to perform in *On Liberty* and in *Considerations on Representative Government*. As a principle of happiness it had no room for nuance; as an ethnical standard it was concerned with 'the subjection of individual spontaneity to external control, only in respect to those actions of each, which concern the interest of other people'[12] i.e. no qualitative distinction is made between types of spontaneity. And yet the whole purpose of *On Liberty* is to champion a *higher* form of spontaneity as the motive force of history, while making the case for the protection of the virtuous from the unvirtuous ... this of course being in the long term interest of the latter, if they did but know it. Meanwhile, *Representative Government* extends the theoretical to the practical where general utility is interpreted by the same virtuous set in their capacity as political representatives and policy makers, an interpretation based no doubt on their own discrimination between lower and higher pleasures. D. P. Dryer makes a similar point in his article[13] when he claims that the principle of utility is not employed by Mill as the 'ultimate appeal on all ethical questions'.[14] Mill, in proclaiming the duty of every man and woman to perfect themselves, is not overriding the principle of utility, he is 'rather maintaining a duty over and above what the principle of utility requires'.[15] The duty to perfect oneself is therefore independent of utility; individuals should not only do that which is conducive to the general good, they also owe it to themselves to pursue their own autonomous self-development in order to attain qualitatively superior forms of character. The 'ultimate principle' therefore becomes the basis for a set of general, social constraints, and the principle of liberty defines the arena of personal freedom as the realm of virtuous self-determination.

It is this distinction between considerations for the general good and the pursuit of personal self-realisation which provide the twin poles drawing Mill's argument one way or the other. In *On Liberty* the discussion gravitates between 'Civil, or Social Liberty: the nature and limits of the power which can be legitimately exercised by society over the individual',[16] and the freedom of the will. And in *Considerations on Representative Government*, as Thompson points out, the debate swings between participation and competence; the former considered in terms of the general welfare, the latter in terms of securing for, government and society, minds of superior character.[17] I believe that in both essays Mill's sympathies lie more with arguments defending the freedom of the will and those who exercise it, than with those solely concerned with general utility. As to his reasons for such a preference I shall now turn to *On Liberty* in an attempt to provide an explanation.

Although Mill seems to state clearly at the beginning of the essay that he did not intend to discuss the 'Liberty of the Will', he nevertheless employed throughout a distinct concept of freedom which assumed a particular solution to the problem of free will

The individual and freedom

within a determined world. Only if we take on board Mill's concept of freedom will we come to appreciate his arguments in *On Liberty* for the cultivation of particular forms of human character. To find his concept of freedom we need to turn to his 'compatibilism'.

In both *On Liberty* and *A System of Logic* Mill identifies a doctrine and its disciples, as major threats to the furtherance of the cause of individual liberty and autonomous self-determination. The threat is 'Owenite social fatalism'. Owen and his followers adopted a social determinism which maintained that we cannot be held responsible for our actions because they are the products of appetites and desires which are in turn conditioned by our characters, characters which are themselves caused by social circumstances which we cannot control. Any suggestion that individuals were capable of spontaneous self-development, and that such 'individuality is one of the leading essentials of well-being'[18] would have been scorned and rejected by Owenite social reformers, indeed:

> spontaneity forms no part of the ideal of the majority of moral and social reformers, but is rather looked on with jealousy, as a troublesome and perhaps rebellious obstruction to the general acceptance of what these reformers, in their own judgement, think would be best for mankind.[19]

Mill wished to distance himself from such doctrines, a desire which is explicable in terms of his disenchantment with Benthamite necessitarianism and his distrust of the accompanying theory which claimed that men were socially manufactured. Human freedom would be impossible in an Owenite system which insisted that all human wants were socially determined, and in which the application of a purely negative liberty would merely remove the limitations to want satisfaction, as long as this satisfaction did not frustrate the wants of others.

In *A System of Logic* Mill confronted this social fatalism and attacked its product, the irresponsible, impotent human actor. The result, as G. W. Smith points out, was a concept of freedom which corresponded with Mill's argument in *On Liberty*.[20] He suggested an alternative to the empiricist compatibilism of Hume, rejecting its claim that the causal origins of an agent's wants are strictly irrelevant to his or her liberty. Mill insisted that agents' characters are the source of their desires and that each of these characters is not solely the product of circumstances causally ascribable only to social conditioning. What Mill wished to suggest was that causal laws were hypothetical and not categorical. Such hypothetical laws would merely 'lay down what will, or will not, occur if intervening causes do not apply'.[21] But of course there will always be intervening causes of one form or another, usually too numerous, too unpredictable and so closely interrelated as to make separate identification, cataloguing and categorisation, almost impossible. We need only look at the variety of social interventions possible in people's lives to appreciate how daunting the task of identifying all such causal effects is. We ourselves are interveners in the affairs of others. The intervention is itself conditioned Mill admitted, but he believed that this would not affect our being able to do what we do. Crucially, Mill then extended our powers of intervention to include ourselves, i.e. he suggested that one of the most important causal antecedents of self-determination is the individual's desire to pursue it. This desire or feeling 'of our being able to modify our character, *if we wish*, is itself the feeling of moral freedom we are conscious of'.[22] In the *Logic* Mill labels this capacity 'self-culture', in *On Liberty* it becomes 'individuality'; in effect, it is Mill's theory of self-determination.

The question of whether Mill's reworking of the compatibilist solution is adequate or not, is not directly relevant to my main purpose. To his own satisfaction, he believed he had equipped himself with a methodology with which to analyse human psychology and social relations, and to formulate a programme of political reform. The problem is that his attention was diverted away from the immediate pursuit of the general good (the expressed aim) to a concern for the life-blood of the polity itself, the intelligentsia. This, I believe, is a direct result of his search for an associationist theory of free will and its goal, a concept of freedom as self-determination. This is the concept that becomes the central concern for Mill in *On Liberty*; it is the capacity realised initially, by a fortunate few who require the protection of the principle of liberty. It is they who are most at risk from the despotism of the majority and they who have most to offer to society if provided with the circumstances allowing them to flourish. It is the desire for autonomous, self-development which for Mill is the basis of the

The individual and freedom

formation of the most authentic human character;

> A person whose desires and impulses are his own – are the expression of his own culture – is said to have character. One whose desires and impulses are not his own, has no character, no more than a steam engine has character.[23]

What Mill went on to assert was that those individuals who had developed the uniquely human capacity of autonomous thought and action were also the only individuals capable of achieving a higher quality of pleasures. Unfortunately, in his own day, Mill noted that only a few had developed the superior faculties conducive to a higher happiness, and that in the majority the 'capacity for the nobler feelings'[24] had died away. That he believed that for most such a capacity had died suggests a pessimistic outlook regarding the generality's ability to recognise the advantages of the more valuable powers of the human intellect, as well as regarding the willingness to respect those who have attained the status of a dissatisfied Socrates. The questions I now wish to tackle are: firstly, what are the characteristics of Mill's self-directing individual? secondly, why should Mill insist that only these individuals were capable of attaining the 'higher pleasures'? and thirdly, why were such individuals specifically singled out by Mill for protection under the principle of liberty?

3   The autonomous individual, happiness and freedom

In *On Liberty* there is ample evidence to suggest that Mill adhered to an ideal of individuality based on his notion of freedom as mastery over character. Several commentators have noted that this picture bears a marked resemblance to the Kantian ideal of freedom as moral autonomy. Gray, in his *Mill on Liberty: a defence*, suggests that Mill absorbed the Kantian view, in neo-Romantic variant, from Von Humboldt.[25] Indeed, Mill quotes or mentions the Baron on several occasions in support of his discussion on freedom and individuality. For example: 'the end of man, or that which is prescribed by the eternal or immutable dictates of reason ... is the highest and most harmonious development of his powers to a complete and consistent whole.'[26] Every individual, given the ability and opportunity, must therefore assert their individuality, that is, their authority over their own development. Only in a situation of liberty can the desire to alter one's character, combined with the expression of this desire through self-amending action, be fully explored. Only by choosing to engage in self-amendment will the individual harness the uniquely human faculties of 'perception, judgement, discriminative feelings, mental activity and ... moral preference.'[27] Such an individual bears a marked resemblance to the 'wise man' of Mill's *Utilitarianism*. This is the only person who, by way of exercising these discriminative and judgemental powers, and combining them with his or her breadth of experience, can discern higher from lower pleasures. Thus for Mill, those who can show that their desires and personal projects are their own, display individuality, and through the pursuit of these desires and the achievement of these projects such individuals can achieve a higher form of happiness, the happiness obtained through the exercise of active human faculties. These are the secondary means and ends which, as Mill pointed out in his essay on Bentham, are the medium through which utility or happiness can be obtained. To succumb to the temptations of habit, routine, and the satisfaction of inferior appetites, all for the sake of a lower happiness, was, he believed, both demeaning and destructive of the ability each of us possesses for self-improvement. Yet he recognised, with regret, that this was the prevailing way of life for the majority. Mill had himself experienced the distinct lack of personal satisfaction which resulted from the direct pursuit of utility, and his emotional response to this revelation is recounted in his *Autobiography*.[28]

Mill therefore clearly believed that the achievement of self-development was both a difficult and an uncommon thing. Many do not know that they are capable of self-amendment, others may attempt to develop the 'nobler feelings' which accompany self-culture and fail in the face of the overbearing weight of conformity and custom; and there are some who Mill believes are capable of pursuing those faculties conducive to higher pleasures, but 'under the influence of temptation postpone them to the lower'.[29] The capacity for self-culture is, for Mill, a fragile desire which in most individuals is stifled before they have the opportunity to employ it. It is generally not through direct opposition or active coercion that the desire is destroyed, more often it is killed 'by the mere want of sustenance'. This is particularly the case, Mill believed, for the 'majority of young persons' in whom the potential for self-development 'speedily dies away if the occupation to which their position in life has devoted them, and the society into which it has thrown them, are not favourable to keeping that higher capacity in existence'.[30] This predicament is made all the worse by the fact that such a sacrifice is not voluntarily made, as most individuals who lose the higher capacity do so without ever being aware of the loss.

In Chapter III of *On Liberty* a recurring theme is that of the debasing effect of modern democratic society on the distinctive endowments of a human being [31] The deadweight of custom and conformity have supplanted the individual desire to exercise discerning and deliberative faculties; the result is a society in which the larger portion of the populace allows the world, or its particular portion of it, to choose for it a plan of life. In doing so the only faculty it exercises is that of 'ape-like' imitation.

The impression the reader is left with after completing Chapter III, and for that matter the whole essay, is of a mass of mediocrity which has 'now fairly got the better of individuality' causing a deficiency of personal impulses and preferences.[32] The individual in such circumstances does not ask 'what would suit my character and disposition? or, what would allow the best and highest in me to have fair play and enable it to grow and thrive?'[33] The inclination of such individuals is to accept what is customary, and shun any sense of the spontaneous and free development of individuality. The majority are satisfied with the present ways of mankind and 'cannot comprehend why those ways should not be good enough for everybody,' hence their suspicion and lack of recognition of the 'intrinsic worth' of individual spontaneity.[34] And once this indifference and mistrust is complemented with the 'Calvinistic theory ... that the one great offence of man is self-will'[35] and its concomitant insistence on obedience, the room left to individual ability is mighty little.

In such an apparently hopeless predicament Mill turns for help to those who have managed, in such hostile circumstances, to preserve, and who continue to assert their desire for self-development. It is these individuals, who in cultivating their particular faculties become valuable to others, it is they who should be allowed the liberty to pursue multifarious experiments in living and to broadcast far and wide 'heretical opinions' without being smothered by social intolerance.³⁶ It is for them that the Principle of Liberty should be applied with all its authority because Mill believed that the future progress of society would rely upon the free exercise of their unique talents; and as I will show, it is they who should be elevated to positions of political authority by appointment and/or election in Mill's democracy of plural voting.

Before tackling this final point I wish to examine briefly Mill's justification for asserting that those proven in their individuality should be protected from the uncultivated generality:

> It is necessary further to show, that these developed human beings are of some use to the undeveloped – to point out to those who do not desire liberty, and would not avail themselves of it, that they may be in some intelligible manner rewarded for allowing other people to make use of it without hindrance.³⁷

Mill believed that through their pursuit of self-culture, free individuals would discover new truths for themselves which in leading to new practices would set examples to those incapable of, or restrained in their own self-development. Only these free agents would be capable of discovering, through their experiments, new and improved practices. It would only be from their ranks that genius would spring, and Mill was not averse to mixing his metaphors when he proclaimed:

> these few are the salt of the earth; without them, human life would become become a stagnant pool ... (and) in order to have them, it is necessary to preserve the soil in which they grow. Genius can only breathe freely in an *atmosphere* of freedom.³⁸

These few are the ultimate in individuality and it is primarily for them that the principle of liberty should be championed. The gift of genius is its originality, and the first service it should perform is to open the eyes of those unoriginal minds, burdened by mediocrity, and reveal to them the higher pleasures gained through aspiring to self-improvement. Mill insisted that if those individuals of 'average intelligence' were capable of any positive quality, it was that of following an initiative. They owed it to themselves to follow the example of those who had confirmed their capacity for self-culture, or, failing that, defer in favour of those persons who had attained superior individuality. For it is they who are the source of social improvement, and general human progress. And as a final

The individual and freedom

warning, Mill reminded his audience that in the greater part of the world the 'despotism of Custom' had overcome the progressive principle of improvement through liberty. Such, then, should be the relationship between the intellectual elite, or that small minority of self-cultivated individuals, and the generality, bound as they are by mediocrity, custom and conformity. And such is the relationship that is carried over by Mill into the sphere of government and politics.

4 The elite, the generality and representative government

It is in his discussion of politics, and particularly of representative democracy, that Mill appears in his most illiberal guise. In his *Considerations on Representative Government* he sought to defend a system of constitutional checks and balances which were meant to achieve two general aims. One was the necessity of securing for society individuals of intellectual excellence so that they might pursue in their own way and in a disinterested fashion the common weal. While the second was the need to prevent the labouring classes from translating their numerical predominance into a majority government, because after all, they were not, Mill believed 'the most highly cultivated' of classes.[39] He recognised that both these aims were difficult to square with his commitment to a universal franchise, but this did not stop him from attempting to formulate a constitutional compromise. Of course it is apparent, especially after reading *On Liberty*, that Mill believed that the generality should be protected from the damaging effects of their own mediocrity; that if only they could be prepared to recognise the progressive tendencies within individuality and allocate those who exhibited such a capacity a proportion of political authority reflective of these superior abilities, then they would surely benefit from the policies which would be the product of such enlightened, disinterested authority.

However, this is not exactly the picture which emerges from the pages of *Representative Government*. The prevailing mood of this essay is characterised partly by a dread fear of the labouring classes and their potentially destructive political power, along with a thinly disguised contempt for the aspiring middle classes, and a suspicion of the motives of the philanthropists. These concerns had

Mill and individuality

already been aired in *On Liberty* where they were coupled with the recommendation that those individuals of confirmed virtue should be encouraged to take positions of authority and influence in the institutions of government. In the essay on Government, however, these worries have direct, practical and political repercussions, both in terms of the democratic structures which Mill believes are required to neutralise the dangers inherent in a system of universal franchise, and with regard to the role of the intelligentsia. The response to their plight is contained in the now familiar suggestion: that there is a need to secure for the men of superior wisdom positions of pre-eminence in the movement for reform. This, I suggest, is a consequence of Mill's commitment to a concept of freedom which views only those of confirmed individuality as 'authentically human'. Those qualities, or something very much like them, which were said to be reflective of self-culture in *On Liberty*, appear again at the beginning of *Representative Government*:

> What ... are the qualities in the citizen individually which conduce most to keep up the amount of good conduct, of good management, of success and prosperity ... those qualities are industry, integrity, justice and prudence (along with) mental activity, enterprise, and courage.[40]

Ideally, the officers of government, 'themselves persons of superior virtue and intellect', would be surrounded by an atmosphere of 'virtuous and enlightened public opinion', but of course in Mill's own day the opposite was the rule, with a generality consisting of 'mere masses of ignorance, stupidity and baleful prejudice'.[41]

In what ways, then, did Mill propose to 'obtain ... for the functions of government the benefits of superior intellect'?[42] One would be through direct institutional recruitment, another through an electoral system of plural voting, and a third avenue would be the inculcation amongst the generality of a positive deference towards 'wiser men'. It is the first of these that immediately strikes one as being remarkably undemocratic. For example, at the head of central government there should be a 'small body, not exceeding in number the members of a Cabinet, who would act as a Commission of legislation, having for its appointed office to make the laws'.[43] The members of the commission would be appointed by the Crown to serve a five year term of office, during which time their purpose would be to frame the laws which the representative

The individual and freedom

assembly would either pass or reject, having 'no power to alter the measure'[44] being only able to refer it back to the commission for reconsideration. The commission would therefore not be answerable to the electorate or to their representatives, only to themselves as disinterested guardians of the public good and to the 'Crown', whatever form that may take (on this point Mill is unclear). This is based on Mill's premise that in 'legislation as well as administration, the only task to which a representative assembly can possibly be competent is *not* that of doing the work',[45] this should be secured for the 'acquired knowledge and practical intelligence of a specially trained and experienced Few'.[46] Unless these functions were clearly demarcated the popular assembly would invariably interfere in the affairs of the administration. 'Even when honestly meant, the interference is almost always injurious' and such a situation is 'at its best ... inexperience sitting in judgement of experience, ignorance of knowledge'.[47]

But such legislative authority is not enough for Mill. He believed that the representative assembly itself reflected the present tendency of civilisation to drift towards collective mediocrity, a process accentuated by all extensions of the franchise. These extensions could only lead to the principal power of a government being wielded by 'classes more and more below the highest level of instruction in the community'.[48] Two ways which would halt and turn back this debilitating trend are suggested by Mill. The first of these is through plural voting and proportional representation; the second is by encouraging the faculty of deference in those of mediocre abilities which should be exercised in favour of individuals of intellectual merit.

Mill's plural voting system was based on the belief that:

> though everyone ought to have a vote – that everyone should have an equal voice is a totally different proposition ... the opinion, the judgement, of the higher moral or intellectual being is worth more than that of the inferior.[49]

Such a being has a claim to superior weight, i.e. a higher number being assigned to their suffrages. Those who are recognised as being intellectually superior would of course possess a greater 'capacity for the management of joint interests',[50] hence the greater weight accorded them in their political representation. For Mill, only a fool would not recognise the efficacy of such a system. An

Mill and individuality

employer, by successfully undertaking his superior function, would understandably obtain two or more votes, because he is more intelligent than the labourer by virtue of the fact that he labours 'with his head, and not solely with his hands'. The same criterion would apply to bankers, merchants, graduates etc.,[51] each allocated a plurality of votes according to the status of their occupations and to the level of their achievement. These arrangements, coupled with proportional representation securing the interests of minorities, would therefore go part of the way towards a parliament 'containing the very *elite* of the country'.[52] Such an elite or 'instructed minority' would 'in virtue of their knowledge, and of the influence it would give them over the rest'[53] wield considerable moral power over the ignorance and incapacity of the generality or 'to speak more moderately', over those of,'insufficient mental qualifications'.[54] Of course, Mill is aware of the danger of those who benefit from a plurality of votes exercising their own class domination. His response to this threat is to urge the parties representing opposed interests to incorporate within their ranks individuals of confirmed virtue, i.e., those generally recognised as being the apogee of human intelligence. By nature Mill assumes that these individuals will be moderate and tolerant in temperament, recommending compromise, consensus and constructive antagonism, in the face of factional demands and destabilising class conflict.[55]

The minority of superior minds is therefore guaranteed a degree of representation and its members a plurality of votes, enabling them, with Mill's blessing, to secure a disproportionate share of influence in government, comforted by the knowledge that those making the laws will be of their ilk. What of the rest of the electorate, do they choose their own representatives from amongst themselves? For Mill such a situation would be disastrous. 'It is so important that the electors should choose as their representatives wiser men than themselves, and should consent to be governed according to that superior wisdom'.[56] 'Once the general tone of the mind of the electoral body, in respect to the important requisites of deference to mental superiority' has been achieved they will obtain for themselves 'men beyond mediocrity' who will 'carry on public affairs according to their unfettered judgement'. Mill is therefore recommending acquiescence in the face of the supposedly incon-

The individual and freedom

trovertible evidence supplied here, and elsewhere, of the natural authority of superior minds. For if the generality are encouraged to believe that the opinions of the 'able man' are usually the right ones, why should they as articulators of wrong opinions have any opinions at all? As we saw in *On Liberty*, for the man of superior intellect to conform to ideas of the inferior is tantamount to intellectual suicide, or as Mill puts it in *Representative Government*, a 'treason against his special office; abdication of the peculiar duties of mental superiority'. Therefore the superior mind must insist on 'full freedom to act as he in his own judgement deems best'. Only under such circumstances can the ordinary individual of average intelligence expect the able representative to act 'for him in the many matters in which he himself is not qualified to form a judgement.'[57]

On the other hand, should the numerical majority impose its mediocre, selfish and short-sighted interests through the representative assembly the result in the long term would be catastrophic for the general good of the community. For Mill, it would not be beyond the capacity of the generality to destroy the shibboleths of a civilised society such as 'realised property', 'knowledge' and 'individuality'. If political authority should fall into the hands of the labouring classes, the 'correct calculation' that distant interests are more worthy than the immediate satisfaction of wants, will be ignored and habitually avoided, and the 'bad parts of ... human nature'[58] will be satisfied at the expense of the higher faculties. These are the unavoidable consequences of unbridled majority class interests, which Mill admitted were the product of most men's *ordinary* life. Their work is routine, motivated by self-interest in its most elementary form, the satisfaction of daily wants; it is never a labour of love which would excite their human sentiments and stimulate their unique faculties. 'Neither the thing done, nor the process of doing it, introduces the mind to thoughts or feelings extending beyond individuals ... in most cases the individual has no access to any person of cultivation much superior to his own'.[59] Hence the generality's tendency to favour passive and contented types, the members of which have no ambition to make any one else happier, or no desire to promote the good of their country or their neighbourhood. In fact, such people have no incentive to improve even themselves in moral excellence. Mill's contempt for such types is total: 'We rightly ascribe this sort of contentment to mere unmanliness[!] and want of spirit'.[60] Part of the solution to this pressing problem is the universal provision of the franchise. But this should not be encouraged just for its own sake. Left to their own devices, those of inferior intelligence will almost invariably pursue short term, class based objectives which will be to the lasting detriment of the community as a whole.[61] For Mill, the inclusion of the generality into the political system serves an educative function, they will be exposed to the influences of superior intellects, recognising the advantages of electing as their representatives men of vision, and accepting the efficacy of a constitution which provides a disproportionate degree of influence to the cultivated minority. Thus;

> A representative constitution is a means of bringing the general standard of intelligence and honesty existing in the community, and the individual intellect and virtue of its wisest members, more directly to bear on the government. and investing them with greater influence in it, than they would in general have under any other mode of organisation.[62]

In effect, positions of real political power should be entrusted to those of greater cultivation who, after all, are more familiar with the ideas and actions conducive to the general interest.[63] Therefore, Mill was of the opinion that the only hope for humankind's continued advance rested with the virtuous, self-cultivating, elite; it was they who would most effectively articulate the true interests of the community as a whole; it was they who should be given a disproportionate amount of influence, for some time to come, in the representative polity in order to carry out their historical task; and it was they who would set an example to the 'less cultivated' of the advantages of pursuing self-development. For their part, the generality would benefit through their deference to and their reverence of their betters, and although possessing one vote per man (and woman), they would learn not to waste it on the likes of themselves, favouring instead individuals of confirmed excellence in their chosen fields, such as their employers and their social and intellectual superiors.

The individual and freedom

5 Conclusion

One of the main purposes of this chapter has been to re-situate several of J. S. Mill's major works around a theme which I believe is common to them all. It was his commitment to a particular form of individuality as the virtuous pursuit of higher happiness via self-determination – which was the result of his critique of orthodox utilitarianism and the subsequent compatibilist solution to the problem of free will and determinism – that underpinned his analysis of freedom, served as the starting point for his critique of representative democracy, and explained his faith in the continued progress of society and in those whom he believed were best equipped to promote it. Certain commentators, in order to avoid the inconsistencies of Mill's application of his theoretical insights, have sought to separate one work from another on the basis that the Mill who wrote *On Liberty* was a different Mill to the one who wrote *Considerations on Representative Government* – Gertrude Himmelfarb is the most celebrated member of this school.[64] Others have chosen to concentrate on *On Liberty*, marshalling Mill's other works behind this 'most eloquent expression of the liberal theory of the open society'.[65] The reasons for such a manoeuvre have depended on which side of the fence the interpreter has sat. On one side, Maurice Cowling focuses on the essay, bringing on other key texts in supporting roles, as a work which reflects its author's 'moral totalitarianism'.[66] While on the other side, 'revisionists' have also rallied behind *On Liberty* as the epitome of all that Mill stood for, claiming that his writings 'contain a coherent and forceful utilitarian defence of liberal principles about the right to liberty' which reaches its definitive expression in the essay.[67]

I believe that putting so much emphasis on *On Liberty* is misdirected, it is only *one* element in a programme for social improvement and individual emancipation. This is in direct contrast to Himmelfarb, whose theory of the 'two Mills' has come under sustained attack, primarily from those of the revisionary camp who wish to maintain that even in his more ostensibly authoritarian works Mill remained committed to the principle of liberty.[68] They insist that the essay is no temporary aberration prompted by the libertarian bidding of Harriet Taylor, and proclaim that Mill's liberal credentials remained intact throughout his mature years.

Mill and individuality

However, my own position is not a revisionary one, I do not seek to rehabilitate Mill as a the true champion of liberty. Much as I agree with those who claim that Mill was no intellectual schizophrenic, I do not share entirely their reasoning. Mill was *for* liberty, but not only as an end in itself. From *The Spirit of the Age* to his *Rectorial Address* to the University of St. Andrews, Mill was deeply concerned by the threat posed by mediocrity to continued social progress.[69] He was constantly at pains to point out that unless society recognised the inestimable value of the pursuit of knowledge (in its widest sense), and sought to protect those individuals who were fortunate enough to pursue it, then social stagnation would be the result. 'A people, it appears, may be progressive for a certain length of time, and then stop: when does it stop? When it ceases to possess individuality.'[70]

I have shown that for Mill 'individuality' meant more than either the freedom to satisfy wants, or the freedom to choose. It is the duty incumbent upon oneself to engage in self-determination and attain qualitatively superior character traits. The principle of liberty was to enable those who wished to explore their capacity for self-development to do so, allowing them the freedom to realise their particular, and by definition, superior talents without restraint, unless of course they harmed the interests of others. At the same time, the principle would enable the virtuous and enlightened to set examples for those less fortunate than themselves, in the hope that the uninstructed, if not able themselves to pursue such a life, would at least be capable of recognising the importance of the agents of ideas to society as a whole.

It is in *On Liberty* where the philosophical and political principles are established which both reinforced Mill's defence of the intelligentsia, and served as the theoretical foundations for the inegalitarian constitutional framework of *Considerations on Representative Government*. These priorities, I would suggest, are not born out of Mill's concern for the majority's present state of ignorance nor his desire for political equality, but derive their preeminence from his belief that civilisation must progress towards the 'good society' and that the guardians of progress are those who have become truly human. Mill was therefore torn between his sympathy for the demand for universal franchise and his belief in the necessity to protect the delicate flower of intellect. But, as I have attempted to show, this dilemma was more than an expression of a subjective clash of allegiance, its roots lie in the attempt to reconcile the depressing predictability of utilitarian necessitarianism with the idealist notion of the autonomous free-agent. When applying this reworked and less stringent utilitarianism to an analysis of the institutions of democratic government, Mill was confronted with very unpromising raw material. The generality, for the foreseeable future, would be incapable of comprehending the complexity and subtlety that characterise the duties of political office, reason enough to place such responsibilities in the hands of the intellectually superior. Further still, once in positions of authority, those gifted with the insights of intelligence should encourage others to obtain the advantages of a cultivated mind; those that already show some inclination in this direction should be given a head start through the provision of more votes and the allocation of responsible posts in the community commensurate with their abilities and talents. Mill admitted that the uninformed generality would continue to have problems unique to their own predicament, he accepted that their demand for the franchise was a legitimate claim, and he recognised that their incorporation in the political system would contribute to their overall education. But he nevertheless insisted that their true, long term interests could only be championed by representatives who are capable of looking beyond the immediate to the future, general good. We may well all be capable of self-improvement Mill proclaimed, but until such time as the conditions which are conducive to universal self-culture exist, we must leave the job of creating those conditions to the small number of individuals already proven in ability. In effect the majority were to be denied full participation in the planning of their own future.

CHAPTER 6

Marx and the individual

1 Introduction

In the following it will be reaffirmed that Marx was motivated by a commitment to revolutionary liberation for social individuals. This commitment developed alongside the elaboration of his science of society which had established that the dynamic of history was not a metaphysical force nor an invisible hand, but the result of actions of individuals in social relations. As was pointed out in the account of Marx's views on human nature, individuals engaged in the reproduction of the conditions of their existence form an integral part, a determining moment of the totality of particular historical epochs. In other words, Marx's view of human progress was based upon the recognition that it was individuals (in social relations) constantly engaged in the innovative re-creation of the material conditions necessary for their continued existence who were the creators of their own history.

As the account unfolds, it will be maintained that Marx's critique of the existing conditions of unfreedom in bourgeois social relations was *not* inspired by an *a priori* sense of injustice nor by a preconceived ethic, but that his constant eschewal of any direct moral or teleological authority (despite his continual use of terms that appear to have either an ethical or a teleological content) was part of a conscious effort on his part to establish the basis for a qualitatively different notion of human liberation and a radically alternative means of achieving it. But, although it will be claimed that Marx's 'ethical' and 'teleological' pronouncements emerged from his critique of existing social relations, and that they did not pre-exist or determine that critique, it will nevertheless be admitted

The individual and freedom

that a strong and consistent image of 'authentic' human existence may well have persisted in Marx's works, just as a 'vision' of communist society stands out in particular texts.

However, such images and visions were not the driving force behind Marx's critical examination of capitalism, and it is a mistake to assume that he began his investigations with a preconceived notion of 'true freedom' or 'communist' community. Neither can it be claimed that Marx applied a principle, or a theory of justice to his analysis of capitalism. All such concepts: morality, justice, *Recht*, rights, etc. were to be understood, according to Marx, not as ahistorical, universal truths or categorical imperatives, but as abstract categories which arise from, and are subsequently employed to regulate, concrete and antagonistic social relations. Therefore, I believe that the search for a universal marxian ethic or a revolutionary principle of distributive justice within Marx's works will always prove to be a fruitless and frustrating endeavour. That such a quest still attracts considerable attention, from both 'defenders' and 'detractors' is evidence of a general misunderstanding. The former are often inspired by the need to defend Marx from those who attack his 'inadequacies', or by the desire to make him applicable to the 'post-capitalist' world. Those who attack do so in the belief that Marx (and by definition marxism) lacks a formulated morality (after they have sought vainly for one) or if he possesses one, it is inadequate or downright dangerous.

Some have viewed the identification by Marx of a human agent in possession of a creative consciousness, exercised in social production, as his response to the traditional dilemma of attempting to establish a theory of freedom which would be compatible with a materialist determinism. As a result it has been claimed that Marx's 'compatibilism' does not escape from similar inconsistencies that accompany a solution such as Mill's, i.e., by attempting to overcome the fatalism of orthodox determinism, compatibilists invariably incorporate (intentionally or unintentionally) evaluative and/or teleological tendencies. In Marx's case the criticism often extends to attempts to discredit the scientific claims made by his social theory by pointing out that he adhered to a non-scientific morality. This is particularly the case with some recent non-marxist accounts echoing traditional opposition, such as those of John Gray and G. W. Smith,[1] which are only reinforced by those

Marx and the individual

who entertain the belief that Marx had a 'Kantian respect for the inviolability of persons',[2] or that he was a moral 'realist' who 'overstressed the importance' of his 'scientific theory'.[3] Others have claimed that the problem of such a supposed inconsistency in Marx's thought originated with the attempt to re-emphasise its idealist and humanist origins, purportedly initiated by the likes of Korsch and Lukacs. In response to this, as we saw in Chapter 3, structuralist marxists, in an effort to avoid what they saw as the confusing and inconclusive consequences of a 'compatibilist' reading of Marx, sought to defend an interpretation which suggested that he jettisoned the 'idealist' baggage of Hegelian theories of alienation in favour of a full blown scientific determinism. Although this approach may well have produced a more internally consistent Marx, it has since been shown by many critics of the 'epistemological break' thesis to be a highly selective and unbalanced account.[4] A far more persuasive analysis points out that throughout his intellectual later life Marx persisted in incorporating a concept of alienation into his examination of political economy, a concept which relied upon a theory of species being and a related analysis of human nature [5] But in reasserting the importance of alienation and species being, the 'continuity thesis' is hounded by the criticism which is based on the belief that these two concepts are linked to an ethic and a telos that Marx himself claimed historical materialism rejected as being relativistic, utopian or ideological.

The problem seems to remain; it would appear from the 'Marx as transcendentalist' critique that his condemnation of capitalism and its exploitation of labour is moralistic and teleological in tone. This approach poses, in one form or another, the following questions: is there a clearly defined morality and/or a telos employed in the writings of Marx? If so what are their origins? If they do exist independently of his social theory do they condition his view of what constitutes an 'authentic' human existence, and if this is found to be the case does this invalidate the *scientific* claims made for historical materialism? Therefore, if this search for a systematic Marxian moral theory is to be successful, it must establish that Marx did have in mind an *a priori* picture of what the fully developed individual would look like, and/or a projection of a future revolutionary and communistic society. It could then be claimed that it was on the basis of such positive evaluations of emancipated individuals and a liberated society that Marx criticised the relations of production based on capital. As a result, Marx could then justifiably be set along side other utopian and moral political thinkers, and applauded or condemned as such, his 'scientific' theory having fallen ignominiously by the wayside.

Alternatively, there are those who claim that Marx studiously avoided categorical statements about 'authentic' human existence and prescriptive pronouncements on communistic society. The reasons given for such avoidance rest on the historical, materialist method which it is claimed Marx employed. Such a method, it is said, overcame the dichotomy that he perceived as artificially present between theory and practice, fact and value, and 'is' and 'ought'. Therefore by purposefully transcending these 'dualist' distinctions and revealing 'universals' for what they are – the legitimating philosophical supports for the dominant ideology – Marx, from this standpoint, did not fall into the same trap as had his contemporaries, the 'ethical socialists', who accepted the ideals of the prevailing morality, or criticised their present application in and on their own terms in an attempt to revolutionise society, or to reform its existing relations in the hope that it would more closely resemble the ends stipulated by those ideals [6] The consequence of such an approach for my examination of individuality in Marx is that we cannot apply morally loaded universalistic categories or concepts to his critique of capitalism or to his purposefully inconclusive projection of post-revolutionary society. However, it will be shown that even if we take such a sympathetic approach to Marx's method, and accept as genuine his claim that he had escaped the clutches of 'bourgeois morality', there is still the nagging incidence of apparently 'ethical' and 'teleological' judgements and proposals throughout his work which requires explanation.

Before assessing the basis of Marx's critique of bourgeois conceptions of freedom, I shall first of all take a short detour in order to address the claims made by those who have sought to encumber Marx with principles of justice, or an ethical system. The reason for such a diversion is that these morally inspired approaches affect our understanding of Marx's view of freedom. If we adopt a position that says Marx applied an 'ideal' of freedom or a teleological vision to his analysis of pre-communist societies then this will invariably condition our perception of the marxian view of freedom. Alternatively, if we accept the radical implications of Marx's historical method, then we will also come to appreciate that his idea of freedom was one unrestrained by predetermined rules or codes, rather, its only boundaries were the limits of each individual's capabilities exercised in a post-capitalist society.

I wish to maintain that Marx never formulated a moral theory, nor did he apply a principle of justice, and that he consistently criticised those who did, in order to distance himself and his understanding of freedom from any charge of idealist speculation. By the same token, it will be admitted that in his haste to escape the clutches of idealist conceptions of *Recht*, Marx never developed a systematic critique of rights, apart from the belief that they were part of the ideological panoply of the bourgeoisie.[7] In effect, he believed that rights could never be applied indiscriminately.

In turning to the *Grundrisse*, it will be suggested that Marx's critical examination of the formal individual freedom and equality coexistent with capitalist relations of production, can only be fully understood if we have in mind his rejection of traditional notions of morality and justice, and his commitment to revolutionary liberation for and by the mass of individualities. It will be admitted that Marx did develop a strong image of 'authentic' human existence and had an idea of what a future communist society might look like, but neither were *a priori*. The community of social individuals was an *a posteriori* protection, a possibility, derived from an analysis of the contradictory nature of capital. The *Grundrisse* is seen as a pivotal work in this respect, incorporating as it does earlier philosophical inquiries within Marx's first extensive examination of political economy.

2 Marx on morality and justice

Over the past decade or so there has been a lively and informative debate over the issue of justice in the writings of Marx. This debate has developed into a three-cornered contest along the following lines. Firstly are those who believe that Marx regarded capitalist relations of production – and the accompanying social relations in general – as unjust. The proponents of this view usually base it on a claim that Marx did possess a theory of distributive justice which was informed by the superior ethic embodied in his communist telos. Secondly and diametrically opposed to this approach, is a position which insists that Marx dismissed any lasting notion of justice and maintained that as a concept it relied upon a particular set of social relations reflective of a contingent mode of production. Those who assert this view believe that Marx rejected normative and evaluative standards as a result of his critique of capitalist relations of production and of the bourgeois concepts and categories which legitimated them. Occupying the middle ground are the third group those who generally accept that Marx did not condemn capitalism on the basis of a post-capitalist notion of justice, but who suggest that he indicted bourgeois society from a superior moral standpoint informed by his vision of communist liberty.

Incidentally, both marxists and non-marxists usually hold one of these three positions. The stances taken by the marxists depend on several criteria: (1) their analysis of the 'true' content of Marx's methodology and ontology; (2) their evaluation of Marx's post-revolutionary society; and (3) perhaps most importantly, their own assessment of whether Marx *needs* a concept of justice or a moral theory to counter-attack those who contest the validity of marxism from a moral perspective informed by a competing ideology. As regards the positions adopted by the non-marxists, this usually depends on the extent and on the basis of their opposition to Marx and marxism, or on the degree of critical sympathy they have for some of Marx's views.

A less hostile non-marxist, Steven Lukes, categorises the various approaches to Marx on justice along the following lines:

(l) Marx thought the relation between capitalist and worker was just (2) he thought it was unjust (3) he thought it was both just and unjust – that is just in one respect and unjust in another (4) he thought it was neither just or unjust.[8]

This particular classification reveals the variety of interpretations that can be derived from the writings of Marx, but it fails to distinguish clearly between those who believe that Marx employed a moral or teleological theory in his evaluation of the iniquities of capitalism, and those who insist that he dispensed with morality altogether. It is this distinction which, I believe, is a far more fruitful one to examine, for if we can establish whether Marx applied an *a priori* normative or evaluative theory in his critique of bourgeois political economy then we can decide on the nature of his approach to justice *per se*, and the implications this approach has for his understanding of individual liberty.

Therefore, I wish to redraw the battle line in such a way that places on one side those who were previously opponents. As a result, writers such as Geras, Cohen and Elster now stand alongside Brenkert, Buchanan and Gilbert, i.e., I group together those that have proposed a Marxian principle of distributive justice with those who believe that Marx applied a preconceived moral theory to his critique of capitalism. In short, I place any non-relative theory of justice or morality which is attributed to Marx opposite the claim that he rejected all such theories. The purpose of this manoeuvre is to reassert what I believe to be Marx's own commitment to an examination of capitalism which does not rely upon a moral foundation, or a hidden theory of justice based on contribution and need, or a prophecy of 'true freedom'. Rather, Marx gained inspiration from his belief that capitalism was based on a set of antagonistic relations of production which would bring about the conditions for a revolutionary transformation. The revolutionary moment itself would be the product of social individuals engaged in the conscious and collective restructuring of social relations in such a way as to allow for the free development of human potentialities. At the same time this revolutionary moment would transcend the artificial division between the moral ideal and practical realisation of human emancipation. To say more than this, Marx believed, would be to indulge in prophesy, a form of speculation he abhorred. I do not wish to claim that such an approach is new, but I believe it more accurately reflects Marx's own position than the assumption which is at the heart of most recent debate on the marxian response to morality, that there is a clear and consistent normative dimension, of one sort or another, in his thought.

Firstly, I shall briefly survey the central claims of those who argue for a marxian moral theory, whether it includes a concept of justice or not. Secondly, Marx~s own critique of socialist distributive justice and idealist communist morality, as well as of more familiar bourgeois forms, will be outlined in order to question the conclusions of the Marx-as-normative-thinker school. This will serve to highlight the conclusions in the final section of the chapter where I suggest that Marx left it to real, active social individuals to

The individual and freedom

transcend the division between the abstract (*a priori* evaluative standards) and the concrete (actual, lived relations between social individuals).

2.1 Marxian justice and communist morality

Marx regarded capitalism:

> as unjust primarily because, as an exploitative system, it does not proportion reward to labour contribution, and because it is not orientated to satisfy human needs, least of all the needs of the producers, within its own productive possibilities.

It is with this that Husami concludes his discussion of Marx on distributive justice,[9] and it is a conclusion which is shared by all those who believe that Marx, especially in the later works (on which they rely almost entirely), applied 'post-revolutionary' standards of distribution in his critique of capitalism. How else, they ask of those who doubt, can we explain the regular occurrence in his writings of words and phrases which condemn capitalism's rapacity? How else can we account for the infamously cryptic statement 'from each according to his abilities, to each according to his needs!'[10] other than as a principle of distributive justice consistent with communist society? Geras believes that this is the only explanation of a 'genuine' paradox in Marx's ideas which is the:

> inconsistency – in his attitude to normative questions. Disowning, when he is not actively ridiculing, any attachment to ideals or values, he is nevertheless quite free in making critical normative judgements, author of a discourse that is replete with the signs of an intense moral commitment.[11]

Geras, along with Cohen and Elster, maintain that Marx 'did think capitalism unjust but he did not think he thought so.'[12] Indeed, Elster claims that Marx 'did not notice' that in the principle 'to each according to his needs' he was invoking an abstract theory of justice – the very thing he thought he was rejecting.[13] Others are less unequivocal,[14] but all are in agreement that Marx was in fact rejecting only narrow, bourgeois notions of justice, and not, it is claimed, justice *per se*. It is with this that the proponents of this view of Marx respond to those who insist that he dismissed *all* concepts of justice, and they reinforce it with their own elaboration of a marxian morality.

The moral theory constructed by these proponents rests on similar principles offered by those who support the idea of a marxian morality, but who claim that it had next to nothing to do with a notion of distributive justice. Both sides proclaim that, whether he knew it or not, Marx applied communistic values of freedom and self-development when condemning capitalism.[15] Both sides then go on to claim that Marx combined an examination of juridical relativism (i.e., the equating of pre-communist codes of justice with historical, contingent social relations) with the formulation of a moral 'realism' (i.e., a morality of the dispossessed, a normative response to exploitation through time which would obtain authority only in a future communist society). It therefore appears inconsistent – and the supporters of marxian justice are surely correct on this point – when those who propound a marxian morality fail to recognise, or refuse to acknowledge, that in practice such a morality would require a number of distributive rules. Later on I hope to show why the grounds on which this argument is based are, to say the least, shaky for both protagonists. For the moment, however, I shall continue my survey of marxian distributive justice.

Supporters of a marxian principle of distributive justice usually make the following claims: (1) Exploitation is robbery, Marx thought, but not by the standards of capitalist society. The capitalist steals 'in some appropriately (marxian) non-relativist sense',[16] (2) The only way we can appreciate fully Marx's attack on capitalism is by accepting that he was applying theories of justice based on contribution and need which originated from his protection of socialist and communist societies; (3) The marxian 'needs principle' is to be understood in terms of the provision, in conditions of material abundance, of those things which satisfy the 'need for the free, all-round development of individuality' that Marx advocates;[17] (4) Marx was therefore a moral realist (or absolutist).

What is the substance of these claims?

The defenders of the first view generally agree that Marx's use of the terminology of robbery suggests that, whether he knew it or not, he was applying a principle of justice to his critique of capitalism. They cite many examples from Marx's writings, one of the most popular being this one from *Capital*, where the surplus product is likened to:

the tribute annually exacted from the working class by the capitalist class. Though the latter with a portion of that tribute purchases the additional labour-power even at its full price, so that equivalent is exchanged for equivalent, yet the transaction is for all that only the old dodge of every conqueror who buys commodities from the conquered with the money he has robbed them of.[18]

The surplus product is said to be 'embezzled, because abstracted without return of an equivalent, from the English labourer ...'.[19] Exploitation is the 'booty pumped out of the labourer ...',[20] while the overthrowing of capitalism will be characterised by the 'expropriation of a few usurpers by the mass of the people. Comments in the *Grundrisse* appear to reinforce those found in *Capital*; Marx talks of *'the theft of alien labour time, on which the present wealth is based"*.[22] Elsewhere, as Husami is at pains to point out, Marx characterised exploitation as '"robbery", "usurpation", "embezzlement", "plunder", "booty", "theft", "snatching", and "swindling"'.[23]

Surely, the argument goes, Marx was not using such terms lightly? Admittedly, he was not averse to occasionally employing emotive rhetoric, but this does not account for all such instances of moral indignation. Neither does Marx's critical evaluation of early capitalist expropriation in terms of the feudal, pre-capitalist forms of justice that such expropriation contravened, explain all the occurrences of the vocabulary of injustice in his work. He may well point out the contradictions between the legitimating theory and the imperfect practice of capitalism, and claim that, at times, the capitalist does break the bourgeois codes of justice which formally recognise, and occasionally uphold, the nominal equality between the exchangers of equivalents, i.e. the buying and selling of labour-power. But once again there are exceptions to this explanation, or so the proponents of a marxian theory of distributive justice wish to suggest. There appear to be instances of Marx condemning capitalism in terms which do not fit easily into any of the above interpretations, neither can they be understood as his reaction to the theft of workers' physical and mental well-being or the embezzlement of their time. In fact, it is claimed, Marx believed that the expropriation of surplus labour value was wrong because it contravened the principles of justice that accompanied his vision of post-capitalist society.

Marx and the individual

The advocates of the second view, that of a marxian theory of justice, believe that Marx criticised capitalism for its injustice from two distinct, though interrelated perspectives. The first of these is based on the structure of the transitory, post-revolutionary, socialist mode of production. The second being a subsequent, and therefore superior, normative principle characteristic of fully developed communism. For both, it is claimed, the evidence lies in the *Critique of the Gotha Programme* (Husami's *'locus classicus'*), indeed this is the only place where Marx appears to propose in any consistent form, post-capitalist forms of justice. The justice of socialism, it is said, can be summarised by the following principle: 'to each proportionally to his labour contribution, after funds are set aside for investment, public goods, funds for those unable to work etc'.[24]

But it must be remembered, Marx the jurist points out, that this principle of justice, and the society from which it springs, have, as their direct antecedent, capitalist society which they emerge from without escaping entirely from its influence.

> In every respect, economically, morally, intellectually, it is thus still stamped with the birth marks of the old society from whose womb it has emerged. Accordingly, the individual producer gets back from society – after the deductions – exactly what he has given it,[25]

that is, the individual's labour time. This is the individual's contribution to the social working day, for which each labourer receives, after the deductions for future production, reserves and social services, a commensurate amount of the social product, or in other words, a share of the 'social supply of means of consumption'.[26] So, although all that is contributed is an individual's labour, and all that is received are individual means of consumption, such an arrangement is still, in principle, a *bourgeois* equal right; it is still, essentially, the same as the exchange of equivalents. Such a development, Marx admits, may be an advance, but it suffers the same fate as all bourgeois equal rights: *'its content* (is) *one of inequality, just like any other right'.*[27] Individuals are unequal in their physical and intellectual capacities, therefore in applying the same standard of labour to all of them, 'it gives tacit recognition to a worker's individual endowment and hence productive capacity as natural privileges',[28] which lead to material inequality. Other material inequalities come into play, for example, as a result of whether the labourer has dependents or not, and if so how many? Such defects are unavoidable if we choose to apply an equal right which treats all as workers and nothing more than workers, and applies a single standard, labour. Nevertheless, such a concept of distributive justice serves its purpose well, according to those who promote it, for it not only condemns capitalism for its distributive injustices, e.g. the income received by capitalists without them working for it and obtained through the exploitation of others,[29] but also paves the way for a 'higher' form of justice which moves beyond the inequality of 'bourgeois' rights (even though they may be 'socialist' rights!)

Just as in capitalism where individual workers are viewed by the capitalist as possessors of the commodity labour power, so in socialism each individual is perceived only as a worker, one whose labour contributes to the social product. The individual is thus regarded only 'from one *particular* side'[30] and not as the multi-faceted human being of developed communism. The individual of communist society therefore requires a principle of justice, so the argument goes, that is responsive to the need for individual self-realisation, hence 'to each according to his needs.' As Van Del Veer suggests:

> Marx was committed to a distribution of dissimilar amounts of goods to different labourers, but the dissimilar distribution should be based not on the different amounts of *labour* contributed but on the varying needs of the labourers.[31]

Of course an amendment proposed by more recent proponents of a marxian theory of justice would be that the individual is qualitatively different in the 'higher' stage of communism, no mere labourer, but a self-realising agent for whom 'labour is no longer just a means of keeping active but has itself become a vital need'.[32] Therefore 'need' in developed communism is more than necessary material consumption, it is a 'right ... to the means of personal development'.[33] This right is unlike any other in that it recognises the inequality that is the result of the heterogeneity of human capacities; each individual is valued for his or her uniqueness. The rewards accruing to individuals who exercise their particular talents, should be evident in the fulfilment which is achieved through their practice.[34] At the same time the right is an equal one in that it recognises the right everyone has to engage in self-realisation. In other words, we are encouraged to believe by the promoters of a marxian morality and system of justice, that there are higher, communist rights which supersede all previous rights.

Consequently, we are therefore led to the third view and the belief that it was on the basis of freedom as self-realisation, with its accompanying telos of communist society and principle of distributive justice, that Marx criticised capitalism. Under bourgeois relations of production, freedom is unevenly and inequitably distributed. Only a small minority of individuals are sufficiently supplied with the means to develop themselves via a form of production which, by nature, necessarily prevents the majority from engaging in self-realisation. 'In capitalist society, free time is produced for one class by the conversion of the whole lifetime of the masses into labour time.'[35]

The writers who support the notion of a marxian theory of justice agree that Marx was motivated by a vision of a future realm of freedom.[36] 'It is ... a universal freedom and self-development that he both envisages and looks forward to at the end of the in.'[37] They also agree that this vision has distributive implications not only in terms of the material wealth which in capitalism is disproportionately in the hands of the bourgeois class, but also with regard to the advantageous conditions necessary for self-realisation, i.e. the 'goods' of freedom. In other words the freedom which is at present monopolised by the capitalist should be universalised, the luxury of self-development should become a generally available good. Marx is therefore proposing, so the argument goes, a superior morality which is attainable through achieving the end of historical necessity, which is of course communism. This morality demands that the community should democratically control the means of production, since only then can the principle of equitable distribution of the 'goods' of self-development be effectively applied.

The success of this marxian morality appears to rely upon an abundance of all those material requirements necessary for the varied needs of self-realisation. Only capitalism can lay the foundations for such a plenitude and only communism can take full advantage of it. For Husami the realisation of the distributive principle of justice based on need 'presupposes material abundance' which is the result of a harmonious relationship between the continually developing productive forces and the changed nature, conditions and attitudes of and about work.[38] However, some who champion marxian distributive justice are sceptical of Marx's occasional claim of the existence of limitless needs supported by a similar level of abundance. Such claims are usually dismissed as being 'absurd'[39] or 'utopian'[40], and an alternative is suggested which goes under the name of 'reasonableness'[41] or 'compromise'.[42] The reasonable compromise is one which, on the one hand, seeks to overcome the potential conflict between individual self-realisation and communal well-being, and on the other, attempts to provide for all a sufficient amount of the material requirements for self-development, without either depriving some or favouring a few.[43] This is rapidly followed up with the rhetorical question: what further justification is necessary for insisting that Marx employed, knowingly or unwittingly, a communist principle of distributive justice? The abolition of scarcity does not bring with it the extinction of justice. Rather, it is to be transformed into a code of mutually acceptable and collectively imposed regulations, mediating between self-developing individuals in a community of 'haves', as opposed to the coercive imposition of rules preserving the privileged minority's monopoly over the means of personal fulfillment.

The logical consequence of the above approach is the unavoidable conclusion of the fourth view, that Marx was a moralist; he was motivated by 'an intense moral commitment'[44] his 'evaluation of capitalist distributive arrangements (was) overwhelmingly *moral*', and such arrangements he viewed as 'morally objectionable'.[45] For another commentator Marx's 'proffering of numerous normative principles' is sufficient evidence of his adherence to 'some absolutist view' of morality.[46] Of its nature and origin Elster is in little doubt; at the heart of Marx's morality is the 'ideal of self-actualisation' which possesses an 'absolute, transhistorical character' not unlike a 'quasi-Aristotelian ideal of the good life for man'[47]; and all is linked to a secularised teleology which has its antecedents in the works of Leibniz and Hegel.[48]

By adopting such positions the proponents of a marxian theory of distributive justice answer in unison to the questions Husami poses himself:

> First, can Marx, consistent with his sociology of morals, use proletarian or post-capitalist standards in evaluating capitalist distribu-

tion? Second, does Marx – his consistency notwithstanding – explicitly or implicitly use these standards in evaluating capitalist distribution?[49]

But of course, comes the unanimous reply, the answer is yes on both counts. Marx, whether he knew it or not, was motivated by a morality of self-realisation, which provided him both with the foundation for a theory of post-revolutionary justice, and with a teleological view of history. History, from this perspective, is the history of freedom's becoming, which when realised is subsequently guaranteed by communism's principles of justice. Marx was therefore still bound to the idealist 'Prometheanism'[50] of his intellectual forebears. Some are more equivocal than others on this point,[51] but all accept that what underpinned Marx's critique of the ideological nature of contingent, historical moralities, and his dismissal of bourgeois rights as so many excuses for exploitation, was a morality of liberation. It then follows that all theories of justice and ethics are historically relative, except, of course, the justice and ethic of the future realm of freedom. These higher normative values, on the contrary, are universal because they accompany the necessary conclusion to human 'prehistory', the triumph of communism.

And it is this belief, that Marx did carry in his intellectual baggage, probably unbeknown to himself, the moral hand-me-downs of his predecessors, that informs the discussion of the marxian moralists (this is despite their reluctance to go the whole hog and embrace a concomitant theory of justice). There are those who go even further, and insist that Marx should be placed amongst the ranks of all the other millennial visionaries of the European tradition. Alan Gilbert, for one, is adamant that Marx did apply a 'single basic moral standard in different historical circumstances',[52] and that Marx and marxists need such a moral stance if they are to fend off the counter-claims of competing systems. Gilbert admits that Marx may well have celebrated the advances made by capitalism in ways that appear to be purely utilitarian – i.e. the victory of capital over previous modes of production is instrumental to the eventual success of the revolution – but it was an instrumentalist perspective that had two sides. On the one hand some of the successes of capital could be classed as intrinsically good, for example, scientific discoveries; on the other, the ultimate

The individual and freedom

aim of 'individual self-realisation' could only be achieved 'at the expense of the contemporary producing classes'.[53] So Marx was prepared to accept the grinding alienation of exploitative economic relations only because it heralded a new beginning which would guarantee universal emancipation.

Indeed, it is from this protected image of the future realm of freedom that Gilbert believes Marx derived his moral theory, his 'eudaimonism: a theory that evaluates activities and states of character by asking how they advance individual happiness and effect the quality of human lives'.[54] In this respect Marx is likened to Aristotle, as both of them had objective conceptions of the good life and judged all existing social relations and levels of individual achievement by this objective standard. In a similar vein, Marx's 'ideal picture of communist social individuality'[55] is identified by commentators such as Brenkert and Buchanan as his evaluative criterion. Buchanan talks of Marx's 'vision of communist society' replacing the earlier notion of species being as the basis for criticising capitalism and for 'grounding the judgement that there is progress in history'.[56] While Brenkert maintains that although Marx may not have consciously formulated a moral theory he nevertheless implicitly applied one when reprimanding capitalism for its excesses.[57] Therefore, regardless of a 'significant body of textual evidence' which suggests that 'Marx simply rejected ethics and morality',[58] it is still 'quite possible to find instances in which he does, in more or less traditional moral ways, criticise society'.[59] And Marx criticised by applying an 'ethic of virtue' much like that of 'the Greeks for whom the nature of virtue or human excellence was the central question of morality'. In other words, Marx was inspired by an ethic of self-improvement and constructed an image of a 'flourishing life' which became in his hands a prescriptive 'ought' enabling him to do what Brenkert believes all such moralists should do, to combine 'moral theory and moral praxis' in order to show 'how society should be changed in the light of the possibilities for such change'.[60]

Brenkert's Marx was clearly a man who was capable of discerning from the march of history a set of moral standards that reflected 'man's fully developed condition' and which also spoke 'directly ... to the earlier less developed conditions in which man finds himself'.[61] In fact, Marx had discovered communist moral standards which were not only the expression of some future 'mature development of human activity', but also the product of an 'entire historical process which leads to the development of that mode of production in which individuals flourish'; he was nothing less than the defender of a 'universalist view of morality'.[62]

But what of Marx himself? How would he have responded to these imputations? I believe that he would have been surprised and not a little outraged at the suggestion that he had formulated, without knowing it, both a communist distributive justice and a revolutionary moral code. And his response might well have been similar to that expressed in his critique of communists, socialists and liberals alike who sought solutions to the practical inadequacies of contemporary society in the realm of ideas. It is to this critique that I now turn, and it is a critique that I believe is directly applicable to modern attempts at equipping Marx with principles of justice and a moral theory.

2.2 Marx against justice and morality

In his preface to *A Contribution to the Critique of Political Economy* Marx recalled his investigation of Hegel's *Philosophy of Right*, which had:

> led to the result that legal relations as well as forms of state are to be grasped neither from themselves nor from the so-called general development of the human mind, but rather have their roots in the material conditions of life, the sum total of which Hegel ... combines under the name 'civil society'.[63]

But, unlike Hegel who had situated civil society within the political state, Marx had maintained that the political and juridical institutions of human society were aspects of the collective productive activity of individuals in pursuit of historically conditioned needs. Once he had come to this conclusion, Marx shifted his attention to the complex phenomenon of human productive activity, and in particular the current mode of that activity, capitalism. As we have already seen, he viewed any mode of production as an intricate totality comprised of many moments, or determinations, each mutually interdependent, but each distinct. Within this totality could be distinguished forms of exchange, distribution and consumption, types of political, moral and religious conviction,

The individual and freedom

but none of them could be understood in isolation from the conditioning influence of the prevailing mode of production, nor could they be separated from the relations of production which each of them in their own way served to regulate. Theories of justice and rights were no different from these other moments, they were just as much determinations of prevailing social relations, and just as reliant for their meaning upon the predominant mode of production. In other words, such determinations existed in a functional relationship with a particular form of production.[64] Justice, rights and morality were therefore all to be understood by Marx in terms of their role as functions of production, and, as the following extracts illustrate, there is little to suggest that he ever wavered from this view.

> This conception of his history thus relies on expounding the real process of production – starting from the material production of life itself – and comprehending the form of intercourse connected with and created by this mode of production, i.e., civil society in its various stages, as the basis of all history ... explaining how all the different theoretical products and forms of consciousness, religion, philosophy, morality, etc., etc., arise from it, and tracing the process of their formation from that basis; thus the whole thing can, of course, be depicted in its totality (and therefore, too, the reciprocal action of these various sides on one another).[65]

Two decades later;

> The justice of the transactions between agents of production rests on the fact that these arise as natural consequences out of the production relationships. The juristic forms in which these economic transactions appear as wilful acts of the parties concerned, as expressions of their common will and as contracts that may be enforced by law against some individual party, cannot, being mere forms, determine this content. They merely express it. This content is just whenever it corresponds, is appropriate, to the mode of production. It is unjust whenever it contradicts that mode.[66]

These two quotes are expressions of the same methodological conclusion: each moment cannot be understood in isolation from the productive conditions which give it meaning, but should be perceived as supportive of, and reliant upon, those conditions. Justice is no different from any other moment in this respect. The justice of a transaction or an institution can only be established if we understand the function it performs within the mode of production. If the function performed is a supportive moment of the continued reproduction of the predominant mode then it (and the transaction or institution) is just. Conversely, an action is unjust if it challenges or is dysfunctional to the existing productive processes. Therefore, following the logic of his earlier critique of idealist abstraction, Marx insisted that there were no ageless forms of justice with which we could judge the conditions of material existence, quite the reverse, each historical epoch was accompanied by a set of standards which reflected in the realm of ideas the functional relationship between the various determinations. In effect, capitalism judged itself by its own juridical standards. Any set of standards which did not fulfil this function were therefore pointless and could be dismissed as being wrong-headed.

Marx could say without equivocation that capitalist exploitation is just and that no injustice accompanied the accumulation by capital of surplus value. By doing so he was signifying his rejection of the view held by a number of socialists that the exchange between capitalist and worker was an unequal one and therefore was unjust. This argument rested on the commonly held assumption that labour was the source of surplus-value and that the capitalist extracted this surplus by paying workers less than the value they had created in the productive process. Marx regarded as erroneous the claim that was central to this argument that workers were due the full value of their labour. If this had been the case then the capitalist was responsible for a remarkable confidence trick. Marx admitted, along with socialists and bourgeois economists, that labour does create value, but he parted company with them when he maintained that the capitalist does not purchase the value created by the worker, i.e. the commodities produced by the labourer; what is purchased is the labour-power of the worker, i.e. the capacity to produce com-modities. As such, labour-power becomes a commodity for the capitalist, as well as for the worker, which has its price, the wage:

> It is the quantity of labour required for its production, not the realised form of that labour, by which the amount of the value of the commodity is determined.
>
> That which comes directly face to face with the possessor of money on the market, is in fact not labour, but the labourer. What the latter sells is his labour-power. As soon as his labour actually begins, it has

The individual and freedom

already ceased to belong to him; it can therefore no longer be sold by him. Labour is the substance, and the imminent measure of value, but *has itself no value*.[67]

What determines the price of labour-power is the amount necessary for the reproduction of that capacity, 'in other words, the value of labour-power is the value of the means of subsistence necessary for the maintenance of the labourer', and the necessary means of subsistence are 'themselves the product of historical development'.[68] The value of the commodity 'labour-power' is therefore, historically determined, conditioned by the degree of development of the forces of production, and, in general, the worker is paid for the commodity at a price commensurate with the cost of its reproduction.[69] For Marx, the transaction of exchanging this commodity for its equivalent is a just one, its price has been charged and paid just like any other commodity, its purchaser using it to create a surplus value which is justly his or hers;

> the seller of labour-power, like the seller of any other commodity, realises its exchange-value, and parts with its use-value ... The use-value of labour-power ... belongs just as little to its seller, as the use-value of oil after it has been sold belongs to the dealer who has sold it.[70]

The purchaser of the commodity has the use of it for a period agreed by the two contracting parties, the labour-power for this time belongs to the capitalist; the capitalist, Marx believed, justly benefits from the fact that it takes only a part of the working day for the worker to produce the value equivalent to the price of the labour-power, while for the rest of the day the worker goes on creating surplus-value, 'this circumstance is, without doubt, a piece of good luck for the buyer, but by no means an injury to the seller'.[71] Even if the capitalist should drive down the price of labour-power, even to the extent of paying less than is required for the socially necessary means for its reproduction, this is not unjust according to Marx. Labour-power is just like any other commodity; if there is an over-supply then the price will drop. This is not to suggest that Marx condones the exploitation of the worker which is the concrete result of this formally free transaction, far from it, rather, he is remaining consistent to his initial view that justice is the functional product of the prevailing relations of production.

Marx and the individual

Marx was also responding to those who suggested that the appropriation by the capitalist of the product of unpaid labour contravened the worker's right to that product. This right had its origins in the works of Locke where it was claimed that the product of human labour is rightfully the labourer's. But the claim was a confused and outdated one when uttered by critics of capitalism because it assumed that an individual's property rights are based on his or her labour. Now this might well have been the case in a society where each individual confronted all others not only as a producer of a commodity, but also the owner of the means of the commodity's production,[72] but in developed capitalism the independent producer/proprietor had been superseded by a system of co-operative labour carried out by propertyless workers, harnessed by means of production owned by a separate class of capitalists. If the old proprietorial right was imposed this would clearly contradict the practice of capitalism which had succeeded in systematically separating the means of production from the labourers. Such a right was therefore an anachronism for Marx:

> Now, however, property turns out to be the right, on the part of the capitalist, to appropriate the unpaid labour of others or its product, and to be the impossibility, on the part of the labourer, of appropriating his own product. The separation of property from labour has become the necessary consequence of a law that apparently originated in their identity.[73]

Marx's conclusion that the traditional labour theory of property was outmoded, and his belief that there was no injustice in the appropriation of surplus-value by capitalists, when combined with his examination of justice in the context of its functional role in society, formed the basis of his attack on all those who were tempted to apply socialist, or communist, juridical standards. Certainly the demand for a 'just wage' made by many socialists reflected a misguided belief that the present, capitalist, form of wealth distribution was both unjust and reformable. For Marx the answer to such demands and charges was straightforward enough; the capitalist is correct in asserting that the present form of distribution is just because it is the only just form of distribution commensurate with the dominant mode of production.[74] To insist otherwise is to misinterpret the relationship between principles of justice and relations of production, and to wrongly assume that

The individual and freedom

these relations are governed by standards of justice. Marx had maintained that 'it was a mistake anyway to lay the stress on so-called *distribution* and to make it the central point'. Distribution, both of the means of consumption and of the conditions of production, is a feature of a particular mode of production, in other words, it is conditioned by the mode of production. As such, Marx believed that it was a fundamental error to claim that a more adequate distribution of the social product of capitalism would rectify the ills of the system, and any oppositional group that took this stance was only deluding itself. Those socialists who had:

> followed the bourgeois economists in their consideration and treatment of distribution as something independent of the mode of production and hence in the presentation of socialism as primarily revolving around the question distribution.[75]

were only taking a retrograde step after the true nature of the conditioning relationship between production and distribution has been established. Therefore, to talk of 'equal right' and 'just distribution' was to employ 'obsolete verbal rubbish', 'ideological and legal ... humbug'.[76] All such talk was based on an artificial inversion of the conditioning effect relations of production have upon juridical concepts. Again, this is not to suggest that Marx is accepting or promoting bourgeois notions of justice, but by the same token he is not applying his own standards of justice to existing circumstances, and he consistently opposed those who did just this.

Equally mistaken, according to Marx, is the view that the capitalist 'robs' the worker in a way that transgresses a non-capitalist conception of justice. Some had suggested that this was Marx's own view, that he was condemning the exploitation of workers from the high ground of post-capitalist justice; how else, it was said, could we hope to explain his emotive use of terms like 'robbery' and 'theft'? Marx's explicit response to these charges can be found in his *Notes on Adolf Wagner* [77] where he admits that he does indeed use such terms in *Capital*, but not in way that signifies an alternative theory of justice:

> In fact, in my presentation, profit is *not* 'merely a *deduction* or "robbery" on the labourer'. On the contrary, I present the capitalist as the necessary functionary of capitalist production, and show very extensively that he does not only 'deduct' or *rob*, but forces the

Marx and the individual

production of surplus value, therefore the deducting only helps to produce; furthermore, I show in detail that even if in the exchange of commodities *only equivalents* were exchanged, the capitalist – as soon as he pays the labourer the real value of his labour-power – would secure with full rights, i.e. the rights corresponding to that mode of production, *surplus value*.[78]

If the labourer had been robbed on the basis of some Marxian principle of justice then it would be nothing short of simple-minded inconsistency for Marx to then say (in this instance, in the same breath) that the surplus-value appropriated by the capitalist is secured 'with full rights'. If this is the case, then Marx was capable of making the same mistake twice, for he goes on to reaffirm in the same document the same position; after noting Wagner's attribution that he held the view 'that "the *surplus value* produced by the labourers *alone* was left to the capitalist employers in an *improper way*"', Marx continues by saying the direct opposite:

> namely, that commodity-production is necessarily, at a certain point, turned into 'capitalist' commodity-production, and that according to the *law of value* governing it, 'surplus value' is properly due to the capitalist, and not the labourer.

Once more we need to remind ourselves of Marx's attitude to justice and the position it holds in his social theory, and resubmit that he was not disagreeing with others on the basis of an alternative theory of justice, rather he was denying the prescriptive authority of oppositional juridical codes. Capitalism did indeed rob the worker, and Marx never tired from repeating this charge when discussing exploitation, but it was a regulated robbery carried out by a class that had secured for itself (probably in contravention of the previous mode's system of justice)[80] monopoly of the means of plundering, i.e. the means of production, at the expense of the labourers who had been completely separated from these very same means. This was an unavoidable consequence of capitalism's success and for this reason Marx had no cause to believe that it was unjust. Wages may well be 'part of the tribute annually exacted from the working class by the capitalist class', but the capitalist purchases more labour-power with part of that tribute, 'even at its full price, so that equivalent is exchanged for equivalent',[81] i.e., it is labour-power and not the labourer that is the purchased commodity. The commodity, its use and its product all remain, in Marx's

139

The individual and freedom

eyes, the rightful property of the purchaser, the capitalist; 'the product is the property of the capitalist and not that of the labourer'.[82]

So, when Marx employed terms such as robbery and theft he was not invoking an alternative theory of distributive justice – as we have already seen, he regarded this as a misguided and retrogressive step – neither was he applying a post-capitalist, communist, juridical standard. Revolution would never succeed if all it attempted to do was to impose on society a set of radical rules and norms, however laudable they might be. Only a transformation of the productive foundations, which, after all, give morality and justice their meaning, would result in the creation of a society in which the social antagonisms that had given rise to the mystification of freedom in the form of morals and rights would be overcome. Genuine human emancipation would be a practical reality and not an abstract, unattainable notion standing above the exploited and the impoverished. Marx believed that the prevailing system of exploitation could never be eradicated by legal and moral means, 'Right can never rise above the the economic structure of a society and its contingent cultural development'.[83] For him communism always remained:

> not a *state of affairs* which is to be established, an *ideal* to which reality [will] have to adjust itself. We call communism the *real* movement which abolishes the present state of things. The conditions of this movement result from the now existing premise.[84]

What was it, then, that motivated Marx to spend a life time examining the basis of human servitude and the possibilities for social and individual emancipation?

Marx did condemn capitalism in no uncertain terms. He recognised it as an outmoded system, riddled with acute contradictions which served to exacerbate the misery, poverty and vacuousness experienced by the vast majority of individuals. And it was these conditions and the contradictions which they exposed which he believed would bring about the eventual collapse of this most dehumanising society. But where is the morality to back up this condemnation? The simple answer is that it is not there. Marx did not question the efficacy of alternative moralities on the basis of his own pre-stated moral theory, neither did he apply systematically a set of formally established standards and values when rubbishing capitalism, quite the opposite. Marx set off on the

Marx and the individual

recharted course he had set himself in 1845 by shedding the speculative moralising of his philosophical compatriots, and whenever the question of justice or ethics reappeared in the subsequent thirty-eight years he applied very similar means to dispel suspicions that he was employing an *a priori* communist morality.

But if Marx was not applying moral criteria to his critique of capitalism what did move him to make such impassioned remarks as the following?

> Within the capitalist system all methods for raising the social productiveness of labour are brought about at the cost of the individual labourer; all means for the development of production transform themselves into means of domination over, and exploitation of, the producers; they mutilate the labourer into a fragment of a man, degrade him to the level of an appendage of a machine, destroy every remnant of charm in his work and turn it into a hated toil ... they distort the conditions under which he works, subject him during the labour-process to a despotism the more hateful for its meanness.[85]

Surely, this can be nothing other then the language of moral indignation? Marx must be judging capitalism from the high ground of communist justice. Not so says the man who insisted that the contradiction between the bourgeoisie and the proletariat will reach a stage when it gives rise to communist and socialist views which will not only 'criticise the conditions of production and intercourse in the hitherto existing world', but will also shatter 'the basis of all morality, whether the morality of asceticism or of enjoyment'.[86] There is little reason not to believe that Marx would have applied to all moral theories the same injunction he levelled at Christianity that 'does not go beyond mere moral injunctions, which remain ineffective in real life'. Indeed the 'ideal' of the 'all-round realisation of the individual' will be made redundant only when 'the impact of the world which stimulates the real development of the abilities of the individual is under the control of the individuals themselves'.[87] The conclusion for Marx was an uncompromising one:

> The communists do not preach *morality* at all, as Stirner does so extensively. They do not put to people the moral demand: love one another, do not be egoists, etc.; on the contrary, they are very well aware that egoism, just as much as selflessness, *is* in definite circumstances a necessary form of the self-assertion of individuals.[88]

The individual and freedom

For some, these conflicting statements are evidence of a fundamental paradox in Marx's approach to capitalism, and one that can only be resolved if we distinguish between Marx's attack on *bourgeois* morality (understood as rights based) and his commitment to a morality of emancipation.[89] But if we do this then I believe we both misinterpret Marx's own understanding of human freedom and overlook the full critical impact of his materialist method on any preconceived notion of the good life. In this context, it is important to recall Marx's comments at the beginning of his only full-scale attack on moral theorising, *The German Ideology*:

> Men are the producers of their conceptions, ideas, etc., that is, real, active men, as they are conditioned by a definite development of their productive forces and of the intercourse corresponding to these, up to its furthest forms ... The phantoms formed in the brains of men are also, necessarily, sublimates of their material life process, which is empirically verifiable and bound to material premises. Morality, religion, metaphysics, and all the rest of ideology as well as the forms of consciousness corresponding to these, thus no longer retain the semblance of independence ... It is not consciousness that determines life, but life that determines consciousness.[90]

What was of primary importance for Marx were relations of production and not theories of justice or morality. For it was the relationship between these relations and the constantly developing forces of production which would lead to the eventual transformation of capitalism, and not any appeal to a moral precept or a juridical principle. Real, active individuals would be the agents of change and not the moralist or jurist who were more likely to hinder radical alternatives than to promote them. Once the origins of morality and justice had been discovered in the contingent, material conditions of existence, Marx believed that their true character would be recognised by the proletarian as 'so many bourgeois prejudices, behind which lurk in ambush just as many bourgeois interests'.[91]

What is clear from Marx's approach to morality is his opposition to the very practice of moralising, the activity of formulating moral theories, regardless of their content. It is not that he rejected the content of bourgeois morality, declaiming against its values and norms, his disagreement is more fundamental than that. If it was just a case of opposing prevailing rules and laws, then we would be correct to expect from Marx an alternative set of norms.

But he never attempted to supply us with his own moral theory with which we could attack the immorality of capitalist exploitation.[92]

Instead, what we have is an indictment of a system which inhibited and distorted the development of a set of unique human characteristics. In its pursuit of wealth for the owners of the means of production, capitalism had utilised capacities which in different circumstances might well serve as the basis for the advancement of the species as a whole. In fact, the economic and social conditions which had generated the most extreme forms of estrangement, at the same time had established the conditions for its eventual abolition. Marx believed that capitalism and capitalists had developed the means by which the human ability for self-determination could be harnessed for the benefit of another, i.e., they had established ways of producing wealth for themselves which took full advantage of the human capacity for the communal reproduction of the means of existence. This system of exploitation, like others before it, had equipped itself with a set of legitimatory morals and rights, reinforced by a theory of justice, which only served to restrain the full expression of human potentialities and reinforce the economic separation of individuals from the means of production. Marx condemned the servitude, exploitation and misery experienced by the majority in such circumstances, but the origins of his indignation were not moralistic; he berated capitalism for its senseless waste of human resources, but he never damned it for its injustice. What did move him was the recognition that the human capacity for self-determination had been alienated from all those who were compelled to sell their labour-power, what did enrage him was the distortion of the human need of community and freedom, and what did anger him was the lack of provision of necessary human requirements such as health, security and shelter. All these are what Allen Wood has correctly called non-moral goods,[93] a set of human needs which are 'actual, objective (though historically conditioned and variable) potentialities, needs and interests', without any moral content, which are worth pursuing for their own sake as expressions of our humanity, as distinct from those moral things which we pursue because we believe (or perhaps more pertinently, others believe) we ought to, and which conform to pre-existing virtues, rights, duties and codes of justice.[94] Only if we adopt this view will we overcome the apparent paradox between

The individual and freedom

Marx's contempt for moral and juridical criticism and his obvious disdain for existing social conditions identified by those who seek to explain it by foisting on him a moral theory, or a concept of justice that he himself made such efforts to denounce as mystification and illusion.

Even if it can be shown that Marx was susceptible to hyperbole when condemning the consequences of capitalism, even if he was not averse to employing the phraseology of moral indignation, what is undeniable is Marx's persistent criticism of all moral theories in themselves. That this criticism, as has been shown, has solid methodological foundations, and is the product of a refutation of all theories that sought to establish a separate and abstract notion of morality and justice, should be contrasted with those isolated, acerbic instances of a personal 'moral outrage' which are clearly the product of individual emotion rather than the expression of an exhaustive, universal ethic. For contemporary commentators to construct an elaborate moral theory from personal indignation and then claim that it is morality marxism has been looking for is to miss the point entirely of Marx's critique of any such formulation. Marx had sought to expose the true conditioning relationship between relations of production and the moral and juridical norms in order to dispel the illusion that such norms were universal, rational and *a priori*. At the same time he arrived at the conclusion that only a revolutionary transformation of the underlying conditions of production, along with the dismantling of their supportive social relations, carried out by those who had hitherto been exploited and alienated, would achieve the ends of freedom, self-determination and community. The next section seeks to develop this theme.

3   The *Grundrisse*, the individual and freedom

It is the *Grundrisse* which, more than any other single work by Marx, reveals the breadth of his analysis of capitalist political economy, elaborating the economic scope of the critique already evident in a nascent form in writings such as the opening chapters of the *German Ideology* and the *Economic and Philosophic Manuscripts*, while at the same time developing the theory of alienation as an expression of the antagonistic relation between labour and capital, thus predating and informing the examination of this crucial relation in *Capital*. In other words the *Grundrisse* is pivotal for anyone interested in both the antecedents to his 'mature' materialist interpretation of history, the essential continuity of his thought, and, perhaps most importantly, the importance his critical observations have for revolutionary action understood as self-determination by social individuals.

It is this last aspect which will be the focus of attention of my discussion. As a negative corollary of the positive pivotal status of this key text, the *Grundrisse* also serves to expose the insupportable nature of the claims made by those who wish to promote the idea that there is a radical disjuncture between the young/early Marx and the mature/late Marx, it also challenges those who would have us believe that Marx solved the riddle of the sands by discovering invariable laws of history which, given time, of their own accord, would bring about the eventual demise of capitalism and herald the new order. This is not to say that the 'authentic' Marx continued to be the hegelian humanist of the early works, or that his thought developed without interruption along the lines mapped out at the beginning of his intellectual career, but that the textual evidence alone shows that Marx was consciously and constantly modifying and reworking his analysis to perform new tasks in the face of new problems.

It is also worth noting at this point that the contemporary functionalist approach (especially that of Cohen)[95] to Marx, which I believe adheres to a version of the 'disjuncture' thesis, makes reference to the *Grundrisse* only as a methodological adjunct to the seminal *Capital* and a preparatory exercise for the definitive 1859 *Preface*.[96] In other words, it contains, in a nascent form, the functional determinism of the later works. In fact it can be maintained that the latter should be regarded only as parts of the general project outlined in the former, and further, that *Capital* and the *Preface* can be more fully understood only if we have a working knowledge of the method employed by Marx in the *Grundrisse*. It was a method which he believed (1) exposed the contradictory nature of capitalist concepts and categories,(2) revealed the antagonistic character of capitalist social relations, based as they are on the appropriation of surplus value, and (3) convinced him that only the labouring classes through revolutionary activity could achieve their own liberation, and that the impersonal laws of history only define *general* and not *inevitable* consequences. This is not to devalue the contribution of *Capital*, rather to suggest that it should not be regarded as the definitive Marxian statement on all aspects of bourgeois relations of production and their historical contingency. Reading *Grundrisse*, on the other hand, offers tantalising insights into areas of Marx's critique undeveloped or entirely absent from other examples of his later work, but which are still situated in the same methodological framework. One such insight is his analysis of individual freedom in the context of bourgeois, 'formal' individuality, and the consequent exposure of this freedom and individuality as the formally proclaimed but concretely unsubstantiated content of capitalist social relations, which are themselves the presupposition for revolutionary human emancipation.

However, on first inspection the *Grundrisse* may appear simply to repeat Marx's previous observations on alienation and to restate the methodological and ontological presuppositions of earlier works, (especially if we rely upon the extracts supplied by those who wish to promote the cause of the uninterrupted continuity thesis, e.g. Kamenka, Avineri, McLellan etc.).[97] For example, with regard to the apparent ontological primacy of individuals, there appears to be little difference between such comments as 'Individuals producing in society – hence socially determined individual pro-duction – is, of course, the point of departure',[98] and, 'As individuals express their life, so they are. What they are, therefore, coincides with their production, both with *what* they produce and *how* they produce.'[99]. The same goes for the incidence of similar passages concerning alienation. But it is in the notebooks of 1857-58 where, for the first time, Marx combined a materialist dialectic with a systematic critique of political economy. Essentially, Marx's exposi-tion of alienation (along with its revolutionary consequences) was to be fully integrated within a detailed examination of the forces and relations of the bourgeois mode of production. This enabled him to identify what he now believed to be both the positive and negative aspects of the contradiction within capital; the contradiction between constantly developing forces of production and the relations of production. For example, this revealed not only the nature of capitalism's negation of past economic formations and social relations, but also its positive tendency to posit the presuppositions for communal production. But there was no 'invisible hand' at work here, this was not the workings out of 'world spirit', or the necessary precondition for the eventual triumph of the *idea* of freedom. For Marx these processes were the result of living labour expended by past and present generations, creating and recreating the conditions of class antagonism in pre-revolutionary society, an antagonism which would accompany and assist the eventual demise of capitalism.

It is also in the *Grundrisse* where Marx evaluates the revolutionary implications of capitalism's constant restructuring of the forces of production in its perpetual pursuit of extracting greater surplus value. In particular it is the increase in the produc-tivity of living labour, i.e. surplus labour time (and the related decrease in necessary labour time) under capital, that as free time in post-revolutionary society will be a major precondition for the liberation of individuals, enabling them to pursue their own consciously determined ends. However, under the guise of capital-ism the increasing productivity of labour serves only to heighten the level of exploitation and the intensity of estrangement experienced by individual workers. The very conditions which are a product of expended labour power, come to oppose the wage labourer as determinants which appropriate labour one-sidedly, so that products are produced not by conscious objectification nor for collective consumption, but for the realisation of their exchange value as commodities for the benefit of the capitalist. Therefore, the forces of production, the materials transformed by these forces, the product which is the result of this process of transformation, and the labour power consumed by commodity production, are all estranged from the individual worker employed by capital. Indeed, within capitalism, knowledge, in the form of science and art incorporated within the forces of production, is perceived by the worker not as a conscious product of collective individuality, but as the property of those forces of production which immediately confront the worker as constant capital in the form of machinery.

So, by incorporating the newly discerned factor of the tendency for the productivity of labour to increase, Marx not only exposes the reason for capitalism's drive for concentration and centralisation – the pursuit of maximising the amount of surplus labour-time extracted from living labour – but also posits the

The individual and freedom

autonomy of the value of free time, i.e., 'releases labour time from its function as the primary condition of wealth, and creates the material conditions for the formation of mass individualities'.[100] The examination of this new factor in the *Grundrisse* was to underpin Marx's analysis of bourgeois economics in *Capital*:

> Fanatically bent on making value expand itself, he [the capitalist] ruthlessly forces the human race to produce for production's sake; he thus forces the development of the productive power of society, and creates those material conditions, which alone can form the real basis of a higher form of society, a society in which the full and free development of every individual forms the ruling principle.[101]

In the following an attempt will be made to follow through some of the introductory observations made above, especially those concerned with Marx's critique of 'bourgeois' notions of freedom and his discussion of individual self-determination that emerges from that critique. This will be done with the understanding that Marx's application of Hegel's dialectic extends to its employment as a technique enabling him to highlight both the positive and negative aspects of contradictions underlying the form of production based on capital; not merely exposing the conflictual nature of prevailing material conditions of production, but also revealing the disjuncture between the form and the content of legitimatory codes of justice and moral principles coexistent with bourgeois social relations.

It was therefore the rational core of Hegel's method which was of interest to Marx[102] and not its mystical or metaphysical shell with its accompanying teleological necessity.[103] It was this objective, materially based and de-mystified application of the method which would lay bare the dynamic laws of bourgeois economy, thus revealing not its universality, but its contingency. Therefore, Marx believed that this would show how contemporary conditions of production are 'engaged in *suspending themselves* and (by the same token were) positing the *historic presuppositions* for a new state of society', giving signs both of its past and what may supersede it, 'foreshadowings of the future'.[104] For Marx it would hopefully be a future of 'universally developed individuals, whose social relations, as their own communal relations, are hence also subordinated to their own communal control'.[105] This was no utopian vision, the evidence of such a future lay within existing social relations which, after all, were the product of past and present generations. It would be the responsibility of future generations to transform the poten-tiality into reality.

In order to construct a picture of what a self-determining social individual might look like, I shall turn first to Marx's critical analysis of the relationship between 'isolated' individuals in bourgeois social and economic relations, focussing particularly on the categories of circulation and money. This will be done with the understanding that such relations are a transitory manifestation of the historical development of the social individual, and that they reveal the possibility of an emancipated existence. So, once the historical nature of relations of production based on capital, and the contingency of the whole network of laws and norms which are supportive of them had been ascertained, Marx believed that the universality claimed by prevailing theories about the individual, either as a rights-bearing moral agent or as a want-maximising, self-interested rational actor, could be effectively debunked.

This leads on to the second part of my discussion which is an elaboration of what I understand to be Marx's tentative and unsystematic appraisal of the post-capitalist society of emancipated social individuals. I believe that Marx meant it to be an equivocal description and that he believed he had a good reason for it being so; to expect anything more substantial is to misjudge the task he set himself and to underestimate the potential ability he believed social individuals possessed to consciously change themselves.

4 The individual, circulation and money

For Marx one of the starkest examples of alienation in capitalist production lay in the process of circulation. This process had not only become a social power viewed by individuals as either a natural or a spontaneous relation, but also had been provided with sets of accompanying laws some of which claimed universality for the process itself, while others sought to enforce its consequences through juridical codes and legal 'rights'. Marx wished to expose the relations of circulation for what they really were: a moment of the contingent exploitative expropriation of surplus value by capital.

Circulation in capitalism, Marx insists in the *Grundrisse*, is

The individual and freedom

exchange, i.e. the mediation of products from particular forms of production in general exchange in the form of exchange value (money). In this way products become commodities produced to realise exchange value. Such a form of circulation has as its fundamental condition a form of production which appropriates the products of labour 'through and by means of divestiture and alienation' for another. Marx goes on to say that;

> circulation as the realisation of exchange value implies: (l) that my product is a product only in so far as it is for others, hence suspended singularity, generality; (2) that it is a product for me only in so far as it has been alienated, become for others; (3) that it is for the other only so far as he himself alienates his product, which already implies (4) that production is not an end in itself for me, but a means.[106]

Under capitalism such a set of relations constitutes an alien social power which appears to the individuals participating in production as an objective, spontaneously arising interrelation, *not* as a transitory facet of a system of production based on the exchange of exchange values which itself is an historical 'moment' of production in general. But this is the very system which, as Marx points out, is the one which 'bourgeois economists' uphold as the basis for individual freedom, who see the ;

> collision of unfettered individuals who are determined only by their own interests – as the mutual repulsion and attraction of free individuals, and hence as the absolute mode of existence of free individuality in the sphere of consumption and exchange.[107]

Meanwhile bourgeois politicians and lawyers construct constitutional and juridical systems which uphold this 'freedom', viewing it as an expression of universal laws of human nature and human society. Nothing, for Marx, could be so absurd and mistaken. Capital may well have established itself as the dominant mode of production, having successfully overcome the barriers of earlier systems of production, but it was incapable of suspending all limits to its complete triumph, or of freeing the majority of individuals, because of the eventually insurmountable barriers which were the product of its own contradictory nature. So, in its 'negation of the guild system etc.'[108] Capital did not set free individuals but only itself through free competition, indeed, Marx says of competition that it is 'nothing more than the way in which the many capitals force the inherent determinants of capital (i.e. the constant pursuit of increased surplus value) upon one another and upon themselves' [109] thereby reproducing forms of production which expropriate labour in the shape of commodities embodying exchange value; as the predominance of capital is the presupposition of free com-petition, so is the free competition between capitals the denial of the free development of individuality. For Marx then, the freedom claimed for the individual in a society of free competition is

> therefore at the same time the most complete suspension of all individual freedom, and the most complete subjugation of individuality under social conditions which assume the form of objective powers, even of overpowering objects – of things independent of the relations of individuals themselves.[110]

According to Marx the process of circulation in capital expressed as the 'free' and 'equal' exchange of equivalents is, therefore, merely the formal epiphenomena of the form of production founded on the creation of exchange value, which relies upon the exploitative relation of 'exchange of *objectified labour* as exchange value for living labour as use value' [111] Marx views this as essential to an understanding of the alienation of labour within relations of production based on capital, in which labour relates to its objective conditions, which, after all, are a creation of labour itself, as alien property. Such a form of exchange has as its presupposition the:

> separation of labour from its original intertwinement with its objective conditions, which is why it appears as mere labour on one side, while on the other side its product, as objectified labour, has an entirely independent existence as value opposite it.[112]

The labour of the individual is therefore posited not as an end in itself, or recognised as an expression of creative human consciousness, but in capital is total alienation, sacrificing the human end-in-itself to an entirely external end.[113] Under such conditions objectification becomes the process of dispossession, erecting an objective power opposite labour which does not belong to the worker but to the 'personified conditions of production, i.e. to capital'.[114] For Marx the labour performed by individuals in social relations is that uniquely human capacity which should be the basis for conscious, creative self-determination, i.e. freedom. However, under capital, the alienated labourer perceives such productive activity in purely instrumental terms, surrendering

The individual and freedom

living labour to capital in exchange for 'objectified labour'[115] in the form of exchange value in the purest form, money. This relationship is part of the elementary precondition of bourgeois society: 'that labour should directly produce exchange value, i.e. money; and, similarly, that money should directly purchase labour, and therefore the labourer'.[116]

In Marx's view, money, as the purest form of exchange value, is the clearest embodiment of the contradiction of that social mode of production corresponding to it, capital. That is, it is both a fact and a relation – a fact as the mode of exchange *par excellence*, and a relation as an expression of exploitation. And yet, as Marx points out, for the bourgeois, money is the epitome of equality, it appears to transcend inequality, particularly in the market where each individual is engaged, apparently on an equal footing, in the exchange of exchange values:

> ... it is in the character of the money relation ... that all inherent contradictions of bourgeois society appear extinguished ... and bourgeois democracy even more than the bourgeois economists takes refuge in this aspect ... in order to construct apologetics for the existing economic relations.[117]

An arrangement only reinforced by those laws which guarantee the fulfilment of contracts based on the exchange of equivalents made by 'equal' and 'free' parties.

Marx's analysis of money in capitalist relations of production therefore provides him with a further opportunity to expose the merely *formal* freedom and equality of individuals expounded by those who posit capitalism as the absolute form of production. Individuals are merely conceived of as exchangers of exchange value both in the form of commodities and labour. Labour power itself becomes a commodity possessing exchange value for both the worker as the 'owner' of living labour capacity, and for the owner of capital in the form of potential surplus value. Once in possession of the 'mediator' of exchange values, money, the individual regards others in the market as mere exchangers of exchange value. Such a relationship becomes, under capital, a formalised social relation; 'i.e. each has the same social relation towards the other that the other has towards him. As subjects of exchange, their relation is therefore that of *equality*'.[118] But this formal equality co-exists with a concrete inequality between the possessors of labour power and the owners of the means of production, which, after all, is the necessary presupposition of relations of production founded on capital.

The *formal* freedom of capitalist circulation and the *formal* equality of the exchange of exchange value, Marx reminds us, are both historically conditioned by capitalist relations of production. Under such a situation the individual is dependent upon a social relation (of capital) which reduces individual activity, individual acts of production, to exchange values. The social bond between individuals is expressed in exchange value, i.e. the individual's own activity has a meaning only insofar as it realises exchange value. The product as a product of objectification is viewed merely as the instrument for engaging in exchange – an attitude further enforced through the development of the division of labour. Each individual's 'private' end is, in such conditions, the production of a general product (exchange value). Each, therefore, possesses in the form of exchange values (money) the 'power' over the activity of others as expressed in the production of exchange value embodied in commodities. In such circumstances:

> activity, regardless of its individual manifestation, and the product of activity, regardless of its particular make-up, are always *exchange value*, and exchange value is a generality, in which all individuality and peculiarity are negated and extinguished.[119]

Such a situation will prevail as long as the presupposition of the predominant mode of production remains the creation of surplus value via the appropriation of labour by the owners of capital. Under these conditions the individual is alienated from both the social character of production and the social form of the product. The relationship between individuals under capital is one of 'indifference' even though the form of production in which they participate is one of social reciprocity and mutual interconnection which exist to a degree hitherto unknown. And yet, 'in exchange value, the social connection between persons is transformed into a social relation between things' [120] It is only when these relations are understood in terms of the antagonistic contradiction on which they are based, that the absence of genuine human freedom and equality become all too apparent.

Marx perceived bourgeois production as the era of personal independence which is founded on objective dependence. It is the

The individual and freedom

era where for the first time 'a system of general social metabolism, of universal relations, of all-round needs and universal capacities is formed', but in which there is the total isolation of individual private interests from those of others.[121] This contradiction will remain as long as the prevailing conditions of capitalist production are perceived by the majority as natural, spontaneous and absolute while the accompanying legal and political structures are viewed as legitimate. However, if we understand these relations as an express-ion of exploitation based on the one-sided expropriation of surplus value by and for capital, and that this condition is itself a contradictory one resting on the antagonistic division between capital and labour, Marx believes that we can identify these relations as the presupposition for a classless society; production based on exchange value is the prior condition of a society of universally developed individuals. Or as Marx himself puts it in his characteristically blunt manner: 'universal prostitution appears as a necessary phase in the development of the social character of personal talents, capacities, abilities, activities'.[122] Capital, in pursuing surplus value, continues to develop and revolutionise the means of production in ways which it hopes will more effectively extract surplus labour. However, the potential of such developments will never be fully realised within capitalist relations of production because, by their very nature, they are not concerned with the satisfaction of the multifarious needs of social individuals, but with the realising of profits for the owners of the means of production. These bourgeois relations, based as they are on private property and the exchange of exchange values, deny the mass of individuals conscious control over those forces of production which are the estranged product of their collective consciousness. Indeed the conditions of production appear as determining the character of labour performed and as consuming the activity of the worker in the process of producing the product which is capital's. However, the growing productivity of the forces of production (and its growing discordance with the increasingly conflictual social relations) is the key to the emancipation of individuals so, when investigating the nature of production under capitalism, Marx adopts the technique which exposes the essential disharmony between its ideal form – bourgeois political economy, and its appearance – concrete forces and relations, and reveals the negative and the positive attributes of the contradictions working themselves out in the bourgeois mode of production:

> Forces of production and social relations – two different sides of the development of the social individual – appear to capital as mere means, and are merely means for it to produce on its limited foundation. In fact, however, they are the material conditions to blow this foundation sky-high.[123]

For Marx the source of surplus value for capital is surplus labour time, which is that productive activity carried out by workers after they have produced sufficient exchange value in the form of commodities necessary for the reproduction of their living labour capacity; hence 'necessary labour time'. Capitalism, in this pursuit of surplus value, employs and constantly redevelops the instruments of production, (i.e. the technology of machinery), in ways that will extract the greatest amounts of surplus labour time, at the same time as reducing necessary labour time. As less 'immediate labour' (perceived by the capitalist as a component of circulating capital) is required to produce greater quantities of products, so the sum of labour objectified in fixed capital expands. More efficient machinery serves this very purpose under capital in that it allows the worker to work a longer part of his or her time for the benefit of capital, 'to work longer for another' than he or she would have done under earlier forms of production.[124] The instruments of production therefore appear to reproduce the relations of production based on capital, i.e. the appropriation of living labour by objectified labour in order to transform the materials of production for the creation of surplus value. So machinery, as both objectified labour and fixed capital, in determining the conditions of living labour, confronts the individual as a 'ruling power' as an 'alien attribute' of capital, and not as the 'accumulation of knowledge and skill, of the general productive forces of the social brain',[125] consciously controlled;[126] 'In machinery, objectified labour itself appears not only in the form of product or of the product employed as means of labour, but in the form of the force of production itself'.[127]

In such circumstances living labour, the 'life expression' of the individual, is to living labour capacity, i.e. the individual worker, an alien activity. But Marx reminds us that although such wage labour appears repulsive and forced[128] it is a transitory aspect of an historical form of production which has inverted the relationship between social labour and its product, the objective conditions of production. Moreover, such an inversion – the private organisation of social production – is an historical and a contingent necessity, 'a necessity for the development of the forces of production solely from a specific historic point of departure, or basis, but in no way an *absolute* necessity of production'.[129] In other words, it is the historical expression of a moment in the development of the forces of production accompanied by a tendential set of social relations which reflect and reinforce, through various means, the expropriation of surplus labour from living labour. Therefore, under capital the worker's activity appears as nothing more than the directing of the machine's work onto the raw materials; the role of supervision and the guarding against interruptions becomes the worker's lot, while the machine exercises the skill, strength and virtuosity. 'The workers activity, reduced to a mere abstraction of activity, is determined and regulated on all sides by the movement of the machinery, and not the opposite';[130] dead labour controls the living. It is through such an inversion that capital increases the productivity of labour, while at the same time striving for the greatest possible reduction of necessary labour. However, these two necessary tendencies of capital are also the presuppositions for the future free development of individualities, but they will remain unrealised presuppositions as long as machinery remains the most appropriate form of the value of fixed capital, subsumed under capital's relations of production.[131]

Within Marx's analysis of the nature of bourgeois 'freedom', and his exposure of the disjuncture between its formal articulation and its concrete expression, rests a picture of what genuine freedom might look like. In other words what is implicit in his critique of capitalist relations of production and what emerges out of his assessment of the contradictions that characterise the development of this mode of production, is the existence of a practicable alternative to the 'spontaneous order' and the 'invisible hand' of the 'disinterested' market. But, in the following section I want to maintain that such an alternative was not an *a priori* construct around which Marx built an elaborate social theory, neither will I subscribe to the claim that the marxism of Marx was based on a number of teleological assumptions, which provided him with a set

Marx and the individual

of superior, end-dependent principles that he subsequently applied to his damning judgement of capitalism. If he had adopted either strategy then we would expect to find an extensive and elaborate defence of one or the other at some stage during his intellectual development. The fact that his own position evolved out of a direct attack on universalist and teleological systems (see especially his condemnation of the idealism of the likes of Proudhon, and his critique of the theory of justice implicit in the Gotha Programme[132] appears to suggest that Marx sought for a novel and radical alternative that he hoped would place the role of system building, in theory and practice, in the hands of the subjects of the system itself – conscious, self-determining, social individuals.

5   Self-determination, social freedom and revolution

Marx's concept of disposable time (free time) is derived from his examination of machinery as fixed capital, particularly in so far as it increases the proportion of surplus labour time to necessary labour time, thus 'enabling labour, through an increase of its productive power, to create a greater mass of the products required for the maintenance of living labour in a shorter time'. This tendency becomes for Marx the condition for the emancipation of labour.[133] As capital strives towards universality and pursues the objective already inherent in its earliest stages of development – the world market and the real subsumption of all society – it encounters barriers in its own nature, which eventually reveal that capital is the greatest barrier to the continued development of the forces of production.[134] Nowhere does this realisation become more apparent than amongst the wage labourers themselves, who hitherto have regarded disposable time as antithetical, in that it is the time in which they produce surplus value for capital.[135] Such disposable time has led to labour's sustained degradation, so that its activity in the process of production appears as 'a complete emptying-out, [of] this universal objectification as total alienation, and the tearing-down of all limited, one-sided aims as a sacrifice of the human end-in-itself to an entirely external end'.[136]

However, with the worsening of the endemic crisis of capitalism, and the increasing inability of capital to control the consequences of such a crisis within existing relations of production, (i.e. the decreasing ability of capital to ride the storm through the concentration and centralisation of the mode of production, the concomitant drive to reduce necessary labour time to a bare minimum, and the reduction of the cost to surplus value of circulation through time and space), workers come to recognise singly and as a class that their separation from the products of their own labour has hitherto been forcibly imposed, and that such a condition had rested on the consistent denial of their own realisation.[137] Subsequently, once this condition of exploitative divestiture and expropriation is understood by those who sell their labour power as being the consequence of the production of surplus value for the owners of capital, and once the relations of production commensurate with commodity exchange are perceived as historical and transient, the overthrow of these relations by the labouring classes becomes for them the imminent and necessary presupposition for the emancipation of the mass of individualities.

With the 'violent overthrow' of capitalism[138] and the concomitant appropriation by the workers of their own surplus labour, disposable time ceases to have an antithetical existence in that its inverted character under capital is suspended and transformed in the conditions of 'communal production' to free time. Under such conditions the individual's act of production confirms both his or her individuality as a conscious objectifying agent, and is recognised as such by others engaged in productive activity, thus confirming the social nature of production. The labour of social individuals is a liberating activity which 'obtains its measure from the outside, through the aim to be attained and the obstacles to be overcome in attaining it'. In communal production the individual, in consciously positing the aim, engages in labour which is self-realisation, 'objectification of the subject, hence real freedom' [139]

This state of affairs is in direct contrast to that described by Adam Smith, who for Marx epitomises the bourgeois economist's (and for that matter bourgeois society's) attitude to labour. Such a view saw all labour as an imposition, 'a curse', which in the time it takes to perform demands a corresponding sacrifice of freedom and happiness, both of which are only fully expressed in the state of 'tranquillity'. Marx admits that this situation may well be true for labour under capital which is, after all, external, forced drudgery,[140] but it is an historical inversion of the actual relationship

Marx and the individual

between the life activity of the individual and its objective conditions. Necessary labour will still be an essential component of communal production (as it is of all previous modes of production), but it will not only be performed for the sake of genuine social need rather than for the owners of the means of production, it will also occupy less of the individual's time as 'social production will grow so rapidly that ... *disposable time* will grow for all'.[141] And it is in the disposable time released by the forces of production that the free development of individuals takes place, employing the means created by those forces for their own ends,[142] which are immediately perceived by the community as contributions to the general, social product.[143] Social worth would therefore be recognised within the activity of production itself and not in the exchange value produced. In the latter, labour is posited as 'general only through exchange', but on the foundation of communal production the 'exchange of products would in no way be the *medium* by which the participation of the individual in general production is mediated'.[144] Under capital the interrelationship between different individual producers is estranged from its immediate, communal, social relation and is transferred to the market where products as commodities represent exchange value, which is realised by capital. However, in communal production, 'communality is presupposed as the basis of production. The labour of the individual is posited from the outset as social labour',[145] and whatever he or she produces is viewed as a particular contribution to the general social product. Marx believes that in such circumstances individuals will reproduce themselves as social individuals[146] and that the wealth of the community will be measured in terms of the 'universality of individual needs, capacities, pleasures, productive forces ... the full development of human mastery over the forces of nature ... the absolute working out of (the individual's) creative potentialities'.[147] The development of all human powers will be regarded as an end in itself, in which individuals will parti-cipate, reproducing themselves *not* in 'one specificity' or through one particular function, but each realising their own 'totality' as a social individual through the all round development of their own capacities.

For Marx the future society of emancipated individuals would require as its precondition, the development of the forces of production by relations of production based on capital. In particular it would be the increasing productivity of labour – and the concomitant increase of surplus labour time, disposable time, free time – under capital that would serve as the necessary presupposition for communal relations of production. Marx's investigation of capital was therefore concerned with the character of those relations of production which generate and develop the productive forces, but which by their very nature are relations which prevent the utilisation of these forces for the benefit of society as a whole. He wished to show how the capitalist mode of production is not a natural, absolute form of production, but one which incorporates within it, in an inverted form, a relationship between labour and its increasing productivity which reveals the necessity for capital's destruction.

It is in the *Grundrisse* that Marx's discussion goes beyond its previous concentration on alienation as the negative condition of a mode of production based on competition, and establishes the positive condition of the new levels of productivity as the basis for human freedom. As such the *Grundrisse* was a watershed for Marx, for it signalled the incorporation of his earlier criticisms of ideology and his analysis of the 'driving forces of history' within a systematic critique of political economy, while at the same time preserving and strengthening his belief in the necessary triumph of a community of emancipated individuals, whose free social development is the precondition for a free society.

6 Conclusion

By developing at some length the argument that Marx did not employ a morality or a theory of justice in his critique of capitalism, I have attempted to show that Marx was committed to a view of human freedom which represented a radical departure from previous and contemporary notions of liberation, one that he believed was untrammelled by codes or conduct that owed their origin to a system of exploitation, a system from which individuals were trying to liberate themselves in the first place. For Marx, the impetus for social emancipation would emerge from the concrete experiences of individuals living and working in social relations and productive processes, and not from the pleas of well-meaning social reformers equipped with a mystified and illusionary 'watertight' moral indignation. I believe that it is still necessary to dispel the impression given by post-marxists (sic) and non-marxists alike that one of the few things salvageable from the wreckage of 'historical materialism' is a marxian moral theory or a revolutionary notion of distributive justice. To entertain such expectations is to commit a disservice to Marx. This is not to suggest that we should return to a marxism that relied upon the kind of vulgar determinism that Marx himself was adamantly dead against. Neither do I wish to give the impression that the conclusions of Marx's critique are faultless. But what I have sought to establish is that Marx explicitly and consciously eschewed any reliance upon speculative *a priorism*: his first attempts at developing a materialist methodology in 1845-46 were based on the premise that before one could discuss the possibilities of human freedom one had to understand the origins of the existing conditions of unfreedom. And once Marx had discovered for himself those origins in the productive activity of previous generations of individuals in social relations, he went on to examine the dynamics of present society in a similar light, believing that the antagonisms and contradictions that drove capitalism ever onwards would also be the presuppositions for a usurpation by the dispossessed.

Lukes is correct in one sense, Marx's future communist society will almost inevitably require a set of norms, standards, codes of conduct (even, perhaps, rights), but as far as Marx was concerned we cannot hope to know their character until we (or more likely a future generation) have established that post-revolutionary society. Marx may well have entertained ideas about these communist ethics, but he always maintained that he was not in the business of imposing a radical morality on contemporary society, only those engaged in the pursuit of revolution and social transformation would discover through their own actions the codes and norms which would govern their activities. For these reasons it is probably right to say that for Marx the communist ethic would remain an unknown quantity until communism itself had been initiated, and, as a necessary consequence of this observation, it would be impossible to apply the unknown morals of communism to the practice of capitalism.

It bears repeating that Marx's notion of freedom is an open

The individual and freedom

one, i.e., it is not confined to any preconceived idea of what individual emancipation *should* be, rather, having recognised that individuals are capable of self-determination, they themselves should be left to discover for themselves the nature of their own liberty and how best it might be pursued. Capitalism as an economic process, as a social system, as a set of moral and juridical standards, in short, as a totality of antagonisms, denied self-determination, but this very systemic denial would eventually give rise to the demand for social emancipation and individual liberty, a demand that Marx believed would only be realised through social revolution.

CONCLUDING NOTE

I began this study by observing that the intellectual legacy of Mill and Marx has to a large extent fuelled many of the ideological conflicts of the twentieth century, I also suggested that this might be no fault of their own, and further, that there may be aspects of their respective systems that could bear comparison. These suggestions are nothing new, in fact they have inspired some to claim that 'Marx and Mill have more in common with each other than either has with the representative thinkers of the next generation, let alone those of our own troubled age'.[1] But full-length comparative examinations are somewhat of a rarity, which is a puzzle considering the number of similar themes that pervade their thoughts. One such common thread which runs through both their writings, and one which was a major preoccupation of this study, is the idea of freedom being something more than the protection of privacy and the respect for autonomy, one that is based on the belief that individuals do have a capacity for self-development, some have termed it perfectibility,[2] accompanied by a tendency to recognise such an ability in others.

This was my starting point. I set out to investigate the origins of each thinker's notions about freedom, attempting to situate them within the scientific theories that both Mill and Marx believed were necessary for an effective understanding of the human condition. What emerged were images of human nature that incorporated capacities for active, voluntary intervention in the conditions of existence, abilities to modify, transform and consciously control our own destinies. It transpired that these capacities for what I called self-determination, were central to the thinkers' theories of human progress. Both believed that history was explicable in terms of the continual, creative and ever-changing pursuit by individuals in social relations of needs and appetites. But they parted company over the character and basis of this capacity for change, and this was to have a crucial impact on their respective views of contemporary society and the means of improving it.

There is no denying that both were convinced that the future would be more rational, harmonious, emancipated and egalitarian than the present, a time in which the productive powers would generate sufficient wealth to enable the large proportion of individuals to enjoy potentialities previously denied them. To this extent they both in their own ways expressed a nineteenth century certainty about continued human progress based on technological and scientific discovery. These developments were clear evidence of the capacities that rational social individuals possessed for working in creative concert with others. Both looked confidently and assuredly to a better, more humane future populated with individuals who through their self-determination, would generate, via collective effort, a qualitatively superior realm of freedom.

Mill and Marx were, arguably, the last of the optimistic system-builders whose respective theories of history convinced them that they were living at a crucial time, where opportunities, if grasped, would lead to a liberating transformation of society. Within a generation of their deaths new approaches to the study of humans and society (often taking as their starting point the writings of Mill and Marx), had succeeded in knocking the shine off the certainty of progress. Weber, for example, had contended that the masses were complacent and resistant to 'improvement' They were potentially destructive of progress and susceptible to the authoritarian charms of the orator. The answer lay with the bureaucratic elites and the enlightened technocrats. Durkheim had expressed the widely held fear – and given it a respectable, sociological foundation – that without the constraints of an extensive moral discipline, both human nature and society as a whole to would be to likely slip into anarchy. From the opposite direction, Freud had highlighted the ambiguities of consciousness. The 'lower' passions that Mill sought to transcend through the cultivation of the 'higher' virtues were identified as crucial aspects of any character formation with their repression viewed as having potentially explosive consequences. The confidence of those who in the nineteenth century had proclaimed the fulfillment of humankind in terms of a liberated social individual, had been superseded by a pessimistic vision of existential isolation, only strengthened by practical experience.

Within that same generation historical events had appeared to put paid to many of the hopes of the century of certainty. The intellectually cathartic experience of the Great War and its international, social economic and political consequences led many to believe that it was the decline into barbarism which had to be avoided and fought against, not the promotion of unpredictable change for its own sake. The faith in continued progress had been dealt a severe blow with the realisation that the products of progress could be employed as agents of mass destruction. Revolutions were extinguished or became bureaucratically vitrified in response to a lack of international reciprocation. Capitalism still had a long way to go before the global totalisation of the class struggle which was now seen by many as the prerequisite for any future success for the proletarian party. Marxists sought either to secure the orthodox anathema of 'socialism in one country' or attempted to salvage what remained of a socialist movement emasculated in the west by reformism and fascism.

But all this was beyond the ken of Mill and Marx who remained clearly of the opinion that once liberated from the wearing constraints of ignorance, poverty and oppression, human agents would lead fulfilling and socially constructive lives, unhindered by the base passions and short-sighted objectives that had been the hallmark of the acquisitive materialism that both of them despised. It is for reasons such as these that some present-day commentators have been inspired to claim that although:

> Marxian theory challenges liberalism, it also affirms and extends certain ethical claims which are at the heart of liberalism: claims about the goods of mutual recognition of persons and self-respect, or a general human capacity for moral personality and individuality.[3]

Others have been prepared to go further:

> Rather than merely repudiating the modern ideal of individuality Marx radicalised it: communism would complete the process of individual emancipation pressed forward by capitalism and liberalism.[4]

But there are several problems with such a linkage which assumes that both thinkers are on the same philosophical continuum. Firstly, it tends to leave out more than it takes into consideration; for example the contrast between Mill's distinct lack of confidence in the labouring class's ability to improve itself on its own terms and with its own intellectual resources, and Marx's unbridled conviction that the proletariat will be the self-appointed champions of the new order. Those who abandon a critical perspective in pursuit of rapprochement will also tend to overlook Mill's rather unscientific faith in the universality of capitalist laws of production, as opposed to Marx's assured belief that these laws were just as contingent as the conditioned forms of distribution. Marx may well have agreed with 'nineteenth century utilitarians on the socially dynamic nature of Western society',[5] but he rejected the reformism propounded by the likes of Mill as being half-hearted and doomed to failure at the hands of the unforgiving market. And while a number of Mill's working class associates seriously contemplated revolutionary insurrection, writing to him for his opinion, he consistently upbraided them for considering such a foolish strategy as a viable alternative to gradualism initiated by a selfless elite.

So although Mill and Marx may well have held similar views of what an emancipated existence might look like, their respective methodologies, theories of human nature and enabling programmes differed considerably. This of course should come as no surprise. It is a conclusion that has usually brought any further comparative discussion to an abrupt halt. Mill and Marx, it has been said, developed theories of liberty which were derived from two quite distinct and opposing intellectual traditions, empiricism and idealism, those great foundational titans of the eighteenth century that battled it out through the nineteenth and are still at loggerheads in the late twentieth.

And in spite of the admission that both thinkers reformulated their own intellectual inheritances in fundamental ways, and that these reformulations intentionally incorporated elements from alternative traditions, it is still often maintained (particularly by critics of both systems) that both thinkers remained true to their original allegiances – Mill to Benthamite utilitarianism, Marx to a materialist Hegelianism. This consistent adherence, it is then claimed, consequently precludes entertaining the view that either thinker may have something to learn from the other. Surely, if the locus of freedom for Mill lies in the capacity for self-culture which initially expresses itself in the realm of ideas and can be explained via a utilitarian reading of the laws of association, then how can we constructively compare it with a marxian notion of liberty that originates in the uniquely human capacity for conscious creative

Concluding note

activity? Or, to put this question the other way around, how can a praxology of emancipation which rests upon the development of a revolutionary class consciousness, and a transformation of the very basis of production, have anything in common with a political philosophy which insisted that individuality needs to be protected from the social and political tyranny of the labouring and middle classes, and further maintained that the prevailing laws of production were universal and efficacious?

If, after recognising the incommensurability of key elements of their systems, we are left with nothing more than the sterile observation that Mill and Marx both ended up with similar notions of liberty as self-determination, then the comparison remains a formal and an uncontentious one. But if we go on to suggest that their analyses may well be employed to highlight the weaknesses of what have become two opposing views of freedom, then maybe the comparison will be a constructive one.

To be less imprecise: with Mill I have sought to claim (particularly in Chapter 5) that his examination of freedom was compromised by his desire that *universal* emancipation should not be pursued at the expense of social stability or the prevailing economic order. This caution – one might more charitably call it prudence – was born out of his exaggerated, but by no means unfounded fear of the 'uneducated generality's' detrimental impact on the delicate flower of liberty, and it was a fear that, as we have seen, informed his limited constitutional reforms in *Representative Government*. It must be remembered that many of the more radical leaders of the labouring classes in the first half of the nineteenth century believed that the first step towards social justice and liberty was a universal suffrage, and that the political power of the working class which would inevitably ensue would be used to initiate a substantial redistribution of wealth via the probable transgression of the hallowed right of private property. Mill was hardly unaware of these tendencies having witnessed the monster demonstrations of Chartism and the birth of an independent labour movement which sought to promote uniquely proletarian aspirations. His fears were that the march of progress would be jeopardised by what he believed were the short term demands of the working classes, and that the source of that progress – new ideas and their originators – would be smothered by middle class mediocrity. It is hardly surprising that Mill had little public support and even less surprising that he never actively courted it, preferring to indulge men and women of confirmed self-cultivation whom he thought would respond favourably to his perceptive observations and reformist proposals.

Mill may well have recognised that the threats to freedom and advancement posed by ignorance and prejudice were the products of poverty and economic disadvantage (evidence to this effect can be found in nearly all of his major works, but especially in *Principles of Political Economy* and *Chapters on Socialism*), but he claimed that via educational reforms, moderate distributional measures and a limited expansion of political representation, such debilitating problems would be substantially solved.[6] However, I believe that as long as Mill stood by this conviction that the prevailing laws of production were inviolate he only compromised his commitment to freedom. Because it was through the operation of these same economic laws that extremes of poverty and wealth were perpetuated, and if we accept Mill's own observation that poverty inhibited the full development of the capacity for self-improvement then we are justified in asking why he persisted in championing the inviolability of the laws of production.

Social reform might properly ameliorate some of the excesses of capitalism, but for Mill the freedom of the market remained paramount. He believed that it was the logical extension of the principle of liberty, the legitimate economic consequence of individual freedom. As he championed the free market of ideas so he defended the free market of commodities:

> The so-called doctrine of Free Trade, which rests on grounds different from, though equally solid with, the principle of individual liberty asserted in this Essay. Restrictions on trade, or production for purposes of trade, are indeed restraints; and all restraints *qua* restraint, is an evil.[7]

Anything more than the minimum of safety-nets smacked of paternalism, the equivalent of the stultifying 'dependency culture' so berated by the present-day right. For Mill, the first signs of self-culture could be detected in the efforts of those freeing themselves from reliance on the cloying charity of others. No amount of well-meaning, but misguided, institutionalised welfare could aid the efforts of the able-bodied, it was up to them themselves to make the right choice to pursue the higher pleasures commensurate with self-development and forego the temptations of immediate appetites.

Mill was faced with a crucial dilemma: how to reconcile the establishment of a minimum of social justice at the same time as promoting individual liberty. This presented a number of problems. Firstly, how to obtain the necessary minor redistribution of the social product without hindering the effective and efficient workings of the market. It must be recalled that although Mill welcomed experiments in co-operative forms of production and foresaw a time when different variants of production would work side-by-side, such alternatives should always be judged by their success in the competitive market. In other words he drew the line at systemic change, believing that 'communism' might well be *one* way ahead (constructively competing with other systems, of course) but for the foreseeable future it should be confined to the level of the manufacturing unit where workers could be managers.[9] In the end I believe that Mill opted for a system which would provide a bare minimum of support, a safety net for those incapable of helping themselves. This was not to include the indigent who had only themselves to blame; the deserted and destitute young, old and infirm were deserving of help but only when it could be shown that all other forms of support, particularly the family, had failed them. If Mill was ever a socialist it was a commitment that was nothing more than experimental.

Secondly, for Mill the pursuit of individual liberty required a set of institutional guarantees and juridical parameters, and perhaps most crucially a general social acknowledgement of the benefits of self-improvement. All three were to be mutually supportive in creating an environment in which liberty could flourish, but the means of achieving it may well have compromised the end. I believe there is a very shaky relationship in Mill's writings between his notion of virtue and his belief in the need for expert guidance and leadership. There are times when the two appear synonymous, for example, when Mill says that only those of confirmed virtue can be said to be truly free,[10] and further that only virtuous people, i.e. those who have controlled their own destinies through the application of self-culture, are suitable candidates for bureaucratic and political authority. The implication is that only those who have already achieved virtue are capable of exercising authority and as a consequence are in a position to appoint successors who exhibit a similar virtue. The danger here is that a particular notion of virtue may well be promoted at the expense of others. This would have an additional effect on the nature and extent of deference. It will be recalled that Mill saw deference as necessary cement for the maintenance of social cohesion, acting both as a means of setting an example to those who would aspire to self-improvement, and as a way of generating respect for those who had attained positions of authority by virtue of their own self-culture. But such deference could just as easily become abstentionism or an excuse or apathy born of economic and social powerlessness.

It has to be remembered that Mill was generally pessimistic about the short and medium term prospects for improvement amongst the labouring and middle classes. He did believe that through modest institutional and procedural reforms, such as improved access to jury service and parish councils, and the extension of the franchise (initially tempered by plural voting), the under-educated generality might be encouraged to adopt a more responsible attitude towards their own lives and the lives of others. As more individuals attained self-improvement so the more participatory society would become. But until such a time the high offices of political and bureaucratic authority would remain in the hands of the meritocratic elite.

Mill was over-protective towards the self-cultivated minority (of which he of course was a member), and by the same token he over-estimated the threat of the ignorant masses. This is a somewhat ironic inversion of what others later saw as the threat posed to multifarious self-development by 'mass culture', itself, arguably, the product of the market relations Mill sought to defend. Control in developed western democracies never did end up in the hands of the 'uncultivate herd', if anything it remained ever more firmly in the grip of the fortunate few who applied their own principles of success and 'virtue' to the rest of society.

In effect Mill failed to appreciate the extent to which adverse economic conditions can mitigate against large numbers of individuals attempting to pursue self-development. In fact he refused to acknowledge the conditioning interdependency between the inequitable distribution of the social product and the prevailing form of production. Distribution might be tinkered with successfully, but the laws of production always remained sacrosanct for Mill. For Marx such an artificial separation epitomised the liberal predilection for abstracting laws from a historically specific mode of production and elevating them to the unimpeachable status of universality. In the process this only served to legitimate the continued expropriation of human potentialities by an economic system which cared little for individual self-determination, preferring the pursuit of profit to the pursuit of personal fulfillment.

But Mill did hit upon something which goes to the heart of all social theories that claim to champion the lot of the unfree. He questioned the emancipatory credentials of all who proclaimed the cause of freedom. To what extent are theories of social emancipation prepared to defend the individual from intrusion and harm? What principles are necessary for the protection of those who wish to pursue lives that may challenge the will of the majority? Can theories which rely upon a determinist notion of human nature or a materialist conception of history leave room for the self-improving human agent? Questions such as these prompted Mill to critically reassess his commitment to Benthamite utilitarianism and to integrate into his own materialist epistemology a conception of free agency. The strains of such a combination were dealt with in Chapter 2. But once Mill had achieved a compatibilist solution to his own satisfaction this formed the basis of his spirited defence of individual liberty. And it was from this that he derived a revitalised utilitarian theory of justice and morality which demarcated and vigorously defended individual sovereignty. If anything can be said to be the positive legacy of Mill it is this.

Can the same be said of Marx? How is it that a critique of capitalism so redolent with a vision of the future realm of freedom failed to construct a set of prescriptive principles to guide the actions of those engaged in the revolutionary struggle? If Marx was so committed to 'universal subjectification' wherein individuals realised genuine self-determination within and through uninhibited social interaction, why did he not also elucidate an accompanying morality. Why no marxian rights to reinforce the enhanced individuation of post-revolutionary society, why the absence of a socialist distributive justice? Lacunae such as these have dismayed those who would otherwise find Marx's analysis appealing, while others, already sceptical of his ambitious claims for dramatic historical change, have quickly seized this alleged inadequacy to reassert their view that revolution will always regard individuals as dispensable if they impede progress towards the new society.

There are those, who, as we have seen, in recognising these shortcomings, sought to develop a marxian morality and, in some cases, a complimentary theory of justice. Chapter 6 included a critical discussion of these normative approaches to Marx and incorporated it in an examination of what I took to be Marx's unique and non-moral understanding of self-determination. This developed the analysis of his understanding of human nature in Chapter 3. Here it emerged that for Marx humans are *homo faber*, they create and recreate the means of their own existence. Such productive activity is pursued within historically contingent relations which define the nature of the activity and condition the circumstances in which that activity is performed. In other words human productive activity, whether it be the immediate production of commodities or other forms of subjectification, both informs the nature of social relations and is in turn given social meaning by those same relations. There is then a circularity of interdependency with the predominant moment being the forces of production.

Marx having equipped himself with these ontological foundations attempted to unravel the complexity of the concrete reality of capitalist political economy. This was to be achieved via abstract categorisation, the 'reproduction of the concrete by way of thought', the only way, Marx believed, 'in which thought appropriates the concrete, reproduces it as the concrete in mind'.[11] Such abstract categorisation comprehended the concrete because it was the *reflection* of the concrete in the mind, in effect approaching its object not from the outside but from the inside. For Marx the concepts that resulted from the process of abstraction contained *and* revealed the underlying dynamic of antagonism within capitalism, the antagonism of labour and capital. It was an antagonism that he believed both explained the content of the hidden laws of capitalism and exposed the composition of bourgeois social relations as mediations, it was for Marx the 'determinate abstraction'.[12] Indeed, bourgeois society was the ever-changing expression of the mediation of the inherently unstable social antagonism, the class antagonism of labour and capital.

Concluding note

From this perspective economic, social, political, moral and juridical phenomena (and the values that underpinned them) are all to be understood in terms of the unifying abstract determination, each demystified as mediations of the concrete antagonistic character of production in class-divided societies. Even those moral and juridical theories which set themselves up as alternatives to contemporary immorality and injustice were just as much reflections and alternative mediations of the *prevalent* relations of production. And I believe that those who have attempted to supply Marxism with a formulated ethic and a theory of distributive justice are merely the modern-day equivalent of the ethical socialists whom Marx regarded as no better than idealists. As far as he was concerned, prescriptive moral theory, whatever its intention or its relationship with the prevailing mode of production, was a product of existing social relations and as a consequence was just as contingent.

The reason that Marx never intentionally articulated a moral theory has two interrelated aspects. Firstly, as outlined above, his method precluded it. In fact it was a method that had its roots in Marx's own rejection of Hegelian idealism and was born out of his dispute with his Young Hegelian contemporaries. Secondly, the application of the method to human history revealed to Marx the 'true' relationship between the abstract and the concrete, between ideas and reality. Active individuals in social relations, collectively pursuing the reproduction of the means of their existence, were the originators of the ideas and norms which gave meaning to their experiences. These ideas and norms might well become 'universalised' governing principles but in reality they were merely transitory mystified abstractions. By the same token any morality Marx may have chosen to construct would have been of a similar character as that proposed by those seeking to legitimate capitalism, i.e. a mediation of existing antagonisms, not a solution to them. Therefore Marx never formulated a morality.

But opponents to this view will insist that Marx's own writings are so liberally seasoned with moral outrage and indignation, that even if he did not intend it, he nevertheless applied normative criteria to his attack on capitalism However, I believe that the use by Marx of morally loaded language can be explained in ways which do not lead to such a conclusion. Language is an inhibiting medium. Whatever the terms used in a discourse they will often be interpreted by others according to prevailing linguistic conventions. This is especially true of terms that are *traditionally* associated with moral sentiment. In the case of Marx those seeking 'evidence' for a marxian morality will find ample supportive material in his writings. Marx was fully aware of the remorseless waste of human resources that had accompanied industrialisation and he was not averse to using emotionally charged language in order to express his personal disgust. His gut-reaction anger was registered using the language available to him, language that he knew would register a similar reaction in his audience. But such rhetorical devices never had any bearing on his metaethic which was an integral part of his methodology and ontology, both of which remained essentially unaltered from when they first appeared in the late 1840s. He con-sistently upbraided those who would use his writings as a source of moral indictments. And he was purposefully vague about the nature of the post-revolutionary world simply because his analysis precluded any such detailed predictions. His 'heroic silence' was always intentional.

Marx might well have possessed a personal set of values that could be viewed as indicative of a 'moral' position, but as far as his analysis of history is concerned such values were never employed as positive prescriptions. The values concomitant with a revolutionary situation would emerge from the experiences of the revolution. Just as Marx left his impressions of future communist society at the level of brief, vague and imprecise notes, so he kept his observations on the values that would exist in such a society to a minimum. The structure and supporting norms of a fully socialised community would be the result of the activities of self-determining social individuals. And it must be remembered that Marx's radical conception of the subjectifying, individuating agent is as open-ended as is the limitless list of possibilities for multifarious forms of human activity, and as such demands that there be no prior normative constraints that might inhibit the free expression of self-realisation.

If Marx was more specific about the distributional principles that might prevail in the transitional 'dictatorship of the proletariat' it was because he saw it as combining aspects of both bourgeois and socialist notions of justice. And since he was more than famil-iar with existing forms of distributional justice he could

Concluding note

project the character of these forms into his picture of the transitional phase. Indeed, it was a phase that he believed he had witnessed, admittedly in an imperfect sense, in the Paris Commune of 1871. But as a *transitional* stage it could not serve as a definitive guide to full communism, and as Marx was twice removed from this eventuality he realised that his projections could, at the most, only be tentative.

Marx's conscious equivocation on the issues of proletarian justice and communist morality was, I believe, the corollary of his conviction that the revolutionary movement would of its own accord establish the social principles commensurate with the unimpeded expression of mutual recognition between self-determining social agents. To say any more than this would be to deny the validity of his whole system of analysis. Furthermore, it would go against his own conviction that only those actively engaged in revolutionising their own conditions of existence would be in a position to comprehend revolutionary values.

If this is the case then it is pointless for 'marxists' to try and formulate something that cannot be found within the vast corpus of Marx, a marxian morality. If marxists wish to discover the nature of such a morality they should either wait for the revolution or participate in a revolutionary movement. The last thing they should do is to remain solely within the rarified environment of Marxist scholarship.

But would the revolutionary project be jeopardised by the recognition of a set of non-moral guarantees that would inhibit the extent to which the subjectifying agent could be restrained by a third party? If mutual recognition is an integral part of the social individual's self-determination then is it possible to codify such a relationship? Is it not possible for even the most liberating and non-violent revolution to inadvertently constrain the actions of some of those who are engaged in the revolutionary project?

Mill believed that his principle of liberty was non-moral, indeed he was convinced that liberty would allow for the fullest expression of moral and non-moral arguments. For him, utility may well have been the litmus test for all moral questions, but this did not mean that as a basis for morality utility was immune to counter-arguments. And if we strip away the residues of laissez-faire political economy and associationist epistemology (amongst

175

other normative aspects of his thought) from Mill's basic argument for liberty, then I believe we are left with a set of value-free principles which would enhance a marxian notion of self-determination. This would not restrict subjectification but strengthen the mutual respect for social individuals that is at the heart of Marx's system. For this is one of the resilient attractions of Marx's analysis of human agency, because not only does it underpin his understanding of history but it also places the subjectifying agent at the head of future change.

A marxist principle of liberty could be a powerful weapon if it were intimately combined with a practical movement for radical change. It would not infer any moral superiority because the life-patterns chosen by emancipated social individuals would be their own. It would not prescribe particular forms of activity because Marx believed that class struggle would reinforce the mutual recognition and co-operative self-determination that are already integral, though deformed, elements of human character. And it might effectively expose the vacuousness of existing claims for liberty made by societies that are inherently unfree, and consistently deny to vast numbers of individuals the opportunity for self-determination.

It is ironic that marxist-inspired revolutions, when writing their constitutions, have usually employed the value-laden language of liberalism, enshrining the familiar bourgeois rights of free expression and freedom to combine within the over-arching rhetoric of socialism. These constitutions have been ridiculed by those who would be glad to see the demise of all quasi-sociallst societies, and rightfully so because the contents of these constitutions have always been hostage to the vagaries of history and the authoritarian whims of an autocrat. But the same might be said of any constitution or bill of rights, regardless of the regime, communist or liberal democratic. For Marx they all performed the same function: the mediation of the antagonism between classes. They reflected the same disjuncture between the concrete and the mystified abstract. Would a marxist principle of liberty shorn of its liberal origins be prone to the same criticism? If combined with the revolutionary practical critique of existing social relations then I think not. A marxian principle of liberty would recognise that self-determination is a genuine human need and that social emanci-

Concluding note

pation and individual freedom are interdependent. In effect, it would protect the social individual from those who would impose their own notion of freedom on others, but by the same token it could be invoked to restrain those who might wish to revert to circumstances which inhibit the expression of self-determination by others.

Much more could be said on this proposal, but it would take an extensive study to do it full justice. Suffice to say that one way forward, I believe, is the constructive, critical comparison between contemporary liberalism and marxism. However, it might be claimed by some who witnessed the dramatic revolutionary events of the recent past that any dialogue between the two ideological titans is now pointless. The upheavals in Central and Eastern Europe may have many unpredictable consequences, but one thing is sure, the argument goes, the citizens of those states often risked their lives for ideals that are very much the progeny of liberalism. Democracy, Justice, Liberty, Rights. A further part of the equation is the demanded liberalisation of economies that had previously been hamstrung by inefficient, corrupt bureaucracies and unbalanced budgeting overburdened by the need for high-tech military parity. Altogether this must surely provide incontrovertible evidence that marxism is no longer a viable alternative, and that lalssez-faire capitalism has proved its resilience?

Such triumphalism has been described by one highly regarded liberal of a Keynesian persuasion as nothing less than 'mental vacuity of clinical proportions'.[13] I am inclined to agree, but for slightly different reasons. Whereas J. K. Galbraith questioned the simple-minded assumptions of those who viewed free-market capitalism as the panacea for the economies of Eastern Europe, I have queried, partly by the use of comparison, the content of a key principle in the liberal panoply as articulated by a member of liberalism's pantheon. The central aim of this study was to encourage a critical re-evaluation of two distinct and highly influential notions of individual liberty. One intended consequence of this comparative study was the conclusion that Marx did have a sophisticated understanding of the nature of personal freedom. And that this conception of liberty was principally born out of a critique of capitalism and its attendant ideological supports. The fact that Marx's critique can and has been effectively applied to those societies which have proclaimed their allegiance to 'democratisation' and the 'socialisation of the means of production' and has exposed these claims as at best unrealised and at worst spurious, is sufficient evidence for its continued relevance. And when turned to those states that have 'prospered' under capital, the critique is still more than capable of revealing endemic unfreedom. One can only hope that liberalism will itself use the opportunity of major political change to openly reassess the foundations of its principles even more thoroughly than before. A heavy responsibility now rests on its shoulders to explain the inevitable social, political and economic dislocations that will undoubtably continue to occur in the newly 'liberalised' societies, in ways that preserve the integrity of the emancipatory vision adopted by the majority of citizens of those same societies.

NOTES

General introduction

1. F. A. Hayek, *The Road to Serfdom*, London, 1944, F. A. Hayek, *Law, Legislation and Liberty*, London, 1982 and R. Nozick, *Anarchy, State and Utopia*, Oxford, 1974 are classic examples of such approaches.
2. C. B. Macpherson, *The Life and Times of Liberal Democracy*, Oxford, 1977 is a good place to start for this perspective.
3. K. Marx. *Capital*, Vol. 1, London, 1977, p. 572.
4. J. S. Mill, *Letters*, ed., H. S. R., Elliot, London, 1910, pp. 346-8. Also see his *Chapters on Socialism*, in *Collected Works*, Vol. 5, Toronto, 1963. It is interesting to note that Mill did have a number of associates, particularly from the nascent labour movement, who linked with the organisations of the 'International' and other campaigns concerned with the promotion of working people's interests. Mill was therefore familiar with the arguments of some of the factions of the revolutionary left, and made several contributions to the debates about the efficacy of insurrection, consistently warning against any such rash misjudgements. Indeed, a full length comparative study of Mill and Marx's involvement in the British labour movement would be of considerable interest to the movement's political historians.
5. The best biographies which deal with the social and historical context of the development of each thinker's ideas are M. Packe, *The Life of John Stuart Mill,*, London, 1954, and D. McLellan, *Karl Marx. His Life and Thought*, London, 1973. There are also interesting accounts by E. August (*John Stuart Mill*, New York, 1975) and B. Nicolaievski and O. Maenchen-Heflen (*Karl Marx, Man and Fighter,*) London, 1936.
6. See Especially *Principles of Political Economy*, Harmondsworth, 1985, Book 2, Ch. 1 and 2, and Book 4, Ch. 7.
7. Marx, Passim!
8. Alan Ryan in *The Philosophy of John Stuart Mill*, London, 1987 and in *J.S. Mill*, London, 1974, provides ample evidence of Mill's own views on the wholeness of his system. Marx in his Preface to *A Contribution to the Critique of Political Economy, Selected Works*, London, 1973, summarises the building o his system.
9. From a 'liberal' perspective the most celebrated critics are Karl Popper, *The Open Society and its Enemies*, Vol. 2, London, 1962, and J. L. Talmon, *The Origins of Totalitarian Democracy*, London, 1961. A recent radical critic of Mill is A. Arblaster, *The Rise and Decline of Western Liberalism*, Oxford, 1984, who in so many words classes Mill as a bourgeois apologist.
10. Isaiah Berlin, *Four Essays On Liberty*, Oxford, 1969, and John Gray, *Mill On Liberty: A Defence*, London, 1983, are both examples of commentators who have isolated *On Liberty* in this way. J. M. Barbalet, *Marx's Construction of Social Theory*, London, 1983 and S. Hook, *Revolution, Reform and Social Justice*, are two amongst many who have taken *Capital* (and often more specifically, Vol. 1) as Marx's definitive statement on historical materialism.

Chapter 1

1 D. F. B. Tucker, *Marxism and Individualism*, Oxford, 1980, p. 3; J. Elster, *Making Sense of Marx*, Oxford, 1969, pp. 4-8.
2 I. Berlin, *Four Essays on Liberty*, Oxford, 1969, pp. 46-8; K. Popper, K. Popper, *The Open Society and its Enemies*, Vol. 2, London, 1962, passim.
3 My reason for preferring the term self-determination will, I hope, become more apparent as the chapters unfold, but it is perhaps worth making a few preliminary remarks. Self-determination in this instance implies several distinct, although interconnected, aspects of human agency. Firstly, I take it to mean the tendency we share with others of expressing, or asserting our particular capabilities and character traits. Secondly, I use the term to characterise the activity of pursuing self-imposed objectives and aims in order to discover personal potentialities. Finally, I understand the pursuit of self-determination in a social sense, i.e. viewing it as the conscious organisation of the objective conditions of existence. John Plamenatz in *Karl Marx's Philosophy of Man*, Oxford, 1975, employed the term self-realisation to express what is in effect, the same concept (see especially pp. 322-56), although my reading of Marx differs from his.
4 S. Lukes, *Individualism*, Oxford, 1973, pp. 69-73.
5 Mill moved from a Benthamite utilitarian psychology to a 'societal' utilitarianism, i.e. he believed he had freed himself, and self-improvers in general from the narrow constraints of a quantifiable balancing of pleasure and pain. However, utility remained the basis for moral judgements and hence social rules, whether these be judicial laws or unwritten norms. I discuss this further in Ch. 5.
6 Throughout I shall employ the terms 'human', 'humanity', 'humankind', etc., in preference to 'man', 'men' and 'mankind'. However, when quoting other authors I shall employ their titles for the species and its members. I have assumed that both Mill and Marx when referring to 'man' or 'men', etc., were following nineteenth-century literary convention and were not signifying intellectual chauvinism. In other words, when dealing with human nature, the individual and freedom, both thinkers were, I believe, referring to men and women. However, this is not to deny that despite their theoretical protestations to the contrary, in private they may well have been conventional examples of Victorian patriarchs. See Mill's *Essays on Sex Equality*, ed., Alice Rossi, Chicago, 1970, for references to Mill's puritanical attitude to sexual relations and his favourable disposition towards sexual abstinency. See Yvonne Kapp's excellent biography of *Eleanor Marx*, London, 1972, especially Vol. 1, for an honest portrayal of Marx the family man. For a useful introduction to the role of women in Mill's and Marx's social theories see L. Goldstein, 'Mill, Marx, and women's liberation', *Journal of the History of Philosophy*, 18 (1980).

Chapter 2

1 J. S. Mill, *Autobiography*, ed., J. Stillinger, Oxford, 1971, p. 132.
2 R. P. Anschutz, *The Philosophy of John Stuart Mill*, Oxford, 1953; H. J. McCloskey, *John Stuart Mill: A Critical Study*, London, 1971; A. Ryan, *J. S. Mill*, London, 1974 and *The Philosophy of John Stuart Mill*, London, 1970.
3 J. S. Mill, *A System of Logic*, Book 6, in *Collected Works of John Stuart Mill*, Vol. 8, ed. J. M. Robson, London, 1974, p. 841.

4 See especially his defence of a clerisy, or administrative/governing elite in his essays on 'Coleridge', 'The Spirit of the Age', 'Civilisation' and 'Representative Government'.
5 J. F. Stephen, *Liberty, Equality, Fraternity*, London, 1874.
6 G. Himmelfarb, *On Liberty and Liberalism: the Case of John Stuart Mill*, New York, 1974.
7 J. M. Robson, *The Improvement of Mankind: The Social and Political Thought of John Stuart Mill*,, London, 1968, p. ix.
8 J. Gray, *Mill on Liberty: a Defence*, London, 1983. C. L. Ten, *Mill on Liberty*, Oxford, 1980.
9 J. S. Mill, *Autobiography*, p. 150.
10 A. S. Ryan, J. S. Mill; G. W. Smith, 'The logic of J.S. Mill on freedom' in *Political Studies*, 28 (1980), pp. 238-52, and 'J.S. Mill on freedom', in *Conceptions of Liberty in Political Philosophy*, ed., Z. Pelczynski and J. Gray, London, 1984.
11 This refers to Mill's broader definition of 'utility' characterised by his comment in *On Liberty*: 'I regard utility as the ultimate appeal on all ethical questions; but it must be utility in the largest sense, grounded on the permanent interests of a man as a progressive being.' *Utilitarianism, Liberty, Representative government*, London, 1910, p. 74.
12 J. Gray, *Mill on Liberty: a Defence* passim.
13 J. S. Mill, *Autobiography*, p. 66.
14 Ibid.
15 Ibid.
16 Ibid., p. 143.
17 Ibid., p. 121.
18 J. S. Mill, 'Essay on Bentham', in *Utilitarianism*, ed. M. Warnock, London, 1962, p. 99.
19 Ibid., p. 103.
20 See V. Haksar, *Equality, Liberty and Perfectionism*, Oxford, 1979.
21 J. S. Mill, *Autobiography*, p. 134. William Whewell and Sir William Hamilton came in for particular criticism as proponents of intuitional philosophy.
22 J. S. Mill, *A System of Logic*, Vol. 1, Book I.
23 J. S. Mill, *Autobiography*, p. 134.
24 J. S. Mill, *A System of Logic*, Vol. 2, Book VI.
25 Ibid., p. 833.
26 J. S. Mill, 'Letter to John Sterling', 20-22 October 1831, in *The Letters of John Stuart Mill*, Vol. 2, ed. H. S. R. Elliot, London, 1910, p. 8.
27 J. S. Mill, *A System of Logic*, Vol. 2, p. i.
28 Ibid., p. 835.
29 J. S. Mill, 'Letter to John Sterling', pp. 8-9.
30 J. S. Mill, *Autobiography*, p. 98.
31 A. Ryan, *J. S. Mill*, p. 41.
32 H. J. McCloskey, *John Stuart Mill: A Critical Study*, p. 42.
33 J. S. Mill, *A System of Logic*, p. 877.
34 Ibid., p. 835.
35 J. S. Mill, *Autobiography*, p. 94.
36 J. S. Mill, *A System of Logic*, p. 836.
37 J. S. Mill, *Autobiography*, pp. 101-2.
38 Ibid., p. 66.
39 J. S. Mill, *A System of Logic*, p. 836.

Notes to pp. 33–43

40 Ibid.
41 Ibid.
42 Ibid., p. 840.
43 Ibid.
44 Ibid. See *On Liberty* for Mill's condemnation of those who, although conscious of a capacity for self-improvement choose to succumb to inferior pleasures and conform to prevailing customs which only further restrict the expression of individuality.
45 Ibid.
46 Ibid., p. 341.
47 Ibid.
48 Ibid.
49 Ibid. p. 896.
50 Ibid., p. 907
51 Ibid., p. 846.
52 Ibid., p. 859.
53 Ibid., p. 850.
54 Ibid.
55 Ibid. An indirect plug, as James Mill's *Analysis of the Phenomena of the Human Mind*, London, 1869, was edited by his son John Stuart, who added to the original text a large number of extensive footnotes which include some interesting asides on the editor's views of human nature.
56 Ibid., p. 853. The Laws of Association are three in number: (1) the law that similar ideas tend to excite one another; (2) the law 'that when two impressions have been frequently experienced (or even thought of) either simultaneously or in immediate succession, then whenever one of these impressions, or the idea of it, recurs, it tends to excite the idea of the other'; (3) the law 'that the greater intensity in either or both of the impressions, is equivalent, in rendering them excitable by one another, to a greater frequency of conjunction.' *A System of Logic*, p. 852.
57 Ibid., p. 856.
58 Ibid., p. 859.
59 Ibid., p. 875.
60 Ibid., pp. 861-2.
61 J. S. Mill, *Auguste Comte and Positivism*, Ann Arbor, 1961, p. 82.
62 J. S. Mill, *Principles of Political Economy*, in *collected Works*, Vol., 2, p. 203.
63 J. S. Mill, *A System of Logic*, p. 864.
64 Ibid., p. 689.
65 Ibid., p. 869. The laws of the formation of character are obtainable, Mill points out, by deduction from the general laws of mind; 'by supposing any given set of circumstances, and then considering what, according to the laws of mind, will be the influence of those circumstances on the formation of character'.
66 Ibid., pp. 869-70.
67 Ibid., p. 869.
68 Ibid., p. 859. Also see F. W. Garforth, *John Stuart Mill's Theory of Education*, Oxford, 1979 for a useful account of the relationship between Mill's study of human nature and its practical purpose.
69 Ibid.
70 Ibid., p. 926.
71 Ibid.

72 Ibid. these pronouncements appear during the course of Mill's enquiry into 'Historical Method', to be employed in an investigation of human progression, and not in his discussion of human nature.
73 J. S. Mill, *Utilitarianism, Liberty, Representative Government*, pp. 248-56. Mill points out the danger of the 'evil disposition' of 'man's selfish interests' in the operation of good government.
74 Ibid., p. 118.
75 Ibid., p. 29.
76 Ibid.
77 Ibid., p. 47.
78 Ibid.
79 Ibid.
80 J. Lively and J. Rees (eds.), *Utilitarian Logic and Politics: James Mill's 'Essay on government; Macaulay's critique and the ensuing debate*, Oxford, 1984.
81 J. S. Mill, *Autobiography*, p. 81.
82 J. S. Mill, *A System of Logic*, p. 859.
83 J. S. Mill, *Utilitarianism, Liberty Representative government*, p. 117.
84 Of particular interest is Mill's allusion to universal good, apparent in uncorrupted human nature: 'If you take the average human mind when still young, before the objects it has chosen in life have given it a turn in any bad direction, you will generally find it desiring what is good, right and for the benefit of all; and if that season is properly used to implant the knowledge and give the training which shall render rectitude of judgment more habitual than sophistry, a serious barrier will have been erected against the inroads of selfishness and falsehood.' *Inaugural Address at St. Andrews University*, London, 1894, pp. 75-6.

Chapter 3

1 K. Marx, *Theses on Feuerbach*, in *Selected Works*, London, 1973, p. 29.
2 K. Marx, Preface to *A Contribution to the Critique of Political Economy*, in *Selected Works*, p. 181.
3 K. Marx and F. Engels, *The German ideology*, in *Collected Works*, vol. 5, London, 1973, p. 54.
4 Otherwise known as *Critique of Hegel's Philosophy of Right*, in *Collected Works*, Vol. 3, London, 1975.
5 See M. Markovic and R. S. Cohen, *Yugoslavia: The Rise and Fall of Socialist Humanism*, Nottingham, 1975.
6 Althusser's response to these imputations was to retreat into the Laager and attempt to invalidate all references to these controversial terms by relying on an ever decreasing number of Marx references.
7 The most notable of these being B. Ollman, *Alienation*, Cambridge, 1976, and I. Mezaros, *Marx's Theory of Alienation*, London, 1975.
8 See E. Kamenka, *Ethical Foundations of Marxism*, London, 1962, and R. N. Berki, *Insight and Vision*, London, 1983 for this kind of perspective.
9 J. Elster, *Making Sense of Marx*, Cambridge, 1985.
10 This probably does a disservice to them both, more so in the case of Engels whose *Dialectics of Nature* (London, 1941) remains the focus of some controversy.
11 L. Althusser, *For Marx*, London, 1969, pp. 155-6.

12 Ibid., p. 158.
13 Ibid., pp. 227-8.
14 B. Ollman, pp. xii-xiv
15 N. Geras *Marx and Human Nature A Refutation of a Legend*, London, 1983, pp. 78-9.
16 Ibid., p. 116.
17 K. Marx, *Theses on Feuerbach*, p. 28.
18 In *Selected Works*, p. 57.
19 This is an argument I pursue at greater length in Ch. 6.
20 See especially V. Venable, *Human Nature: The Marxian View*, London, 1946, and G. A. Cohen, *Karl Marx's Theory of History. A Defence*, Oxford, 1978.
21 K. Marx, Preface to *A Contribution to the Critique of Political Economy*, p. 182.
22 Ibid.
23 Ibid., p. 181.
24 This claim forms the basis of S. Avineri's investigation in his *The Social and Political thought of Karl Marx*, Cambridge, 1968.
25 K. Marx, *Economic and Philosophic Manuscripts*, London, 1973, pp. 116-17.
26 Ibid., p. 118.
27 K. Marx, *Theses on Feuerbach*, p. 29.
28 K. Marx and F. Engels, *The German Ideology*, p. 54.
29 K. Marx, *Capital*, Vol. 1, London, 1977, pp. 20-1.
30 Preface to *A Contribution to the Critique of Political Economy*, pp. 182-3.
31 Cf. *Economic and Philosophic Manuscripts*, pp. 106-19 and *Grundrisse*, London, 1973, pp. 162, 196, 452-8.
32 Marx to Engels, 24 April 1867, in *Selected Correspondence*, London, 1934, p. 217.
33 Marx to Annenkov, 28 December 1846, in *Selected Correspondence*, Moscow, 1975, p. 31.
34 Marx, *Grundrisse*, p. 515.
35 Marx, *Capital*, Vol. 1, p. 668.
36 K. Marx, *Capital*, Vol. 1, pp. 457-8.
37 Ibid., p. 458.
38 K. Marx, *Theories of Surplus Value*, part 2, London, 1975, p. 118.
39 See L. Seve, *Man in Marxist Theory*, Brighton, 1978.
40 K. Marx and F. Engels, *The German Ideology*, pp. 77-8.
41 Op. cit.
42 Ibid., p. 23.
43 Ibid., p. 91.
44 K. Marx and F. Engels, *The German Ideology*, p. 41.
45 See A. Negri, *Marx Beyond Marx*, South Hadley, Mass., 1984, whose reading of Marx's *Grundrisse* develops this theme, as does R. Gunn in 'Marxism and philosophy: a critique of critical realism', in *Capital and Class* 37 (1989).
46 K. Marx and F. Engels, *The German Ideology*, p. 31.
47 See A. Heler, *The Theory of Need in Marx*, London, 1976, for a discussion of this issue.
48 K. Marx and F. Engels, *The German Ideology*, pp. 41-2.
49 Ibid., p. 42.
50 Ibid., p. 43
51 Ibid..
52 Ibid., p. 44
53 Ibid., p. 45

54 Ibid.
55 Ibid., pp. 31-2
56 Ibid., p. 87.
57 K. Marx, *Theses on Feuerbach*, p. 28.
58 K. Marx and F. Engels, *The German Ideology*, p. 58.
59 K. Marx, *Critique of Hegel's Philosophy of Law*.
60 K. Marx, *Theses on Feuerbach*, p. 28.
61 K. Marx and F. Engels, *The German Ideology*, p. 53.
62 Ibid.
63 Ibid., pp. 53-4.
64 Ibid., p. 39.
65 Ibid., pp. 35-6
66 Ibid., p. 437.
67 Ibid., p. 438.
68 Ibid., p. 36-7 and p. 41.
69 K. Marx, Preface to *A Contribution to the Critique of Political Economy*, p. 181.
70 K. Marx and F. Engels, *The German Ideology*, pp. 35-6.
71 Letter to Annenkov, p. 37.
72 Ibid.
73 K. Marx, *Grundrisse*, p. 85.
74 K. Marx, *The Poverty of Philosophy*, p. 135.
75 K. Marx, *Grundrisse*, p. 85.
76 Ibid., p. 86.
77 Ibid.
78 Ibid., p. 85.
79 Ibid., p. 85-6.
80 Ibid., p. 87.
81 Ibid., p. 88.
82 Ibid.
83 Ibid., p. 87.
84 Ibid., p. 100-8.
85 Ibid., p. 100.
86 Ibid., p. 101.
87 Ibid.
88 Ibid., p. 101-2.
89 Ibid., p. 88.
90 Ibid., p. 265.
91 Ibid., p. 472.
92 Ibid., p. 422.
93 Ibid., p. 160.
94 Ibid., p. 687.
95 Ibid., p. 512.
96 Ibid. As apt today with reference to 'market socialism' as it ever was!
97 Ibid., p. 676.
98 Ibid., pp. 493-4.
99 K. Marx, *Capital*, Vol. 1, p. 174.
100 Ibid.
101 Ibid.
102 Ibid., pp. 173-4.
103 Ibid., p. 173.
104 Ibid., p. 179.

105 Ibid., p. 571.
106 N. Geras, *Marx and Human Nature*, London, 1983, pp. 79-80.
107 K. Marx, *Capital*, Vol. 1, pp. 570-1.
108 Ibid., p. 570.
109 K. Marx and Engels, *The German Ideology*, pp. 409-12.
110 Ibid., p. 410.
111 Ibid.
112 K. Marx, *Capital*, Vol. 1, p. 571.
113 K. Marx and F. Engels, *The German Ideology*, p. 31.
114 K. Marx, *Grundrisse*, p. 83.
115 K. Marx, *Capital*, Vol. 1, pp. 20-1.

Chapter 4

1 This definition of Promethean is taken from A. Walicki, 'The Marxian conception of freedom' in Z. Pelczynski and J. Gray (eds.), *Conceptions of Liberty in Political Philosophy*, London, 1984, p. 225.
2 R. J. Arneson, 'Democracy and liberty in Mill's Theory of Government', *Journal of the History of Philosophy*, 20 (1982), passim.
3 M. Hollis, 'J. S. Mill's Political Philosophy of Mind', *Philosophy* 47 (1972), pp. 340-1.
4 W. Thomas, *Mill*, Oxford, 1985, p. 108.
5 S. Lukes, *Marxism and Morality*, Oxford, 1985, p. 63.
6 A. MacIntyre, *A Short History of Ethics*, London, 1967, p. 214.

Chapter 5

1 Op. cit.
2 Op. cit.
3 J. S. Mill, *Utilitarianism, Liberty, Representative Government*, pp. 72-3.
4 Stephen, *Liberty, Equality, Fraternity*, Cambridge, 1967. I. Berlin, 'Two Concepts of Liberty' and 'John Stuart Mill and the Ends of Life' in *Four Essays On Liberty*, Oxford, 1969; H. J. McCloskey, *John Stuart Mill: a critical study*, London, 1971; T. Honderich, 'The Worth of J. S. Mill on Liberty', *Political Studies*, 22: (1974).
5 J. S. Mill, *Utilitarianism, Liberty, Representative Government*, p. 74.
6 C. L. Ten, *Mill on Liberty*, Oxford, 1980; Gray, *Mill on Liberty: A Defence*, London, 1983; J. Berger, *Happiness, Justice, and Freedom*, London, 1984.
7 J. S. Mill, *Utilitarianism, Liberty, Representative Government*, pp. 120-1.
8 J. Gray, *Mill on Liberty: a Defence*, p. 10.
9 *A System of Logic*, p. 841. Also, see P. M. Smart, 'Mill on Human Nature' in *Politics and Human Nature*, ed. I. Forbis and S. Smith, London, 1983.
10 See especially the work of D. G. Brown, 'Mill on Liberty and Morality', *Philosophical Review*, 81 (1972); 'What is Mill's Principle of Utility?', *Canadian Journal of Philosophy*, 3 (1973); "Mill and Harm to Others' Interests', *Political Studies*, 26 (1978). Also Lyons, 'Mill's Theory of Morality', *Nous*, 10 (1976); 'Mill's Theory of Justice', in A. I. Goldman and J. Kim (eds.), *Values and Morals*, Dordrecht, 1978; 'Liberty and Harm to Others', *Canadian Journal of Philosophy*, Supp. Vol. 5, (1979).

11 See C. L. Ten, *Mill on Liberty*, pp. 42-51; J. Gray, *Mill on Liberty: A Defence*, pp. 19-48; and J. Berger, *Happiness, Justice, and Freedom*, Ch. 3.
12 J. S. Mill, *Utilitarianism, Liberty, Representative Government*, p. 74.
13 D. P. Dryer, 'Justice, Liberty, and the Principle of Utility in Mill', *Canadian Journal of Philosophy*, Sup. vol. 5, (1979).
14 J. S. Mill, *Utilitarianism, Liberty, Representative Government*, p. 74.
15 D. P. Dryer, 'Justice, Liberty, and the Principle of Utility in Mill', *Canadian Journal of Philosophy*, Supp. Vol. 5 (1979).
16 J. S. Mill, *Utilitarianism, Liberty, Representative government*, p. 65.
17 D. F. Thompson, *John Stuart Mill and Representative Government*, Princeton, 1976.
18 J. S. Mill, *Utilitarianism, Liberty, Representative government*, p. 115.
19 Ibid.
20 G. W. Smith, 'The Logic of John Stuart Mill on Freedom', *Political Studies*, 28 (1980); 'J. S. Mill on Freedom', in Z Pelczynski and J. Gray (eds.), *Conceptions of Liberty in Political Philosophy*, London, 1984.
21 G. W. Smith, 'J. S. Mill on Freedom' p. 189.
22 J. S. Mill, *A System of Logic*, p. 841.
23 J. S. Mill, *Utilitarianism, Liberty, Representative Government*, p. 118.
24 Ibid., p. 24.
25 Gray, Mill on Liberty, p. 78.
26 J. S. Mill, *Utilitarianism, Liberty, representative government*, p. 115.
27 Ibid., p. 116.
28 J. S. Mill, *Autobiography*, Chapter 5.
29 J. S. Mill, *Utilitarianism, Liberty, Representative Government*, p. 9.
30 Ibid., pp. 9-10.
31 Ibid., p. 116.
32 Ibid., p. 119.
33 Ibid.
34 Ibid., p. 115.
35 Ibid., p. 119.
36 Ibid., p. 93.
37 Ibid., p. 122.
38 Ibid.
39 Ibid., p. 279.
40 Ibid., p. 188.
41 Ibid., p. 193.
42 Ibid., pp. 317
43 Ibid., pp. 237.
44 Ibid.,
45 Ibid.
46 Ibid., p. 241.
47 Ibid., pp. 231-2.
48 Ibid., p. 266.
49 Ibid., p. 283.
50 Ibid., p. 284.
51 Ibid., p. 285.
52 Ibid., p. 265.
53 Ibid., p. 269.
54 Ibid., p. 243.
55 Ibid., p. 265-7.

56 Ibid., p. 319.
57 Ibid., p. 322.
58 Ibid., p. 254.
59 Ibid., p. 216.
60 Ibid., p. 214.
61 Ibid., pp. 192-3, pp. 250-2, p. 302.
62 Ibid., p. 195.
63 Ibid., p. 217.
64 G. Himmelfarb, *On Liberty*.
65 C. L. Ten, *Mill on Liberty*, p. 1.
66 M. Cowling, *Mill and Liberalism*, Cambridge, 1963.
67 J. Gray, *Mill on Liberty: a defence*, p. 14.
68 See C. L. Ten, *Mill on Liberty*, Ch 9, and J. C. Rees, 'The thesis of the two Mills', *Political Studies*, 25 (1977).
69 J. S. Mill, *The Spirit of the Age*, Chicago, 1942, and 'Rectorial Address', in William Knight (ed.), *Rectorial Addresses, University of St. Andrews*, London, 1894.
70 J. S. Mill, *Utilitarianism, Liberty, Representative Government*, p. 128.

Chapter 6

1 J. Gray 'Philosophy, Science and Myth in Marxism', in *Marx and Marxisms*, ed. G. H. R. Parkinson, Cambridge, 1982; 'Marxian Freedom, Individual Liberty, and the End of Alienation', in E. Frankel Paul *et al.* (eds.), *Marxism and Liberalism*, Oxford, 1986. G. W. Smith, 'Sinful Science? Marx's Theory of Freedom From Thesis to Theses', *History of Political Thought*, 2 (1981) and 'Marxian Metaphysics and Individual Freedom' in *Marx and Marxisms*, ed. G. H. R. Parkinson, Cambridge, 1982.
2 R. A. Kocis, 'An Unresolved Tension in Marx's Critique of Justice and Rights', *Political Studies*, 34 (1986). also see the 'Wittgensteinian' perspective on Marx offered by G. Kitching in *Marx and the Philosophy of Praxis*, London, 1988.
3 A Gilbert, 'An Ambiguity in Marx's and Engels's Account of Justice and Equality', *The American Political Science Review*, 76 (1982).
4 See for example A. Callincos, *Althusser's Marxism*, London, 1976, M. Kelly, *Modern French Marxism*, Oxford, 1982, E. P. Thompson, *The Poverty of Theory*, London, 1976 and T. Benton, *The Rise and Fall of Structural Marxism*, London, 1984.
5 B. Ollman, *Alienation* Cambridge, 1976; I. Meszaros, *Marx's Theory of Alienation*, London, 1975; S. Avineri, *The Social and Political Thought of Karl Marx*, Cambridge, 1968.
6 See works by A. Wood, T. Skillen, D. P. H. Allen and T. Carver, amongst others.
7 I agree with Lukes on this point. See his *Marxism and Morality*, Oxford, 1985, pp.61-70.
8 Ibid., p. 48.
9 Z. I. Husami, 'Marx on Distributive Justice', *Philosophy and Public Affairs*, 8 (1978), p. 48.
10 K. Marx, *Critique of the Gotha Programme* in *The First International and After*, ed., D. Fernbach, Harmondsworth, 1974, p. 347.
11 N. Geras, 'The Controversy About Marx and Justice', *New Left Review*, 150 (1985), p. 84.
12 Ibid. p. 70 and G. A. Cohen, 'Freedom, Justice and Capitalism', *New Left Review*,

126 (1981), p. 12.
13 J. Elster, *Making Sense of Marx*, Cambridge, 1985, p. 222.
14 D. Van De Veer, 'Marx's View of Justice', *Philosophy and Phenomenological Research*, 33 (1972-73).
15 N. Geras, *Marx and Human Nature. Reputation of a Legend*, London, 1983, pp. 71-2; A. E. Buchanan, *Marx and Justice*, London, 1982, pp. 14, 48; 'The Marxian Critique of Justice and Rights', *Canadian Journal of Philosophy*, Supp. Vol. 7 (1981); G. G. Brenkert, *Marx's Ethics of Freedom*, London, 1983, 'Freedom and Private Property in Marx', *Philosophy and Public Affairs*, 8 1979); A. Gilbert, 'Historical Theory and the Structure of Moral Argument in Marx', *Political Theory*, 9 (1981), p. 192, 'An Ambiguity in Marx's and Engels's Account of Justice and Equality', *The American Political Science Review*, 76 (1982) p. 343.
16 G. A. Cohen, Review of *Karl Marx* by A. Wood in *Mind*, 42 (1983), p. 443.
17 Z. I. Husami, 'Marx on Distributive Justice', *Philosophy and Public Affairs*, 8 (1978), p. 61.
18 K. Marx, *Capital*, Vol. 1, p. 546.
19 Ibid., p. 573.
20 Ibid., p. 559.
21 Ibid., p. 715.
22 K. Marx, *Grundrisse*, p. 705.
23 Z. I. Husami, 'Marx on Distributive Justice', p. 45.
24 J. Elster, *Making Sense of Marx*, p. 229.
25 K. Marx, *Critique of the Gotha Programme*, p. 346.
26 Ibid.
27 Ibid., p. 347.
28 Ibid.
29 Ibid., pp. 344-5.
30 Ibid., p. 347.
31 Van De Veer, 'Marx's View of Justice', *Philosophy and Phenomenological Research*, 33 (1972-73), p. 373.
32 K. Marx, *Critique of the Gotha Programme*, p. 347.
33 N. Geras, 'The Controversy about Marx and Justice', *New Left Review*, 150 (1985) p. 60.
34 Z. I. Husami, 'Marx on Distributive Justice' p. 34.
35 K. Marx, *Capital*, p. 496.
36 E.g. Van De Veer, 'Marx's View of Justice', p. 377 and Z. I. Husami, 'Marx on Distributive Justice', p. 61.
37 N. Geras, 'The Controversy about Marx and Justice', p. 72.
38 Z. I. Husami 'Marx on Distributive Justice', p. 61.
39 N. Geras, 'The Controversy about Marx and Justice', p. 82.
40 J. Elster, *Making Sense of Marx*, p. 231.
41 N. Geras, 'The Controversy about Marx and Justice', pp. 82-3.
42 J. Elster *Making Sense of Marx*, p. 233.
43 Ibid., pp. 231-2, p. 233 and N. Geras, 'The Controversy of Marx and Justice' pp. 82-3.
44 N. Geras, Ibid., p. 84.
45 Z. I. Husami, 'Marx on Distributive Justice', pp. 78-9.
46 D. Van De Veer, 'Marx's View of Justice', p. 384.
47 J. Elster, *Making Sense of Marx*, p. 219.
48 Ibid., pp. 107-9.
49 Z. I. Husami, 'Marx on Distributive Justice', p. 47.

50 L. Kolakowski, *Main Currents of Marxism*, Vol. 1, Oxford, 1978, pp. 412-14.
51 Cf. N. Geras, 'The controversy about Marx and Justice; p. 85 with Z.I. Husami, 'Marx on Distributive Justice', pp. 55-6.
52 A. Gilbert, 'Historical Theory and the Structure of Moral Argument in Marx; *Political Theory*, 9 (1981), p. 174, A. Gilbert, p. 343.
53 A. Gilbert (1981), p. 177.
54 Ibid., p. 192.
55 A. Gilbert, (1982), 'An Ambiguity in Marx's and Engels's Account of Justice and Equality; *The American Political Science Review*, 76 (1982), p. 343.
56 A. E. Buchanan, *Marx and Justice, The Radical Critique of Liberalism*, London, 1982, p. 14.
57 G. G. Brenkert, *Marx's Ethics of Freedom*, London, 1983.
58 Ibid., p. 9.
59 Ibid., p. 15.
60 Ibid., p. 18, p. 22.
61 Ibid., p. 76.
62 Ibid., p. 79.
63 In *Selected Works*, London, 1973, p. 181.
64 See Allen, Skillen and Wood for similar approaches.
65 K. Marx and F. Engels, *The German Ideology*, p. 53.
66 K. Marx, *Capital*, Vol. 3, London, 1977, pp. 339-40.
67 K. Marx, *Capital*, Vol. 1, pp. 502-3.
68 Ibid., p. 167, p. 168.
69 Ibid., pp. 168-72.
70 Ibid., p. 188.
71 Ibid.
72 Ibid., p. 547.
73 Ibid.
74 K. Marx, *Critique of the Gotha Programme*, p. 344.
75 Ibid., p. 348.
76 Ibid., pp. 347-8.
77 Allen and Wood also make this point.
78 K. Marx, *Notes on Adolf Wagner* in T. Carver, *Karl Marx. Texts on Method*, Oxford, 1975, p. 186.
79 Ibid., p. 219.
80 Marx appeared to be well aware that this would have been the case; see *Grundrisse*, p. 634 and *Capital*, vol. 1, p. 713.
81 K. Marx, *Capital*, Vol. 1, p. 546.
82 Ibid., p. 180.
83 K. Marx, *Critique of the Gotha Programme*, p. 347.
84 K. Marx and F. Engels, *The German ideology*, p. 49.
85 K. Marx, *Capital*, Vol. 1, p. 604.
86 K. Marx and F. Engels, *The German Ideology*, p. 419.
87 Ibid., p. 292.
88 Ibid., p. 247.
89 Lukes, *Marxism and Morality*, Oxford, 1985, pp. 27-47.
90 K. Marx and F. Engels, *The German Ideology*, pp. 36-7.
91 K. Marx and F. Engels, *Manifesto of the Communist Party* in *Collected Works*, Vol. 6, pp. 494-5.
92 See Skillen, passim.
93 A. W. Wood, *Karl Marx*, London, 1981, pp. 126-30, 'The Marxian Critique of

Justice' in M. Cohen *et al.* (eds.), *Marx, Justice and History*, Princeton, 1980, and 'Marx on Right and Justice: A Reply to Husami', *Philosophy and Public Affairs*, 8 (1979).
94 A. W. Wood *Karl Marx*, pp. 126-8.
95 G. A. Cohen, *Karl Marx's Theory of History. A Defence*, Oxford, 1978.
96 K. Marx, Preface to *A Contribution to the Critique of Political Economy*.
97 S. Avineri, *The Social and Political Thought of Karl Marx*, Cambridge, 1968, E. Kamenka, *The Ethical Foundations of Marxism*, London, 1962. D. McLellan, *The Thought of Karl Marx*, London, 1971, *Marx's Grundrisse*, London, 1971 and *Karl Marx. His Life and Thought*, London, 1973. B. Ollman, *Alienation*, Cambridge, 1976.
98 K. Marx, *Grundrisse*, p. 83.
99 K. Marx and F. Engels, *The German Ideology*, pp. 31-2.
100 B. Badaloni, 'Marx and the Quest for Communist Liberty', in *The History of Marxism*, Vol. 1, (ed.), E. J. Hobsbawm, Brighton, 1982.
101 K. Marx, *Capital*, Vol. 1, p. 555.
102 Marx to Engels, 14 January 1858, and Marx to Kugelman, 6 March 1868, in *Selected Correspondence*, pp. 93, 187.
103 K. Marx, *Capital*, Vol. 1, p. 29. See also T. Carver's 'Marx and Hegel's *Logic*', in *Political Studies*, 24 (1976), pp. 57-68.
104 K. Marx *Grundrisse*, p. 461.
105 Ibid., p. 162.
106 Ibid., p. 196.
107 Ibid., p. 649.
108 Ibid.
109 Ibid., p. 651.
110 Ibid., p. 652.
111 Ibid., p. 515.
112 Ibid.
113 Ibid., p. 488.
114 Ibid., p. 831.
115 Ibid., p. 462.
116 Ibid., p. 225.
117 Ibid., pp. 240-1.
118 Ibid., p. 241
119 Ibid., p. 157.
120 Ibid.
121 Ibid., p. 158
122 Ibid., p. 163.
123 Ibid., p. 706.
124 Ibid., p. 701.
125 Ibid., pp. 693-4.
126 I am well aware that the distinction between circulating and fixed capital, and variable and constant capital is one that is not developed by Marx in *Grundrisse* to the level of sophistication present in *Capital*, Vol. 2 (see especially pp. 216-31), but I do not think that this effects my discussion detrimentally.
127 Ibid., p. 694.
128 Ibid., p. 611.
129 Ibid., pp. 831-2.
130 Ibid., pp. 692-3.
131 Ibid., p. 701.

Notes to pp. 157–177

132 See *The Poverty of Philosophy* and *Critique of the Gotha Programme*.
133 K. Marx, *Grundrisse*, p. 701.
134 Ibid., p. 410.
135 Ibid., p. 708.
136 Ibid., p. 488.
137 Ibid., p. 463.
138 Ibid., p. 750.
139 Ibid., p. 140.
140 Ibid., p. 463.
141 Ibid., p. 708.
142 Ibid., p. 706.
143 Ibid., p. 171.
144 Ibid.
145 Ibid., pp. 171-3.
146 Ibid., p. 832.
147 Ibid., p. 488.

Concluding note

1 G. Lichtheim, *Marxism*, London, 1974, p. 404.
2 Haksar, *Equality, Liberty and perfectionism*, Oxford, 1979.
3 Gilbert, 'Democracy and individuality', *Social Philosophy and Policy*, 3 (1986) p. 19.
4 J. Miller, *History and Human Existence. From Marx to Merleau-Ponty*, Berkeley, 1979, p. 13.
5 G. G. Brenkert, 'Max Critique of Utilitarianism' in *Marx and Morality, Canadian Journal of Philosophy*, Sup. Vol. 7 (1981), pp. 219-20.
6 See Kurer, 'John Stuart Mill on Government Intervention' in *History of Political Thought*, 10, 3 (1989) for an examination of Mill's motives for recommending intervention.
7 *On Liberty*, p. 150.
8 Ibid., Ch. 5. Also see S. Hollander's exhaustive 2-volume examination of the social and political ramifications of Mill's political economy in his *The Economics of John Stuart Mill*, Oxford, 1985.
9 *Principles of Political Economy*, Book 2, Ch. 1 and Book 4, Ch. 7.
10 *A System of Logic*, p. 841.
11 *Grundrisse*, p. 101.
12 See A. Negri's *Marx Beyond Marx*, South Hadley, Mass. 1984, for an illuminating exposition on this aspect of Marx's method.
13 J. K. Galbraith, 14th Encyclopaedia Britannica Lecture, University of Edinburgh, 24 January 1990.

BIBLIOGRAPHY

1 Works by Mill and Marx
These are listed in alphabetical order.

John Stuart Mill
Auguste Comte and Positivism, Ann Arbor, 1961. Michigan University Press.
Autobiography, ed. J. Stillinger, Oxford University Press, 1971.
Bentham, in *Utilitarianism*, ed. M. Warnock, Collins, Glasgow, 1977.
Chapters on Socialism, in *Collected Works*, Vol. 5, ed. J. M. Robson, University of Toronto Press, 1967.
Civilisation, in *Collected Works*, Vol. 18, ed. J. M. Robson, University of Toronto Press, 1877.
Coleridge, in *Collected Works*, Vol. 10, ed. J. M. Robson, University of Toronto Press, 1969.
Inaugural Address delivered to the University of St Andrews, 1 February 1867, Longmans, Green, Reeder and Dyer, 1867.
Letters of John Stuart Mill, ed. H. S. R. Elliot, Longmans, London, 1910.
Principles of Political Economy, Penguin, Harmondsworth, 1985.
The Spirit of the Age, University of Chicago Press, 1942.
The Subjection of Women, Dent, London, 1929.
A System of Logic, in *Collected Works*, Vols. 7 and 8, ed. J. M. Robson, University of Toronto Press, 1974.
Utilitarianism, Liberty, Representative Government, Dent, London, 1910.

Karl Marx
Capital, in 3 volumes, Lawrence and Wishart, London, 1977.
Critique of the Gotha Programme, in *The First International and After*, ed. D. Fernbach, Penguin, Harmondsworth, 1974.
Critique of Hegel's Philosophy of Law, in *Collected Works*, Vol. 3, Lawrence and Wishart, London, 1975.
Economic and Philosophic Manuscrips of 1844, Lawrence and Wishart, London, 1973.
The German Ideology with F. Engels, in *Collected Works*, Vol. 5, Larence and Wishart, London, 1973.
Grundrisse, Penguin, Harmondsworth, 1973.
The Holy Family, with F. Engels, Progress Publishers, Moscow, 1975.
Manifesto of the Communist Party, with F. Engels, in *Selected Works*, Lawrence and Wishart, London, 1973.
The Poverty of Philosophy, Progress Publishers, Moscow, 1976.
Preface to *A Contribution to the Critique of Political Economy*, in *Selected Works*, Lawrence and Wishart, London, 1973.
Selected Correspondence, Progress Publishers, Moscow, 1934.
Selected Correspondence, Progress Publishers, Moscow, 1975.
Theories of Surplus Value, in 3 volumes, Lawrence and Wishart, London, 1975.
Thesis on Feuerbach, in *Selected Works*, Lawrence and Wishart, London, 1973.

Bibliography

2 Other works

Allen, D. P. H. 'Does Marx have an Ethnic of Self-Realization?' *Canadian Journal of Philosophy*, 10 (1980), pp. 377-86.

Allen, D. P. H. 'Marx and Engels on the Distributive Justice of Capitalism', *Canadian Journal of Philosophy*, Supplementary Vol. 7 (1981), pp. 221-50.

Althusser, L. *For Marx*, Allen Lane, London, 1969.

Anschutz, R. P., *The Philosophy of John Stuart Mill*, Clarendon Press, Oxford, 1953.

Arblaster, A. *The Rise and Decline of Western Liberalism*, Basic Blackwell, Oxford, 1984.

Arneson, R. J. 'Democracy and Liberty in Mills' Theory of Government', *Journal of the History of Philosophy*, 20 (1982), pp. 43-64.

August, E. *John Stuart Mill*, Charles Scribner's Sons, New York, 1975.

Avinerie, S. *The Social and Political Thought of Karl Marx*, Cambridge University Press, 1968.

Ayer, A. J. Introduction to *The Logic of the Moral Sciences*, Duckworth, London, 1987.

Badaloni, B. 'Marx and the Quest for Communist Liberty' in E. J. Hobsbawn (ed.), *The History of Marxism*, Vol. 1, Harvester Press, Brighton, 1982.

Barbalet, J. M. *Marx's Construction of Social Theory*, Routledge and Kegan Paul, London, 1983.

Benton, T. *The Rise and Fall of Structural Marxism*, Macmillan, London, 1984.

Berger, J. *Happiness, Justice, and Freedom*, University of California Press, Berkeley, 1984.

Berki, R. N. *Insight and Vision*, Dent, London, 1983.

Berlin, I. *Four Essays on Liberty*, Oxford University Press, 1969.

Brenkert, G. G. 'Freedom and Private Property in Marx', *Philosophy and Public Affairs*, 8 (1979), pp. 122-47.

Brenkert, G. G. 'Marx's Critique of Utilitarianism', *Canadian Journal of Philosophy*, Supplementary Vol. 7 (1981), pp. 193-220.

Brenkert, G. G. *Marx's Ethics of Freedom*, Routledge and Kegan Paul, London, 1983.

Brown, D. G. 'Mill on Liberty and Morality', *Philosophical Review*, 81 (1972), pp. 133-59.

Brown, D. G. 'What is Mill's Principle of Utility?', *Canadian Journal of Philosophy*, 3 (1973), pp. 1-12.

Brown, D. G. 'Mill and Harm to Others' Interests', *Political Studies*, 26 (1978), pp. 395-9.

Buchanan, A. E. 'The Marxian Critique of Justice and Rights', *Canadian Journal of Philosophy*, Supplementary Vol. 7 (1981), pp. 269-306.

Buchanan, A. E. *Marx and Justice. The Radical Critique of Liberalism*, Methuen, London, 1982.

Callincos, A. *Althusser's Marxism*, Pluto Press, London, 1976.

Carver, T. *Karl Marx. Texts on Method*, Basil Blackwell, Oxford, 1975.

Carver, T. 'Marx - and Hegel's *Logic*', *Political Studies*, 24 (1976), pp. 57-68.

Carver, T. 'Concepts, Logic and Interests: Individualism and Marx's *Capital*', unpublished.

Cohen, G. A. *Karl Marx's Theory of History. A Defence*, Oxford University Press, 1978.

Cohen, G. A. 'The Labor Theory of Value and the Concept of Exploitation', in M. Cohen, T. Nagel and T. Scanlon (eds.), *Marx, Justice, and History*, Philosophy and Public Affairs, Princeton University Press 1980.

Cohen, G. A. 'Freedom Justice and Capitalism', *New Left Review*, 126 (1981), pp. 3-16.

Cohen, G. A. Review of *Karl Marx* by A. Wood, *Mind*, 42 (1983), p. 443.

Bibliography

Cowling, M. *Mill and Liberalism*, Cambridge University Press, 1963.
Cumming, R. D. *Human Nature and History*, University of Chicago Press, 1970.
Dearlove, J. and P. Saunders, *Introduction to British Politics*, Polity Press, Cambridge, 1984.
Dryer, D. P. 'Justice, Liberty, and the Principle of Utility in Mill', *Canadian Journal of Philosophy*, Supplementary Vol. 5 (1979), pp. 63-73.
Dunayevskaya, R. *Marxism and Freedom*, Pluto Press, London, 1975.
Duncan, G. *Marx and Mill*, Cambridge University Press, 1973.
Duncan, G. and J. Gray 'The Left Against Mill', *Canadian Journal of Philosophy*, Supplementary Vol. 5 (1979), pp. 203-29.
Elster, J. *Making Sense of Marx*, Cambridge University Press, 1985.
Fletcher, R. (ed.) *John Stuart Mill: a logical critique of sociology*, Nelson, London, 1971.
Frankel Paul, E., F. A. Miller Jr., J. Paul and J. Ahrens (eds.) *Marxism and Liberalism*, Basic Blackwell, Oxford, 1986.
Fromm, E. *Marx's concept of Man*, F. Ungar, New York, 1961.
Garforth, F. W. *John Stuart Mill's Theory of Education*, Martin Robertson, Oxford, 1979.
Gaus, G. F. 'Mill's Theory of Moral Rules', *Australian Journal of Philosophy*, 58 (1980), pp. 265-79.
Geras, N. *Marx and Human Nature. Refutation of a Legend*, Verso, London, 1983.
Geras, N. 'The Controversy about Marx and Justice', *New Left Review*, 150 (1985), pp. 47-87.
Gilbert, A. *Marx's Politics: communists and citizens*, Martin Robertson, Oxford, 1981.
Gilbert, A. 'Historical Theory and the Structure of Moral Argument in Marx', *Political Theory*, 9 (1981), pp. 173-205.
Gilbert, A. 'An Abiguity in Marx's and Engels's Account of Justice and Equality', *The American Political Science Review*, 76 (1982), pp. 328-46.
Gilbert, A. 'Democracy and Individuality', *Social Philosophy and Policy*, 3 (1986), pp. 19-58.
Goldstein, L. 'Mill and Marx, and Women's Liberation', *Journal of the History of Philosophy*, 18 (1980), pp. 319-34.
Gould, C. *Marx's Social Ontology*, MIT Press, Cambridge, Mass., 1978.
Gray, J. *Mill on Liberty: A Defence*, Routledge and Kegan Paul, London, 1983.
Gray, J. 'Marxian Freedom, Individual Liberty, and the End of Alienation', in E. Frankel Paul, F. D. Miller Jr., J. Paul and J. Ahrens (eds.), *Marxism and Liberalism*, Basil Blackwell, Oxford, 1986, pp. 160-87.
Gunn, R. 'Marxism and philosophy: a critique of critical realism', *Capital and Class*, 37 (1989), pp. 87-116.
Haksar, V. *Equality, liberty and perfectionism*, Oxford University Press, 1979.
Halevy, E. *The Growth of Philosophic Radicalism*, Faber and Faber, London, 1972.
Hayek, F. A. *The Road to Serfdom*, Routledge and Kegan Paul, London, 1944.
Hayek, F. A. *Law, Legislation and Liberty*, Routledge and Kegan Paul, London, 1982.
Heller, A. *The Theory of Need in Marx*, Allison and Busby, London, 1976.
Himmelfarb, G. *On Liberty and Liberalism*, Knopf, New York, 1974.
Hollander, S. *The Economics of John Stuart Mill*, in 2 volumes, Basil Blackwell, Oxford, 1985.
Hollis, M. 'J. S. Mill's Political Philosophy of Mind', *Philosophy*, 47 (1972), pp. 334-47.
Honderich, T. 'The Worth of J. S. Mill *On Liberty*', *Political Studies*, 22 (1974), pp. 463-70.

Bibliography

Hook, S. *Revolution, Reform, and Social Justice*, Basil Blackwell, Oxford, 1976.
Husami, Z. I. 'Marx on Distributive Justice', *Philosophy and Public Affairs*, 8 (1978), pp. 42[79.
Kamenka, E. *The Ethical Foundations of Marxism*, Routledge and Kegan Paul, London, 1962.
Kapp, E. *Eleanor Marx*, Virago, London, 1972.
Keat, R. 'Individualism and Community in Socialist Thought', in J. Mepham and D-H. Ruben (eds.), *Issues in Marxist Philosophy*, Harvester Press, Brighton, 1981.
Kelly, M. *Modern French Marxism*, Basil Blackwell, Oxford, 1982.
Kitching, G. *Marx and the Philosophy of Praxis*, Routledge, London, 1988.
Kocis, R. A. 'An Unresolved Tension in Marx's Critique of Justice and Rights', *Political Studies*, 34 (1986), pp. 406-22.
Kolakowski, L. *Main Currents of Marxism*, Vol. 1, Oxford University Press, 1978.
Korsch, K. *Marxism and Philosophy*, Monthly Review Press, New York, 1970.
Kurer, O. 'John Stuart Mill on Government Intervention', *History of Political Thought*, 10 (1989), pp. 457-80.
Letwin, S. R. *The Pursuit of Certainty*, Cambridge University Press, 1965.
Lichtheim, G. *Marxism*, Routledge and Kegan Paul, London, 5th Impression, 1974.
Lively, J. and J. Rees (eds.) *Utilitarian Logic and Politics: James Mill's 'Essay on Government', Macaulay's critique and the ensuing debate*, Clarendon Press, Oxford, 1984.
Lukács, G. *History and Class Consciousness*, Merlin Press, London, 1971.
Lukes, S. *Individualism*, Basil Blackwell, Oxford, 1973.
Lukes, S. *Marxism and Morality*, Oxford Universtiy Press, 1985.
Lyons, D. 'Mill's Theory of Justice' in A. I. Goldman and J. Kim (eds.), *Values and Morals: essays in honor of William Frankena*, Charles Stevenson and Richard Brandt, P. Reidel, Dordrecht, 1978.
Lyons, D. 'Liberty and Harm to Others', *Canadian Journal of Philosophy*, Supplementary Vol. 5 (1979), pp. 1-19.
Lyons, D. 'Mill's Theory of Morality', *Nous*, 10 (1976) pp. 101-20.
McCloskey, H. J. *John Stuart Mill: a critical study*, Macmillan, London, 1971.
MacIntyre, A. *A Short History of Ethics*, Routledge and Kegan Paul, London, 1967.
McLellan, D. *Marx's 'Grundrisse'*, Macmillan, London, 1971.
McLellan, D. *The Thought of Karl Marx*, Macmillan, London, 1971.
McLellan, D. *Karl Marx. His Life and Thought*, Macmillan, London, 1973.
Macpherson, C. B. *The Life and Times of Liberal Democracy*, Oxford University Press, 1977.
Macpherson, C. B. *The Political Theory of Possesive Individualism*, Oxford University Press, 1977.
Magid, H. M. 'Mill and the Problem of Freedom of Thought', *Social Research*, 21 (1954), pp. 43-61.
Marcuse, H. *Reason and Revolution*, Routledge and Kegan Paul, London, 2nd edition, 1955.
Markovic, M. *From Affluence to Praxis*, University of Michigan Press, Ann Arbor, 1974.
Markovic, M. and R. S. Cohen *Yugoslavia: The Rise and Fall of Socialist Humanism*, Spokesman Books, Nottingham, 1975.
Mepham, J. and D. H. Ruben *Issues in Marxist Philosophy*, Vol. 4, Harvester Press, Brighton, 1981.
Meszaros, I. *Marx's Theory of Alienation*, Merlin Press, London, 1975.
Miller, J. *History and Human Existence, From Marx to Merleau-Ponty*, University of

California Press, Berkeley, 1979.
Nicolaievski, B. and O. Maenchen-Heflen *Karl Marx, Man and Fighter*, J. B. Lippincott, London, 1936.
Negri, A. *Marx Beyond Marx*, South, Hadley, Bergin and Garvey, South Hadley, Mass., 1984.
Nozick, R. *Anarchy, State and Utopia*, Basil Blackwell, Oxford, 1974.
Ollman, B. *Alienation*, Cambridge University Press, 2nd edition, 1976.
Packe, M. *The Life of John Stuart Mill*, Secker and Warburg, London, 1954.
Plamenatz, J. *The English Utilitarians*, including 'Mill's Utilitarianism', Basil Blackwell, Oxford, 1949.
Plamenats, J. *Karl Marx's Philosophy of Man*, Oxford University Press, 1975.
Popper, K. *The Open Society and its Enemies*, Vol. 2, Routhledge and Kegan Paul, London, 1962.
Rees, J. C., A Re-reading of Mill on Liberty', *Political Studies*, 8 (1960), pp. 113-29.
Rees, J. C. 'Was Mill for Liberty', *Political Studies*, 14 (1966), pp. 72-7.
Rees, J. C. 'The thesis of the two Mills', *Political Studies*, 25 (1977), pp. 369-82.
Robson, J. M. *The Improvement of Mankind*, Routledge and Kegan Paul, London, 1968.
Roemer, J. (ed.) *Analytical Marxism*, Cambridge University Press, 1986.
Rossi, A. (ed.) *Essays on Sex Equality*, University of Chicago Press, 1970.
Ryan, A., *The Philosophy of John Stuart Mill*, Macmillan, London, 1970.
Ryan, A. *J. S. Mill*, Routhledge and Kegan Paul, London, 1974.
La Selva, S. V. 'Selling Oneself into Slavery: Mill and Paternalism', *Political Studies*, 35 (1987), pp. 211-33.
Seve, L. *Man in Marxist Theory*, Harvester Press, Brighton, 1978.
Skillen, A. 'Workers Interests and the Proletarian Ethic; Conflicting Strains in Marxian Anti-moralism', *Canadian Journal of Philosophy*, Supplementary Vol. 7 (1981), pp. 155-70.
Smart, P. M. 'Mill and Human Nature', in I. Forbes and S. Smith (eds.), *Politics and Human Nature*, Frances Pinter, London, 1983.
Smith, G. W. 'The Logic of J. S. Mill on Freedom', *Political Studies*, 28 (1980), p. 238-52.
Smith, G. W. 'Sinful Science? Marx's Theory of Freedom From Thesis to Theses', *History of Political Thought*, 2 (1981), pp. 141-59.
Smith, G. W. 'Marxian Metaphysics and Individual Freedom', in G. H. R., Parkinson (ed.) *Marx and Marxisms, Philosophy* Supplementary Vol. 14 (1982), pp. 229-42.
Smith, G. W. 'J. S. Mill on Freedom', in Z. Pelczynski and J. Gray (eds.), *Conception of Liberty in Political Philosophy*, Athlone Press, London, 1984, pp. 182-216,
Stephen, J. F. *Liberty, Equality, Fraternity*, Cambridge University Press, 1967.
Stephen, L. *The English Utilitarians*, Vol. 3, 'John Stuart Mill', Duckworth, London, 1900.
Talmon, J. L. *The Origins of Totalitarian Democracy*, Mercury Books, London 1961.
Ten, C. L. *Mill on Liberty*, Oxford University Press, 1980.
Thomas, W. *Mill*, Oxford University Press, 1985.
Thompson, D. F. *John Stuart Mill and Representative Government*, Princeton University Press, 1976.
Thompson, E. P. *The Poverty of Theory*, Merlin Press, London, 1976.
Tucker, D. F. B. *Marxism and Individualism*, Basil Blackwell, Oxford, 1980.
Van de Veer D. 'Marx's View of Justice', *Philosophy and Phenomenological Research*, 33 (1972-73), pp. 366-86.

Bibliography

Venable, V. *Human Nature: The Marxian View*, Denis Dobson, London, 1946.
Walicki, A. 'The Marxian Conception of Freedom', in Z. Pelczyniski and J. Gray (eds.), *Conceptions of Liberty in Political Philosophy*, Athlone Press, London, 1984, pp. 217-42.
Williams, G. L. *John Stuart Mill on Politics and Society*, Fontana, London, 1976.
Williams, G. L. 'Mill's Principle of Liberty', *Political Studies*, 24 (1976), pp. 132-40.
Wolff, R. P. *The Poverty of Liberalism*, Beacon Press, Boston, 1968.
Wood, E. M. *Mind and Politics. An Approach to the meaning of liberal and socialist individualism*, University of California Press, Berkeley, 1972.
Wood, A. W. 'Marx on Right and Justice: A Reply to Husami', *Philosophy and Public Affairs*, 8 (1979), pp. 267-95.
Wood, A. W. 'The Marxian Critique of Justice', in M. Cohen, T. Nagel and T. Scanlon (eds.), *Philosophy and Public Affairs*, Princeton, 1980.
Wood, A. W. *Karl Marx*, Routledge and Kegan Paul, London, 1981.

INDEX

Althusser, L., 49, 51-2, 59, 183 n. 6; *see also* Marx, epistemological break; Marxism, structural-functionalist
Anschutz, R. P., 22
Arneson, R. J., 92
Avineri, S., 146

Bauer, B., 54
Bentham, J., 45, 105
 and utilitarianism, 23, 27-8, 92, 98, 102
 Marx on, 83-5
Berger, J., 99
Berlin, I., Sir, 98-9
Brenkert, G. G., 52, 123, 132
Buchanan, A. E., 52, 123, 132

Cohen, G. A., 52, 123-4, 145; *see also* Marxism, analytical
communism, 2-3
Comte, A., 37-9, 91
Cowling, M., 114

Dryer, D. P., 101
Durkheim, E., 164,

Elster, J., 18, 52, 123-4, 130; *see also* Marxism, rational choice
Engels, F., 49, 51, 54, 59-60, 86, 183 n. 10

Feuerbach, L., 52, 54, 60, 65, 69
Frankfurt School, 49
free market, 2, 168, 177
freedom, *see individual authors*
Freud, S., 164

Galbraith, J. K., 177
Geras, N., 51-2, 83, 123-4; *see also* Marxism, humanist
Gilbert, A., 123, 131-2
Gray, J., 23, 99, 104, 118

Hayek, F. A., 18
Hegel, G. W. F., 5, 62, 64, 70, 76, 130, 147-8

The Philosophy of Right, 133
 see also idealism
Helvetius, C. A., 84
Himmelfarb, G., 114
Holbach, P. H. D., Baron d', 84
Honderich, T., 98
Humboldt, W., Baron von, 104
Hume, D., 38, 102
Husami, Z. I., 52, 124, 127, 129-30; *see also* Marxism, humanist

idealism
 English romanticism, 28, 45, 104
 Hegelianism, 12, 49, 54, 56, 58-9, 62, 65, 86, 119, 145, 166
 Marx and, 5, 11-12, 19, 57, 119, 130, 135, 145, 157, 166
 metaphysical philosophers, 46
 Mill and, 26, 28, 37, 116
 speculative philosophy, 85-6; *see also* Hegel

Kamenka, E., 146
Kautsky, K., 51
Korsch, K., 49, 119

Leibniz, G. W., 130
liberalism, 2-4, 16, 177
Locke, J., 137
Lukács, G., 49, 119
Lukes, S., 19, 94, 122, 161

Macaulay, T. B., Lord, *Essay on Government*, 45
McCloskey, H. J., 22, 98
MacIntyre, A., 94
McLellan, D., 146
Marx, K.,
 bourgeois society, 53, 55, 65, 117, 129, 146, 149; *see also* capitalism
 Capital, 5, 9, 13, 49, 58, 64, 74, 81-3, 86, 125-6, 138, 145-6, 148
 capitalism, 54, 56-7, 78, 80, 82-4, 86, 93, 118-62 *passim*; *see also* bourgeois society
 circulation, 149, 158, 191 n. 126

199

Index

civil society, 54, 133
classes 58, 68
    capitalists, 135-7, 139-40, 143, 145, 147, 150-1
    workers, 135-7, 139, 144-5, 147, 158
communal production, 158-9
Communist Manifesto, 49, 52
communist society, 118-19, 121-2, 127, 129, 131, 161, 174
Contribution to the Critique of Political Economy, 54, 59, 133
Critique of the Gotha Programme, 9, 127
Critique of Hegel's Philosophy of Law, 48, 54, 63
dictatorship of the proletariat, 91, 174
Economic and Philosophical Manuscripts, 48, 54-8, 81, 144
epistemology, 53, 67, 87
epistemological break, 49-88 *passim*, 119, 145; *see also* Althusser
free will and determinism, 2, 11-12, 60, 62, 78, 118-19, 145-6, 161
on freedom, 1-16 *passim*, 118, 129, 142, 144, 151, 158, 161, 178
    formal, 152-3, 156
    as a moral good, 129
    as a non-moral good, 143
    mutual recognition, 2, 14, 21, 93, 175-6
    self-determination, 1, 7, 11, 14, 16, 18, 68-9, 71, 80, 90, 93, 144-5, 148, 151, 162-5, 171-2, 175-6, 180 n. 3
    self-development, 125, 129-30, 143, 163
    self-improvement, 132
    self-realisation, 129, 158, 174
    revolution, 7, 15, 50, 57, 68, 87-8, 91, 93, 117, 119-21, 123, 126, 144-6, 162, 167, 174-5
The German Ideology, 48, 53-4, 57, 64-5, 69, 74-5, 78, 81, 84, 86-7, 142, 144
Grundrisse, 9, 13, 48, 59-60, 64, 74, 81-2, 86, 121, 126, 144-9, 160
The Holy Family, 60
on human nature, 1-16 *passim*, 21, 48-88 *passim*, 90-4, 117, 119, 140-50, 172, 180 n. 6
alienation, 2, 11, 13, 49-50, 55-7, 59-60, 62, 80, 119, 143-4, 146, 149-51, 153, 157, 160; *see also* estrangement; fetishism
consciousness, 21, 48, 67-71, 118, 142
essence, 49, 55-8, 60, 62-4, 69
estrangement, 55, 60, 68, 143, 147
fetishism, 49, 55
needs, 21, 66, 72, 82, 87, 125, 128, 130, 143, 176
species being (*gattungwesen*), 11, 54-6, 62, 63, 119,
on individuality, 18-21, 48-88, 117-62 *passim*
on justice, 117-162 *passim*
    distributive justice, 123-8, 130, 138, 161, 171-3
    exploitation, 125-6, 143-4
    feudal justice, 126, 190 n. 80
    functional nature of, 134-9
    juridical relativism, 125
labour, 88, 119, 151, 155, 158-60
    division of, 61, 63, 77
    labour power, 56, 80, 126, 128, 135, 147, 152, 158
on methodology, 9, 10, 14, 122, 144, 146, 174
    abstraction, 63-5, 67, 73-7, 80-1, 83-4, 86-7, 118, 124, 135, 172
    empiricism, 62, 65, 69
    materialism, 71, 86, 118, 120, 142, 145-6, 166
    dialectical, 48-9
    historical, 58-9, 62, 119, 161
    scientific socialism, 58-9, 79
    theory and practice, 7, 14, 53, 63, 120
money 149, 152-3
on morality, 13-14, 68, 71, 94, 117-62 *passim*; 171-8
    bourgeois morality, 142
    communistic values, 125, 127-8, 130, 132-3, 137-8, 140-2, 161, 171, 175
    'eudaimonism', 130, 132; *see*

Index

also Gilbert
moral 'realism', 125
Recht, 118, 121
rights, 13, 50, 94, 118, 121, 127-9, 134, 137-8, 140, 142-3, 149, 161, 171
teleology, 11, 118-20, 122, 129-31, 148, 156-7
nature, physical, 66-8, 70-2, 82, 159
Notes on Adolf Wagner, 138
ontology, 122, 146, 172, 174; *see also* human nature
on political economy, 5, 54, 58, 62, 73-4, 76-80, 82-6, 119, 122, 146, 154, 160, 172
private property, 7, 55, 60, 154
production
    forces of, 49, 53, 56, 67, 73, 79, 146-7, 154, 157-9, 172
    means of, 154
    mode of, 67, 71, 74, 122, 134, 138, 158
    relations of, 54, 60, 80, 121-3, 144, 146, 153-60
on progress, 5, 117, 164-5
on reason, 62
social relations, 11-13, 21, 48-9, 53-8, 60-1, 66, 72-3, 78-80, 83, 85, 87-8, 91, 117, 121-3, 132, 134, 144-6, 148, 152, 154, 160, 172, 176
socialist society, 126, 128
Theories of Surplus Value, 61
Theses on Feuerbach, 49, 53, 57-8, 70, 86-7
value, 56, 68, 80
    exchange value, 150-5
    surplus value, 135-7, 139, 145, 149, 153-5, 157-8
Marxism, 2-4, 16
    analytical, 50; *see also* Cohen
    humanist or ethical, 51, 58-9, 87, 117; *see also* Geras; Husami
    rational choice, 18, 50; *see also* Elster
    structural-functionalist, 49, 52, 59, 86, 119, 145; *see also* Althusser; Poulantzas
Marxism-Leninism, 48
Mill, James
An Analysis of the Phenomena of the Human Mind, 38, 182 n. 55
Marx on, 85
Mill, J. S.
    Art and Science, 24-5; *see also* Mill on methodology
    Autobiography, 24, 27, 105
    Chapters on Socialism, 168
    Considerations on Representative Government, 9, 24, 96-7, 100-1, 108-9, 112, 114-15, 167
    epistemology, 25, 98
    associationism, 99, 103, 175
    free will and determinism, 10-11, 23-4, 26-7, 32-3, 37-8, 45-7, 101-2
    causal determinism, 103, 171
    compatibilism, 10, 97 100 103 114, 171
    freedom, 1-16 *passim*, 164-78 *passim*
    ethology, 21, 26, 37, 40-1, 47, 182 n. 65
    moral freedom, 36, 103-4
    mutual recognition, 2, 14
    negative, 97-9
    positive, 97, 99
    the Principle of Liberty, 107, 114-15
    self-culture, 34, 36, 91, 93, 98, 103, 105, 107, 109, 116, 166, 168-70
    self-determination, 1, 14, 16, 25-6, 31, 96-7, 101-3, 114-15, 163-5, 180 n. 3
    self-development, 7, 99, 101, 105-7, 163, 169-70
    self-improvement, 10, 20, 22-3, 28, 31, 35-6, 47, 91, 93, 97, 105, 107-8, 116, 169-71, 182 n. 44
    and virtue, 100-1, 114, 169
    of the will, 101
    on human nature, 22-47, 90-116 *passim*, 183 n. 84
    faculty of speculation, 42
    instincts, 42-5
    pleasures, 104-5
    principle of association, 21, 27, 29, 38-9, 42, 44, 166, 182 n. 56

Index

self-interest, 43, 91, 112, 183 n. 73
social sympathy, 43-4; *see also* utilitarianism
on individuality, 18-47 *passim*, 96, 99, 102-8, 112, 114-15; *see also* freedom
on justice, 43-4, 169, 171
on the labouring classes, 165, 167, 179 n. 1
and liberalism, 114
On Liberty, 9, 12, 23-6, 43, 46, 92, 95-7, 100-4, 106, 108-9, 112, 114-15, 182 n. 44
on methodology, 9-10, 12, 14, 26
empiricism, 25, 98, 166
General Science of Society, 36
materialism, 95, 71; *see also* epistemology
on morality, 14, 43-4, 46, 98-9, 112, 171, 175
and political economy, 6-7
Principles of Political Economy, 168
on progress, 5, 20, 107-8, 114-15, 164-5, 183 n. 72
on reason, 35, 104
Rectorial Address, 115
on representative democracy, 15, 95, 100, 106, 108-116
the Cabinet, 109
and class domination, 108, 111-12
the Commission of legislation, 109
the Crown, 109
the franchise, 107-11, 113, 115, 170
political authority, 12, 15, 23-4, 26, 91, 96, 103, 107-9, 112, 166-7, 169-70, 181 n 4
proportional representation, 110-11
'revisionist' interpretations of, 99-100
The Spirit of the Age, 115
A System of Logic, 5, 9, 12, 22, 24-5, 28, 30-3, 36, 41-2, 45-7, 95, 99, 102-3
Tidology, 37
utilitarianism, 11, 20, 23, 25-8, 30-2, 35, 38, 43, 45-6, 92-3, 97-101, 114-16, 166, 171, 180 n. 5, 181 n. 11; *see also* Bentham
Utilitarianism, 9, 12, 23, 43, 46, 95, 97, 105

Nozick, R., 18

Ollman, B., 51
Owen, R., 102
and the 'utopianists', 33

perfectability, 163
Philosophical Radicals, 27
Popper, K., 19
Poulantzas, N., 49; *see also* Marxism, structural-functionalist
Proudhon, P., 74, 157

Ryan, A., 22, 24

Saint-Simonians, 5, 30, 91
Smith, A., 158
Smith, G. W., 24, 102, 118
Stephen, J. F., 23, 98
Stirner, M., 54, 141

Taylor, H., 114
Ten, C. L., 23, 99
Third International, 49
Thomas, W., 92
Tucker, D. F. B., 18

utilitarianism, 12, 18, 50, 78, 83-5, 166; *see also* Bentham; Mill

Veer, Van de, D., 128

Weber, M., 165
Wood, A., 143

Yugoslavia, 49